Ch
to r
ww
wv

THE PREMIERSHIP IN FOCUS

THE PREMIERSHIP IN FOCUS

Celebrating 15 years of the Premier League with BBC TV's *Football Focus*

MARTYN SMITH

BBC
BOOKS

This book is published to accompany the BBC television series *Football Focus*.

Published in 2007 by BBC Books,
an imprint of Ebury Publishing.
A Random House Group Company

10 9 8 7 6 5 4 3 2 1

Commissioning editors Christopher Tinker and Vivien Bowler
Production controller Katherine Hockley

Produced for BBC Books by Butler and Tanner Ltd
Editing, design, layout, printing and binding by Butler and Tanner Ltd, Frome, Great Britain
Editor Julian Flanders
Designer Lyn Davies
Picture researcher Julian Flanders
Index Indexing Specialists (UK) Ltd

To buy books by your favourite authors and register for offers visit **www.rbooks.co.uk**

PICTURE CREDITS

All photographs © Empics (PA Photos) except the following: BBC pages 7, 11, 17, 25, 31, 39, 43, 53 (left), 67, 71, 73, 81, 86, 95, 109, 110, 119, 123, 133, 137, 145 (both), 151, 154, 160, 165, 179, 184, 193, 197 (both), 200, 202, 208; Hulton-Getty page 6; Martyn Smith pages 19, 53 (right), 59, 62 (bottom), 75, 147, 203, 207, 212, 215, 200.

ACKNOWLEDGEMENTS

Lots of colleagues at the BBC have helped with the research and writing of this book and I would like to thank all the presenters, commentators, reporters, pundits and producers who have once again let me plunder their thoughts and memories.

I'm especially grateful to Phil Bigwood and Claire Donohoe-Lane in the *Match of the Day* office for their advice and assistance and for providing such a superb directory enquiries service and to Steve Boulton and all the *Football Focus* team for their help and time.

Thanks also to Julian Flanders for once again being a terrific editor to work with on this book and to everyone in the BBC Sport Library and in Current Operations for their help with the many tapes that were viewed. Also to Danny Garlick and Kirsty Locker for all their massive support in recent years.

My friends have also been very patient while I've spent several months absorbed with this project. Jay Ramirez has kept me relaxed and Edward Lidster managed to cope with all my moans and groans while establishing his own career as a theatre designer.

It always fascinates me to see how football connects people in so many different forms and locations. When we were in South Africa filming for *Sport Relief* in 2006 we had just spent time with people who were living in some horrendous conditions in cramped homes and caring for relatives who were suffering from AIDS and yet there, in the midst of the poverty, were Premiership football shirts being worn by the kids and a poster tacked up on a post to let everyone know that Robbie Fowler had just returned to Liverpool.

My late friend Peter Malzer followed Arsenal throughout his life, regardless of the continent he was working on, and would take great joy in baiting his West Ham and Forest supporting sons, Nick and Alexander, as George Graham and Arsène Wenger led the North London side to an incredible run of success.

At the other end of the supporting scale my uncle, Alan Smith, had his ashes scattered on the pitch of non-league Chelmsford City after more than 60 years following them, all the while remaining stoic and optimistic despite the many seasons of frustrations and disappointments. His elder brother Stan has racked up almost 70 years as a regular supporter and it is the devoted fans like them who help the game stay vibrant at the lower reaches.

This book is dedicated to all of the above, to my parents, Mike and Nettie Smith, and to the sporting futures of Lucy, Callum and Coralie Smith.

Contents

Introduction

It was appropriate that former Arsenal goalkeeper Bob Wilson was the first presenter of *Football Focus* in 1974 as his club had been an integral part of the BBC's football coverage since it began 80 years ago, mainly because their ground was close to the BBC's transmitter at Alexandra Palace in North London.

Arsenal's 1-1 draw with Sheffield United was the first match commentary to be broadcast on radio on 22 January 1927, while football first appeared on television on Wednesday 15 September 1937 when the cameras went behind the scenes at Highbury as part of a magazine show called *Picture Page*.

The following day football appeared in the *Radio Times* as a separate show for the very first time. At 3.40 p.m.,

Football at the Arsenal began and the great broadcaster, John Snagge, welcomed viewers as he stood on the pitch accompanied by Gunners' manager George Allison.

A year later another milestone was reached with the televising of a live match, once again from Highbury. It was the Charity Shield game between Arsenal and Preston North End on 26 September 1938 and was covered by just two Super Emitron cameras, which were placed in the centre of the back row in the top tier of the West Stand with the commentators alongside.

Despite the fact that his team was on the pitch, George Allison became the first television summariser working with commentator Tod Rich from Somerset. The programme went on air at 5.24 p.m. At that time there were thought to be fewer than 4,000 television sets in Greater London and only a handful outside. Unfortunately just 23 minutes later at 5.47 it stopped and the transmission was faded out as the weather had become so bad that the picture quality was unwatchable. It was short and sweet, and the television revolution had begun.

When the television service re-opened in 1946 after the war, the BBC were keen to begin showing football as soon as possible but were still only able to televise matches that took place within 20 miles of Alexandra Palace which, once again, limited them to broadcasting London-based games. There were now believed to be about 15,000 television sets in the area and live football resumed from Barnet on the afternoon of Saturday 19 October 1946, when the home team took on Wealdstone in the Athenian League.

The First Highlights

The Coronation in 1953 saw a big rise in the number of television sets purchased and the man who was in charge of that broadcast, Peter Dimmock, was also now Head of Sport. In 1954 he and sports editor Paul Fox began to build on the increasing popularity of televised sport by launching a new midweek magazine programme, *Sportsview*. It was the first regular show to feature football match highlights, profiles and news stories as well as reports from other sports.

Such was the programme's popularity that in the following year they introduced a Saturday evening programme aimed mainly at football fans. Presented by the BBC's football commentator, Kenneth Wolstenholme, beginning on BBC1 at 10.15 p.m. on Saturday 10 September 1955, *Saturday Sports Special* was a revolutionary new show that contained film reports and match action from around the UK.

The Arsenal players go through their paces in front of a BBC camera at Highbury for the very first time in September 1937. Commentary was provided by John Snagge (far left) and Arsenal manager George Allison, who went on to work as the first ever expert summariser.

The series ran for six years and was supplemented in October 1958 by the launch of *Grandstand* but it eventually ended because broadcasting was led, as ever, by new technology. *Saturday Sport Special* comprised of short match reports that had been shot on 16mm film, which then had to be processed in time for transmission. As there was usually only one camera in operation at matches it meant that occasionally, and embarrassingly, the winning goal might be scored while the film was being changed.

When videotape and the reality of multi-camera coverage developed, the programme died a natural death. Viewers could still see midweek highlights in *Sportsview* as well as the occasional live European competition, but in general 1961 to 1964 were barren years for football fans until BBC2 was launched and *Match of the Day* began. Football, even then, was seen as a means of encouraging viewers to watch a new service.

'Welcome to *Match of the Day*'

On 22 August 1964 Kenneth Wolstenholme's opening link was recorded pitchside from Anfield. 'Welcome to *Match of the Day*, the first of a weekly series coming to you every Saturday on BBC2. As you can hear we're in Beatleville for this Liverpool versus Arsenal match.' Ken was joined by his summariser, Walley Barnes, who previewed the game.

Liverpool were the defending champions, the ground was full and the first ever *Match of the Day* goal came when Ian Callaghan crossed to Roger Hunt who hooked the ball into the top left-hand corner with a right-footed volley. Liverpool won 3-2, although only an estimated 20,000 viewers actually saw the show.

As new transmitters opened the reach increased and new technology began to make an impact with the introduction

Left Kenneth Wolstenholme warms up for his first appearance on *Match of the Day* which was broadcast from Anfield on 22 August 1964 on BBC2.

Above right Jimmy Hill (left) and Bob Wilson in action on the set of *Match of the Day* during the mid-1970s.

of instant replay facilities in 1966 and the fledgling colour TV service in subsequent years.

Match of the Day switched to BBC1 at the start of the 1966–67 season and *Grandstand*'s 'Football Preview', presented by Sam Leitch, began two years later as did ITV's two new regular football programmes. With Jimmy Hill as Head of Sport at LWT they launched *On the Ball* on Saturday lunchtimes and *The Big Match* on Sunday afternoons, both fronted by Brian Moore.

By August 1970 the standard *Match of the Day* format was in place with the new and now iconic theme tune, the highlights of two matches per show and the Goal of the Month competition. By then David Coleman was in the presenter's chair, although Jimmy Hill switched channels and became the main anchor for the start of the 1973–74 season. With John Motson and Barry Davies as the main commentators the classic *Match of the Day* line-up was established.

At the beginning of the 1974–75 season the BBC decided to revamp their lunchtime coverage and *Football Focus* began. Bob Wilson made the brave decision to step straight from the Arsenal goal and into the presenter's chair and he remained there for 20 years. In the early days *Focus* ran for 15 or 20 minutes each week but its player and manager features and studio interviews were instrumental in raising their profiles and helping to create nationally known figures.

Football league highlights proved to be a competitive battleground for the BBC and ITV during the 1980s with the two organisations alternating Saturday evening and Sunday afternoon highlights for four years from 1980–81.

Each side was allowed to show seven live Division One matches from the start of the 1983–84 season with ITV opting for Sunday afternoons and the BBC broadcasting theirs on Friday evenings, beginning with Manchester United's 4-2 win over Tottenham on 16 December 1983.

Live Sport Takes Over

With live sport being seen as the way forward the Saturday night highlights shows were dropped from the start of the 1986–87 season with the BBC switching its resources to covering live matches on Sunday afternoons and *Match of the Day* only rarely appearing on the Saturday evenings of FA Cup weekends.

Manchester United players celebrate one of their four goals against Tottenham in the BBC's first live match in December 1983. These two sides served up several thrilling games in the early days of live broadcasts.

The last four-year contract to cover league games ran from 1988 to 1992 and was won exclusively by ITV, leaving the BBC with just the FA Cup and England highlights which they shared with the new satellite operator BSkyB.

After several years of speculation it was announced in February 1992 that a new, breakaway FA Premier League was going to be formed. ITV were expected to win the TV rights but the BBC and BSkyB combined to place a counter bid and had strong influence within the new organisation. There was bitterness felt by many club chairmen at the way in which ITV had favoured big clubs during the previous contract. In May 1992 the rights were decided and each club had one vote. BSkyB were awarded live matches on Sundays and Mondays and the BBC gained the Saturday night highlights as part of a five-year, £304m deal. The two companies also joined forces to sign a new £72m, five-year deal to cover FA Cup and international matches leaving ITV

with rights to the newly formed Football League and the League Cup. *Match of the Day* was back full time and *Football Focus* also returned on a weekly basis. Now with access to a wealth of goals and match action the reinvigorated programme moved into the next phase of its life as the Premiership began in August 1992.

Roots of the Premier League

More than a century after it had been created in 1888 the Football League was looking increasingly like an idea that had outlived its time and the First Division clubs were restless for change. The game's image had suffered in the 1970s and 1980s and even though Liverpool, Everton and Nottingham Forest had produced some wonderful football and dominated the domestic and European scene, the downsides had all too often become front-page news.

Hooliganism, falling crowds, the banning of British clubs from European competitions, poor facilities and crumbling stadiums were all still problems and the names of some grounds were now more synonymous with tragedies and loss of life as the game struggled to recover from Heysel, Bradford and Hillsborough.

Football's image was badly tarnished in front of millions of TV viewers in the 1970s and 1980s. The riot at Kenilworth Road after the FA Cup sixth round match between Luton and Millwall in March 1985 was one of many incidents that highlighted the problem.

The upsurge in football's popularity after Italia 90 began to change the image of the game in England and the Taylor Report proposed the expensive conversion of all First Division grounds into all-seated stadiums, but it was the overseas leagues in Italy, Spain and Germany that were attracting the world's biggest names, including an increasing number of British players.

Paul Gascoigne's footballing passion, exhibited to the full during Italia 90, went a long way to restoring the sport's popularity.

Television money had also become much more important as the Football League began to recognise its commercial value. It had only received £6.3m for a two-year agreement in 1986, but everything changed when ITV increased that to £44m over four years when they won exclusive rights in 1988.

Even then there had been talk of a breakaway super league but the clubs were all pursuaded to sign the collective deal, although the seeds for change had been sown and many of the chairmen were keen to form a new structure. The catalyst was the arrival of satellite television with the airtime available for regular live matches to be broadcast and on 17 July 1991 the teams in Division One signed the Founder Members' Agreement which established the principles of a new commercially independent Premier League.

Incredible Rise in Value

The following year the clubs resigned from the Football League and on 27 May 1992 the FA Premier League was formed with the freedom to negotiate its own sponsorship, television and radio deals. The first Sky television agreement was worth £191m over five seasons with the BBC's highlights deal and overseas contracts boosting the total to £304m, an incredible rise in the value of the product.

The new league, led by a chairman and a chief executive, was committed to reducing in size from 22 to 20 with each club having one equal vote for rule changes and contracts. Half of the money raised in contract negotiations is shared equally between the clubs, 25 per cent is linked to where the teams finish in the league and the remaining 25 per cent is paid according to the number of TV appearances each season.

The top two sides in the final league table qualify automatically for the UEFA Champions League with the third and fourth placed teams going into the final qualifying round and the fifth-placed team qualifying for the UEFA Cup along with the winners of the FA Cup and League Cups. When the Premier League came into existence the Football League re-organised itself into Divisions One, Two and Three.

Premier League matches are now shown on television in 204 territories and are especially popular in Asia. In China alone audiences can reputedly run to more than 100 million as the game continues to grow in popularity and the world's top names keep signing up. But back in August 1992, when the players lined up to play in the competition for the very first time, there were many who thought that all that had really happened was a change in name. How wrong they were...

The Last League Season

Howard Wilkinson led Leeds United to the final title of the old Football League, their first since 1974. The Yorkshire club finished four points ahead of Manchester United with Sheffield Wednesday in third place. Luton Town, Notts County and West Ham were the three relegated sides who missed out on the new adventure. Gary Lineker was the leading scorer with 28 league goals for Tottenham and was also voted Player of the Year with the Manchester United pair of Gary Pallister and Ryan Giggs collecting the PFA awards for Player and Young Player of the season.

Leeds United players celebrate with the last ever Football League Division One Championship trophy at Elland Road in May 1992.

FF 1992-93

Spurs striker Teddy Sheringham was the Premier League's top scorer in its first season. His total of 22 included one for Nottingham Forest against Liverpool in the first live televised BSkyB match.

Programmes

On the day that the Premier League kicked off, 15 August 1992, *Football Focus* was still part of *Grandstand*. It was usually in the opening segment of the programme although the durations varied. Now in his 19th season in the presenter's chair, Bob Wilson was joined by Gary Lineker as his regular pundit for the first few weeks, and by a variety of guests for the remainder of the season when Gary left to play in Japan. The show was presented from the *Grandstand* set with Steve Rider sitting a few feet away from Bob and linking into his section each week.

After a four-year gap, *Match of the Day* returned on Saturday nights fronted by Desmond Lynam and joined by regular pundits Alan Hansen and Trevor Brooking. The show reverted to the classic format of extended highlights from three main games, but as well as extra analysis, viewers were also able to see the goals from all the other matches.

Presenter
Bob Wilson

FOOTBALL FOCUS

Pre-season

The summer's main transfer news came on 26 July when Southampton's 21-year-old striker Alan Shearer moved to Blackburn Rovers for a new British record fee of £3.6m after scoring 23 goals in 118 league games for the South Coast team.

Other big money switches saw Paul Stewart join Liverpool from Tottenham for £2.3m, Arsenal's David Rocastle move to current champions Leeds for a club record £2m and Chris Waddle return to English football when he exchanged Marseille for Sheffield, joining Wednesday for £1m.

Watford's promising young goalkeeper, David James, signed for Liverpool in June and the former Arsenal boss, Don Howe, became Chelsea's coach after resigning as manager of Coventry where he was succeeded by Bobby Gould.

There were also some changes to the rules for the new Premiership. Referees would now wear green strips rather than the traditional black, each team had a choice of three substitutes, including one goalkeeper, and half time was extended to 15 minutes.

August 1992

Alex Ferguson, Manchester United's manager, was interviewed on the first *Focus* of the season to talk about his new front man, Dion Dublin, who had cost him £1m from Cambridge United. 'We did get involved in Alan Shearer, but when it came to the actual transfer fee for a 21-year-old, we just felt that as Dion Dublin was an alternative we've possibly got the better value.'

Dublin failed to score on his debut against Sheffield United, but Brian Deane entered the history books as the scorer of the first Premiership goal when his header put the Blades 1-0 up against Manchester United after just five minutes. Dave Bassett's

Premiership managers start of 1992–93

Team	Manager	Team	Manager
Arsenal	George Graham	**Manchester United**	Alex Ferguson
Aston Villa	Ron Atkinson	**Middlesbrough**	Lennie Lawrence
Blackburn Rovers	Kenny Dalglish	**Norwich City**	Mike Walker
Chelsea	Ian Porterfield	**Nottingham Forest**	Brian Clough
Coventry City	Bobby Gould	**Oldham Athletic**	Joe Royle
Crystal Palace	Steve Coppell	**QPR**	Gerry Francis
Everton	Howard Kendall	**Sheffield United**	Dave Bassett
Ipswich Town	John Lyall	**Sheffield Wednesday**	Trevor Francis*
Leeds United	Howard Wilkinson	**Southampton**	Ian Branfoot
Liverpool	Graeme Souness	**Tottenham Hotspur**	Peter Shreeves
Manchester City	Peter Reid*	**Wimbledon**	Joe Kinnear
			*player-manager

side won 2-1, but lost five of their next six games.

Shearer's first two league goals for Blackburn came on his debut in their 3-3 draw at Crystal Palace and he spoke to *Focus* in the trophy room at Ewood Park that week. 'I chose Blackburn because I feel that they are going places backed by Jack Walker. If I'd just wanted to make money I could have made a killing abroad, but it felt right to go to Blackburn.'

Defending champions Leeds made a good start in the sunshine, beating Wimbledon 2-1, while Arsenal lost 4-2 at home to Norwich in front of a large painted mural of fans at a redeveloping Highbury. They had been 2-0 up but, as Tony Gubba said in the commentary, 'the scoreline proved to be as much an illusion as the cardboard supporters'.

The following day saw the first live televised BSkyB game when Nottingham Forest beat Liverpool 1-0 thanks to Teddy Sheringham's left-foot shot from the edge of the box. Unfortunately for Forest fans they won only two more of their next 20 games, even suffering a 5-3 defeat at Oldham, which prompted Brian Clough to say that his team were so bad that even his granny could have scored against them.

At the end of the first week Norwich were top on goal difference from Coventry, as the only clubs to win both openers. They had beaten Chelsea 2-1 at home with an extraordinary winner from Mark Robins. The ball came in high over his right shoulder as he ran into the box and he volleyed over the keeper with the outside of his right foot.

Having taken one point from their first three games Dublin's last-minute winner gave Manchester United their first win, at Southampton, while Terry Phelan moved from Wimbledon to Manchester City for £2.5m, a British record for a full back.

In the same week Eric Cantona struck a hat-trick as Leeds demolished Tottenham 5-0, Aston Villa lost at Everton to a spectacular long-range curling shot by Mo Johnston and QPR went to the top of the league for the first time since October 1987 when they won 1-0 at Coventry.

The month ended with Sheringham moving to Tottenham for £2.1m and Norwich in first place having beaten Forest 3-1. It was their fourth successive defeat and Clough's worst start in 17 years.

September

Tottenham were helped by Sheringham's first goal for the club as they finally collected three points after three draws and two

defeats, beating Sheffield United 2-0, but there was some shocking luck for Dublin who broke a leg in Manchester United's 1-0 win over Crystal Palace and was out for the rest of the season.

Manchester City's first goal of their three at Sheffield Wednesday was an unusual one as a consequence of the new rule outlawing passes back to the goalkeeper. Roland Nilsson was adjudged to have played the ball directly to Chris Woods and the visitors were awarded an indirect free kick six yards out. Despite nine Wednesday players on the line they were unable to stop Peter Reid nudging the ball to David White who drove it in.

On the second weekend Norwich went two points clear when they recovered from two down to win 3-2 at Chelsea and a week later they extended their lead, beating Sheffield Wednesday when Rob Newman headed the only goal of the match. Chris Armstrong scored twice from John Salako crosses as Crystal Palace beat Everton 2-0 to register their only win in the first 17 games and four months of the season.

Dean Saunders had moved from Liverpool to Aston Villa for £2.3m and scored twice in Villa's 4-2 victory over his old team, although the match is mainly remembered for Reds' Israeli striker Ronnie Rosenthal's famous miss. He rounded the keeper, was on the edge of the six-yard box with a completely open goal... and hit the bar!

October

The biggest premiership win of the season came when Blackburn thrashed Norwich 7-1. Shearer's pace and cross created the first for Roy Wegerle and Tim Sherwood headed the second. Another Shearer cross set Wegerle up for the third, he then produced stunning control and a chip of his own to make it 4-1,

Gordon Cowans' direct free kick made it five, Stuart Ripley placed the sixth from the edge of the box and a Shearer header completed the rout.

After 11 games the table had an unexpected look as Blackburn led with 24 points, one ahead of Norwich with Coventry on 21 and QPR 20. Manchester United were in sixth place, level on 19 points with Aston Villa.

A week later Norwich were back on top having beaten QPR 2-1 and Ian Rush went past Roger Hunt's club record for Liverpool when he notched his 287th goal in their 2-2 draw at Old Trafford.

Blackburn restored their lead following a 0-0 draw with Manchester United who then ended their run of five successive draws by losing 1-0 at home to Wimbledon. Lawrie Sanchez, the only surviving member of their 1988 Cup-winning side, touched on Terry Gibson's free kick to produce one of the biggest upsets of the season.

At the end of the month Everton lost 3-1 at home to Manchester City to go into bottom position. It was their seventh defeat in nine games and the glory years of Howard Kendall's first spell in charged seemed a very long way away.

November

The first Arsenal feature of the season saw Gerald Sinstadt interview a relaxed George Graham at their training ground. He explained that he had bought John Jensen, the Danish international with a semi-Keegan perm and a bad moustache, to be a 'midfield general' and ballwinner as, in Alan Smith, Kevin Campbell, Paul Merson, Ian Wright and Anders Limpar, he already had so many potential goalscorers.

That afternoon they went top, beating Coventry 3-0, to notch their sixth successive win, but Graham's goalscoring calculations then misfired as they scored a paltry 18 goals in their remaining 27 games of the season to finish as the lowest scorers in the Premiership with 40 goals.

On the second weekend of the month Norwich regained the lead after a 3-2 victory at Oldham thanks to Mark Robins' hat-trick and last-minute winner, and a fortnight later they moved four points clear following a 2-1 win over Sheffield United.

Manchester United had dropped to tenth place when they lost 1-0 at Aston Villa having gone seven games without a win. With only five victories from their first 15 matches it was hard to see how they could be title contenders, but Alex Ferguson finally had cause to celebrate when they found winning form against Oldham to start them on the run that would change their season and help establish the destination of the first Premiership trophy as they took 26 points out of a possible 30.

Instrumental in that spell was the signing from Leeds of Frenchman Eric Cantona who

Below Alex Ferguson's greatest ever signing? Frenchman Eric Cantona joined Manchester United from Champions Leeds in November 1992 and provided the spark that ignited United's unstoppable drive for the title.

Commentator John Motson

John Motson's first football commentary on the BBC came in December 1969 when he described the second half action of Everton against Derby County for Radio 2. In October 1971 he made his *Match of the Day* debut on Liverpool's 0-0 draw with Chelsea. A permanent and iconic fixture in the BBC's commentary team ever since, Motty has been behind the microphone at more than 500 Premiership matches for *Match of the Day* and Radio Five Live.

'My favourite Premiership goal that I commentated on came in August 1996 when I was at Plough Lane to describe David Beckham's astonishing shot from the halfway line for Manchester United against Wimbledon. If I was picking one outstanding overall player he would also be from the same club as I'd have to go for Ryan Giggs for his endurance and loyalty. He was there when it started and is still there now as one of the elite band who have played in every season of the Premier League.

Although Manchester United and Arsenal dominated the league until Chelsea came along, the match that really stands out for me as a commentator was when Blackburn lost at Liverpool on the day that they won the Championship. It was amazing to see them celebrating despite having just conceded a goal.

One of the biggest changes in the last 15 years is that the Premiership has become a brand as opposed to a league and this has upped the quality of football to way above that of the old Division One, where we never have had the glitz and the glamour. Another thing that has changed are the grounds and stadiums. We started out post-Hillsborough with all the terraces outlawed under the

Taylor Report. In many ways they are now more like theatres with a lot more comfort and convenience, although the loss of the terracing has meant that the fans are possibly less vocal.

The last 15 years have been great for those who got in and survived, but more difficult for the clubs who have been in the top flight but have now dropped down. Some of those clubs have little chance of going back up as the financial gulf gets ever bigger.'

moved from Elland Road to Old Trafford for £1.2m. Ferguson was convinced he had made a crucial purchase, telling *Focus,* 'I hope he gives us goals. Sometimes strikers need a challenge and I think and hope that Brian McClair and Mark Hughes will relish it. It's part of a footballer's make-up to be on edge and I think that's better for them.'

At the other end of the table Oldham got their fourth win of the season in their 17th attempt when they beat a hapless Middlesbrough 4-1. Having been one up from a Willie Falconer header Boro conceded three in the next ten minutes. Manager Lennie Lawrence described it as 'absolute, total ineptitude'. It was to be the pattern of the season though, as his defence conceded 74 goals, more than any other side.

Still stuck firmly at the bottom, Nottingham Forest took their record to just 11 points out of a possible 51 when they lost 1-2 at home to Southampton. There was no joy either for Steve Coppell who saw his Crystal Palace side thrashed 5-0 at Liverpool. It was to be their biggest defeat of the season and left them just a point above Forest.

December

In their opening match of the month Norwich scored twice in the last 15 minutes to beat Wimbledon 2-1 and go eight points clear, a terrific and unexpected achievement for such a small club. At 22, the Canaries' striker Mark Robins was the leading scorer with the leading club and looked to be the buy of the season. 'I'd like to think that I do more than just score goals, but that's what I do best.' Although one of the first players to shine in the Premiership he had been with Manchester United, but after only starting 27 matches at Old Trafford moved to East Anglia when Norwich paid £800,000 for him in August.

His new manager, Mike Walker, was a big fan. 'Look at Rush and Lineker, they don't do a lot of build-up play, but what they've been bought for and why they're worth a lot of money is that they've got that knack of putting the ball in the net and that's priceless.' He scored 11 goals in his first 16 appearances but the goals dried up, although he still finished the season as the club's leading Premiership scorer with 15.

Meanwhile the title-holders, Leeds, suffered their first home defeat since 13 April 1991 when bottom club Forest shocked everyone with a 4-1 win.

Having won just one out of their first 17 matches Palace astonished their fans by winning five in a row during December to earn Steve Coppell the Manager of the Month award. They began with goals from Chris Armstrong and Gareth Southgate in a 2-0 win over Sheffield United and added the scalps of QPR, Leeds, Wimbledon and Middlesbrough.

With 11 goals in 16 games Norwich striker Mark Robins, seen here in action against his old club at Old Trafford, was the leading scorer with the leading club in December 1992.

Pundit Ian Wright

Ian Wright joined Arsenal from Crystal Palace in 1991 and was their leading scorer for six consecutive seasons. After spending a year with West Ham he retired in 2000 having scored 113 Premiership goals. His sons, Shaun and Bradley Wright-Phillips, have both followed him into the game.

'For me the best player to play with was Dennis Bergkamp. He was the total professional and had the right approach to his diet, training and lifestyle. We worked well together because we were two completely different animals. He was cold, calculating and precise, a clinical genius. I was at the other end, in your face, always going for the chances and it worked perfectly with him in just behind me. Peter Schmeichel was a great quality keeper, the finest I played against because of his incredible presence and will to win, and Des Walker was the toughest defender. He was quick, strong and studied the forwards. He always knew my runs but was very undervalued as a player as he didn't speak to the press.

It didn't feel any different when Division One became the Premier League but in the season before it began I had scored 29 league goals and all of a sudden they didn't seem to count towards the records that people focus on. Had it started a year before I would have had a massive total.'

Manchester United moved third when they beat Norwich 1-0 at the start of the worst spell for the Norfolk club who took just three points from a possible 18. Then, in a hard-fought derby, Ipswich inflicted the first home defeat of the season on the leaders when Chris Kiwomya and Gary Thompson each scored to move the promoted team into sixth spot. Norwich remained top but with a telling goal record of 34 goals for and 34 goals against.

Mark Bright's strike at Hillsbrough against QPR gave Sheffield Wednesday their first win in eight games and was the start of an unbeaten run of ten matches for Trevor Francis' team that included eight wins and took them into fourth place. Meanwhile, Leeds slipped to just above the relegation zone when they went down 3-1 at Blackburn to a brace from Shearer and one by Jason Wilcox.

Manchester United ended the year with the biggest win of their season when they put five past Coventry and moved second, three points behind Norwich who drew 0-0 at Elland Road.

January 1993

On 9 January Manchester United beat Tottenham 4-1 to top the Premier League table for the first time, on goal difference from Norwich. They went one up when Lee Sharpe's backheel released Denis Irwin who crossed for Eric Cantona to score with a looping header. Cantona also provided a perfect chip over the defence to let Irwin in for the second and within two minutes Brian McClair had added a third. Tottenham's keeper Erik Thorstvedt looked stunned when Paul Parker's first goal for the home team made it 4-0 before Nick Barmby headed a late reply.

Norwich missed their chance to return to the top the next day when they lost to Nigel Worthington's only goal of the season at Sheffield Wednesday, but a week later a 1-1 draw at home to Coventry saw them return to pole position while Blackburn beat Oldham 1-0 to go third. It was the start of a run of seven defeats in eight games that put pressure on their manager Joe Royle.

The following afternoon Aston Villa became the latest club to lead the table when they beat

Middlesbrough 5-1, their biggest win of the season, but on Monday evening Manchester United made it three leaders in three days when they beat fellow championship challengers QPR 3-1 at Loftus Road.

Ipswich finally ended Manchester United's near three-month unbeaten run when they won 2-1 at Portman Road. A tale of two keepers saw Peter Schmeichel charge out to counter the danger from a long ball fired over Steve Bruce's head. But he missed it and left Chris Kiwomya with an open goal. Frank Yallop's shot was deflected in for the second but Brian McClair tapped in six minutes from the end to add some pressure. The home team claimed the points thanks to a brilliant close-range reaction save by keeper Clive Baker from Mark Hughes.

Southampton's 2-0 win against Aston Villa gave the Saints some breathing space at the bottom and meant yet another change at the top when Norwich beat Everton 1-0 at Goodison Park to inflict the first of four straight defeats for Howard Kendall and his men.

February

Manchester United and Aston Villa both won at the start of the month to fill the top two places. United beat Sheffield United 2-1 while Ron Atkinson's Villa put two past Ipswich to start them on a terrible spell where they only won two of their remaining 16 games.

Paul Ince was profiled on *Focus* and allowed the cameras and David Davies to interview him at home in his living room, something that is almost unimaginable in today's game where most players are only allowed to speak at the training grounds or team hotels. Ince had joined Manchester United from his home club West Ham in 1989 when his mentor, John Lyall, was sacked.

It was put to him that his 'transformation from a self-confessed East End tearaway into a family man of Cheshire could hardly have been more rapid or more consciously achieved'. He agreed, 'I've learned to channel my emotions and I think that's led to an improvement in my game. I won't change overnight but I'm working on it.'

Lyall remembered that he was 'marvellously motivated, as a young lad in his early teens he showed great skill and after training would ask for a ball to continue to practise volleys and diving headers when the others would practise basic passing'.

It was Aston Villa's turn to lead the table when Ray Houghton scored the only goal of the game at Chelsea on 13 February. Two days later the home team's manager, Ian Porterfield, was sacked and replaced by former local favourite David Webb

Tottenham were in a great run of form and their fourth consecutive win came with a 4-0 thrashing at home to Leeds with Teddy Sheringham scoring his first hat-trick for the club. It was suitable revenge for earlier in the season when the Yorkshire side had won 5-0.

Sheffield Wednesday moved into fourth place behind Aston Villa, Manchester United and Norwich after recording their seventh successive league win, 2-1 at Manchester City. Trevor Francis' gamble of using Paul Warhurst as a makeshift striker was still paying off as he scored for the fourth consecutive match.

One of the saddest announcements of the season came the following day when England's legendary World Cup-winning captain, Bobby Moore, died of cancer at the tragically young age of 51.

March

Chelsea started the month with their first win in 13 games when Graham Stuart put the

Editor Philip Bernie

Philip Bernie was the Editor of *Football Focus* for the first three seasons of the Premiership and has edited many other shows, including *Grandstand, Onside,* and *Sports Personality of the Year.*

'When the Premiership started we knew it was going to be pretty big. It was a great relief and excitement to have football back on the BBC and *Focus* returned on a full-time basis with Bob Wilson still at the helm. He was very dedicated, conscientious and terrific to work with as he was so passionate about football and had good strong views about it.

We had a very small team and *Focus* was very much the poor cousin to *Match of the Day*, although we had some good film-makers. However, as it was the kick-start to *Grandstand* it often got reduced or lost because of other events in the show, although its significance grew during the 1990s. I loved editing it but it was stressful

and for a while we had no autocue because of cost cuts which was very difficult for Bob.

The Premiership started with two great stories which were terrific for the football shows. Manchester United finally won the league, having just lost out to Leeds the previous year, and it was amazing to have that as the big story for the first year as they were the biggest club with the larger fan base. The other was that the biggest sleeping giant, Newcastle, was being revived by Kevin Keegan and he was brilliant for us as he was so honest and emotional and encouraged that flamboyant attacking style.

We introduced Gary Lineker as a pundit and then worked out a strategy to develop him as a presenter and gave him training on TV and radio. It was clear that he had something, although he had to work on techniques such as autocue, but he's a bright guy and a good learner and people shouldn't underestimate just how hard he worked.'

ball through David Seaman's legs to score the only goal of the game against Arsenal. It was only Chelsea's seventh goal in the same period. Blues fans then had the added pleasure of seeing Tottenham concede six against Sheffield United the next day. Manchester United returned to the head of the table, two points ahead of Villa, when headers by Hughes and McClair secured them victory at Anfield to leave Liverpool three points outside the relegation zone.

In a season where form was erratic and results hard to predict no one should have been surprised when bottom beat top as Oldham's Neil Adams headed the only goal of the game against United, although they remained top on goal difference when Villa couldn't break the deadlock against Tottenham the following night.

There was yet another change when Norwich went to Nottingham and beat Forest 3-0 to reclaim the Premiership lead for the first time in two months, but three days later the merry-go-round spun again with Norwich losing 3-0 at Wimbledon, Villa beating Sheffield Wednesday 2-0 and United being held 1-1 in the Manchester derby.

The next top of the table clash saw East Anglia hold off the Midlands when John Polston scored the only goal for Norwich against Aston Villa to give the Canaries top spot for the eighth time that season.

At the other end there was a crucial win for Sheffield United at Coventry. The winner was route one at its best. Keeper Alan Kelly punted the ball down the pitch, it bounced once and Adrian Littlejohn volleyed it over the head of Steve Ogrizovic.

April

Despite Oldham's season-long relegation struggle only Manchester United and Blackburn scored more league goals than the Latics and their biggest win came when they defeated Wimbledon 6-2. On the same

weekend Forest lost 1-0 to Villa and Ron Atkinson's side yet again led the table with Manchester United moving second a point behind and a point above Norwich who they beat 3-1 at Carrow Road.

Norwich manager Mike Walker was left fuming when his side effectively blew their championship chances in the next game, losing 5-1 at Tottenham. 'If we play like that we'll struggle to finish in the top ten never mind the top three.'

Tony Daley's first goal in a year was enough for Villa to win at Arsenal and when they also took all three points against Manchester City they had lost just once in their past 11 games to leave them a point behind with three to play. But that was to be the end of their good form and they imploded, losing all three.

Crystal Palace still had a slim chance of escaping relegation when they met the leaders at Selhurst Park, but in the second half Ryan Giggs' cross from the left found Hughes who volleyed the first goal. He was unmarked despite the nine Palace players in the box. Ince scored the second and opened a four-point gap with two games left.

Manchester United's first title since 1968 began to look more likely when Villa were

Above Ryan Giggs – one of the young stars of Manchester United's first title for 26 years. But honours were even in the Manchester derby at Maine Road when the teams drew 1-1 in late March.

Opposite A disastrous first season in the Premiership ended in relegation for both Nottingham Forest and Crystal Palace. The two teams shared the points in a 1-1 draw at the City Ground at the beginning of March.

beaten 3-0 at Blackburn. Further west, United's great rivals Liverpool were also having a good finish to the season and defeated Leeds 2-0 to break into the top six after five straight home wins moved them from 15 to fifth in six weeks.

May

Aged 58 Brian Clough announced that he would be retiring at the end of the season after 18 years as manager of Nottingham Forest. Jimmy Hill joined Bob on *Focus* to look back at Clough's long managerial career and pay tribute to his many achievements. Jimmy felt that 'from the public's point of view he just added spice to their lives for so long; he's an entertainer'.

With two games to play Manchester United were on 78 points, four ahead of Aston Villa with Norwich a further six back in third place. Middlesbrough, Forest and Oldham filled the relegation spots with 40 points apiece although Sheffield United on 43 and Crystal Palace with 45 were still in the danger zone.

Above Oldham's Nick Henry scores the winner against Villa and hands the title to Manchester United.

Right An emotional Brian Clough salutes the City Ground crowd. Clough retired as manager of Nottingham Forest after a sparkling 18-year career.

Final League Table

Team	P	W	D	L	F	A	Pts
Manchester United	42	24	12	6	67	31	84
Aston Villa	42	21	11	10	57	40	74
Norwich City	42	21	9	12	61	65	72
Blackburn Rovers	42	20	11	11	68	46	71
QPR	42	17	12	13	63	55	63
Liverpool	42	16	11	15	62	55	59
Sheffield Wednesday	42	15	14	13	55	51	59
Tottenham Hotspur	42	16	11	15	60	66	59
Manchester City	42	15	12	15	56	51	57
Arsenal	42	15	11	16	40	38	56
Chelsea	42	14	14	14	51	54	56
Wimbledon	42	14	12	16	56	55	54
Everton	42	15	8	19	53	55	53
Sheffield United	42	14	10	18	54	53	52
Coventry City	42	13	13	16	52	57	52
Ipswich Town	42	12	16	14	50	55	52
Leeds United	42	12	15	15	57	62	51
Southampton	42	13	11	18	54	61	50
Oldham Athletic	42	13	10	19	63	74	49
Crystal Palace	42	11	16	15	48	61	49
Middlesbrough	42	11	11	20	54	75	44
Nottingham Forest	42	10	10	22	41	62	40

Leading Goalscorers league only

Teddy Sheringham	Tottenham Hotspur	22*
Les Ferdinand	QPR	20
Dean Holdsworth	Wimbledon	19
Mick Quinn	Coventry City	17
Alan Shearer	Blackburn Rovers	16
David White	Manchester City	16
Ian Wright	Arsenal	15
Brian Deane	Sheffield United	15
Matt Le Tissier	Southampton	15
Mark Hughes	Manchester United	15
Eric Cantona	Manchester United	15†
Mark Robins	Norwich City	15

* including 1 for Forest   † including 6 for Leeds

Forest and Middlesbrough were the first to be relegated. Sheffield United ruined Clough's farewell appearance at the City Ground, winning 2-0. He gave commentator Barry Davies a big hug during an emotional post-match interview and said he would be spending more time with his grandchildren. Middlesbrough also made the drop even though they won 3-2 at Sheffield Wednesday.

On 2 May Nick Henry became the man who handed the title to Manchester United for the first time in 26 years when he scored the only goal in Oldham's win at Villa Park, making it impossible for Ron Atkinson's team to catch his former club. As well as making Alex Ferguson the first manager to win league titles in Scotland and England the goal also gave Oldham a slim chance of survival.

The following day, the first ever Premiership Champions beat Blackburn 3-1 at Old Trafford and Rick Parry, Chief Executive of the Premier League, presented the trophy to Steve Bruce and Bryan Robson as their former manager Sir Matt Busby stood smiling in the stand.

With just the final relegation spot to be decided Sheffield United won 2-0 at Everton to guarantee their survival and Oldham pulled off an incredible escape by winning two games in four days. Having beaten Liverpool 3-2 they ended up on the right side of a 4-3 scoreline against Southampton on the final day of the season as Crystal Palace lost 3-0 at Arsenal and went down on goal difference.

There were a couple of final farewells. Nigel Clough scored his dad's last-ever goal for Forest in a 2-1 loss at Ipswich. He moved to Liverpool for £2m a few weeks later and Frank Clark succeeded Clough senior in the manager's office. And David Webb was sacked as Chelsea manager despite taking them to 11th spot. He was replaced by Glenn Hoddle who, having led Swindon to the Premier League, now moved to Stamford Bridge as player manager.

Awards

Footballer of the Year
Chris Waddle, Sheffield Wednesday

PFA Player of the Year
Paul McGrath, Aston Villa

PFA Young Player of the Year
Ryan Giggs, Manchester United

Honours List 1992–93

Premier League Champions
Manchester United

Runners-up Aston Villa

Relegated Crystal Palace, Middlesbrough, Nottingham Forest

Promoted Newcastle United, West Ham United, Swindon Town

FA Cup Winners Arsenal

League Cup Winners Arsenal

League Cup
Arsenal lifted the trophy for the second time in their history time when they beat Sheffield Wednesday 2-1 in the final at Wembley with goals by Paul Merson and Steve Morrow.

FA Cup
In a repeat of the League Cup final Arsenal once again beat Sheffield Wednesday although this time they needed two attempts when the first game finished 1-1 after extra time. Ian Wright put Arsenal ahead after 21 minutes but David Hirst restored parity 40 minutes later.

In the replay Ian Wright again scored first, Chris Waddle levelled the scores then, in the last minute of extra time, Andy Linighan, who had been playing with a broken nose and finger for most of the game, headed the winner for Arsenal to claim the FA Cup for the sixth time.

FF 1993–94

The new management team at White Hart Lane featured two former players, Osvaldo Ardiles (left) and Steve Perryman. They had a good start with three wins in their first four matches, but things went downhill from there.

Programmes

The beginning of the new season marked Bob Wilson's 20th year as the presenter of *Football Focus* and he was accompanied each week by a different footballing guest.

The opening *Focus* featured reports on two former team-mates who were now leading Premiership clubs in the capital. Glenn Hoddle had steered Swindon to promotion the previous season but was then poached by Chelsea. Up in North London Ossie Ardiles had succeeded Peter Shreeves as Tottenham manager and he had another former player, Steve Perryman, as his assistant. 'I believe that football is an art not a science and it should be played that way,' said Ardiles. 'We [Steve and I] have different styles; I am more of a romantic. If you leave it to me I would play a goalkeeper, six midfielders and five front players. He's much more down to earth and that will help me very much.' Presumably Steve also helped Ossie to avoid picking 12 players to start the match.

Presenter
Bob Wilson

Pre-season

This season the teams were playing in the renamed FA Carling Premiership and using squad numbers for the first time. The main transfers had been Brian Deane moving across Yorkshire to Leeds from Sheffield United for a club record £2.9m, Peter Beardsley returning to newly promoted Newcastle from Everton for £1.4m and Roy Keane joining Manchester United from Nottingham Forest for £3.75 m.

August 1993

Peter Beagrie scored the first goal of the new season at Southampton where Everton won 2-0, newcomers Newcastle, Swindon and West Ham all lost their opening matches, Blackburn won 2-1 at Chelsea, and Nigel Clough scored both goals on his Liverpool debut against Sheffield Wednesday.

The most unusual pre-match warm up came at Villa Park where Ron Atkinson had arranged for the tenor Renato to sing a few bars of Puccini in the changing room. It seemed to work as they beat QPR 4-1 but, despite the encouragement of fellow Argentinian Ricky Villa who was watching from the stands, Ardiles lost his first home match as Tottenham manager when Ian Wright's goal, three minutes from time, gave Arsenal a 1-0 victory.

Manchester United opened their title defence with a 2-0 win at Norwich and in their next game Roy Keane scored twice on his home debut with Mark Hughes getting the third from a classic Ryan Giggs run and cross in a 3-0 win against Sheffield United.

At the end of the first week life looked rosy for Howard Kendall when Tony Cottee scored a hat-trick for Everton who went top by beating Sheffield United 4-2. All three goals were from close range with a volley, a tap in and a header, but neighbouring Liverpool moved above them on goal difference when they won 5-0 at Swindon. It was the first time they had reached top spot since Graeme Souness became manager.

Three days later Chelsea, Southampton and Newcastle all recorded their first wins of the season. Chelsea beat QPR 2-0, Matt Le Tissier scored twice for the Saints as Swindon conceded five for the second game in a row and Kevin Keegan tasted managerial victory for the first time at this level when Malcolm Allen's chip was deflected over Neville Southall in Newcastle's 1-0 win against Everton.

The first managerial casualty came at the end of the month when, having started the season with a draw and three losses, Peter Reid was sacked by Manchester City after three years in charge, despite having finished ninth the previous season. He was replaced by Oxford's manager Brian Horton. For the other strugglers a 0-0 draw with Norwich gave Swindon their first point and first clean sheet in their fifth match. In contrast Liverpool made it four wins in five when they beat Leeds 2-0. Ian Rush scored his 200th goal for the Reds although it probably wasn't his classiest as it went in off his nose after the ball flicked up off his foot. John Lukic, the Leeds goalkeeper that day, had also been in goal for Arsenal when Rush scored his first for Liverpool 12 years before.

September

Manchester United beat West Ham 3-0 to open up a three-point lead at the top of the table while on the same day Horton's reign at their local rivals got off to a good start when Manchester City won 3-1 at the Premiership's early season whipping boys, Swindon. Across the Pennines an extraordinary second 45 minutes saw Sheffield Wednesday and Norwich draw 3-3, despite the match being goalless at half time. The home team scored three in 11

minutes only for Norwich to rally with three of their own in the next 13.

The defending champions suffered their first league defeat in 17 matches when they lost 1-0 to Chelsea. Gavin Peacock, Hoddle's new signing from Newcastle, scored after Peter Schmeichel was unable to hold Steve Clarke's shot. Also ending a record, albeit an unwanted one, were Leeds. After 24 league games without success Howard Wilkinson's team finally won away from home when they beat Southampton 2-0 at The Dell.

The Merseyside derby at Goodison Park on 18 September was even livelier than usual when Everton defeated Liverpool 2-0 to condemn them to a fourth loss in five games. When Mark Ward's shot went through a funnel of seven red shirts to open the scoring Steve McManaman and Bruce Grobbelaar reacted by having a playground-style scrap. At one point McManaman briefly shoved his goalkeeper in the face with both hands after being grabbed by the chin and pushed away. Their moods weren't improved when Tony Cottee took the ball round the keeper and nutmegged Mark Wright for the second.

A week later Everton suffered one of their heaviest ever home defeats when, despite having gone one up against Norwich, they lost 5-1. Efan Ekoku demonstrated superior pace and finishing to score four and there was also gloom in the red side of the city as Liverpool's 1-0 loss to Chelsea meant that they had completed their first pointless September for 90 years.

October

After nine games Manchester United led the table with 22 points, three ahead of Arsenal, with Aston Villa, Wimbledon and Leeds all on 16.

As the surprise package of the season so far, Wimbledon were featured on *Focus* with

Glenn Hoddle was appointed player-manager of Chelsea in the summer of 1993. Early season form was poor but things picked up after the signing of striker Mark Stein from Stoke.

Malcolm Allen scored Newcastle's winner against Everton to secure Kevin Keegan his first win as manager in the top flight.

their manager Joe Kinnear resenting the criticism that they were an unsophisticated long ball side. 'You've still got to have quality, balls have to be delivered really well and people don't give us credit for the type of balls that we deliver that hurt the opposition. It is too easy to say we just lump it into the middle.'

Just as Kinnear was talking about his talented players he was flattened by members of the first-team squad who rugby tackled and bundled him to the ground. As he recovered, out of breath and laughing, he added, 'the spirit is still the same, [they're] still a lovely bunch'.

Somehow it was hard to imagine the same scene at Manchester United who moved five points clear of Arsenal with a 3-2 win at Sheffield Wednesday. Leeds' good form continued when the two Garys put four past

Wimbledon. Speed brilliantly volleyed the first from Rod Wallace's cross, McAllister lifted a free kick over the Dons' wall and then he and Speed each added a second.

There was more woe for Everton who were leading Tottenham 2-1 with two minutes remaining at White Hart Lane but allowed the Darrens Anderton and Caskey to score and secure an unlikely win. It was, however, the start of a dreadful run for Ardiles' side who won only two of their next 23 games.

At the bottom of the table the pattern was already set after just ten matches. Sheffield United were 18th with nine points, just above Wednesday and Oldham who each had seven. Below them were Southampton on four points and, bottom and still without a win, Swindon who had just three. Four of them were still in the bottom five at the end of the season.

Presenter Bob Wilson

Goalkeeper Bob Wilson joined Arsenal in 1963 and retired 11 years later having won the European Fairs Cup in 1970 and the League and FA Cup Double in 1971. He had been a BBC pundit during the 1970 World Cup finals and was asked by Sam Leitch, the Head of Sport who also fronted the Saturday *Football Preview*, to join the BBC as a regular analyst when he retired.

'I first began presenting *Football Preview* in 1974 when it was renamed *Football Focus,* although I knew that it was a huge risk as no player had ever before gone straight into presenting. It was very demanding but being a recent former player helped enormously as I was able to get access to the teams.

The BBC did their utmost to keep me when I was headhunted to present ITV's football coverage. My last show was particularly memorable. It was the first of the 1994–95 season, live from Old Trafford. Alex Ferguson was on with me and when I finished I went into the scanner where the producer, John Shrewsbury, said to me, "You belong here, you've been here 20 years."

There have been two outstanding goalkeepers in the Premiership so far. I was coach to David Seaman for 15 years so have that obvious loyalty, but I couldn't split him and Peter Schmeichel as both are true greats. Just look at the trophies they won and the number of international caps they have between them and, despite having very different styles, no one has matched them.

Of course there are some really good keepers around. Petr Cech and Jens Lehmann are the best in the Premier League at the moment. Lehmann is technically better but players are aware that they can get to him by standing on his toe or roughing him up at corners. I also have massive admiration for Shay Given at Newcastle who is not the ideal size for a goalie but counters that with fantastic reactions and fast feet, and I think he's shown extraordinary consistency.

The game has become very different in the past few decades but I think that Arsène Wenger has probably changed the face of British football more than most. I played eight games as an amateur for Arsenal, turning up in my duffle coat and scarf in my first year. I would teach all day and train at night and on the day I made my Arsenal debut against Forest I had already refereed a game at Wormwood Scrubbs.

Arsène's players are obviously far better prepared than that. His philosophy is youth, power, pace, technique and he strongly believes that his team should be giving entertainment to the fans. He has brought a new technical attitude, changed the diets and drinking habits, and bought a lot of intelligent overseas players at a time when he couldn't afford to pay the prices that clubs were demanding for British ones.'

Bob Wilson saves at the feet of Nottingham Forest's Colin Addison at Highbury in 1963 – it was his first season at Arsenal.

Norwich won 2-1 at Chelsea to go second, and Liverpool registered their first league win since August and scored their first league goal in six games when they beat Oldham 2-1. It was also Robbie Fowler's first goal in the Premiership. Manchester United's 1-0 win at Everton stretched their lead to nine points when Lee Sharpe scored with the team's only shot on target. Leeds and Blackburn drew 3-3 but the match marked a return to form for Alan Shearer after an injury as he scored a hat-trick.

With Newcastle's promotion a lot of attention was focussed on their 22-year-old striker Andy Cole who had scored 26 goals in 25 games. Kevin Keegan was a huge fan of the latest hero to wear the famous No. 9 shirt. 'He's got electric pace, good feet, scores goals but is willing to work hard as well. If he carries on with the same attitude and willingness to learn he could be anything.' Keegan's assessment was pretty good as Cole went on to win five Premierships titles, two FA Cups, the League Cup and the Champions League and become the second highest scorer in the history of the Premiership. Unfortunately for Kevin all the glory and most of the goals came during his time at Manchester United.

When Coventry lost 5-1 at QPR their manager Bobby Gould immediately resigned. He told Bob Wilson on *Focus* the following week that he had had three chairmen in three months and 'didn't feel that the relationship with the new chairman, Brian Richardson, would work'. Phil Neal succeeded him as caretaker manager at Highfield Road.

Having been dropped for three games, Matt Le Tissier returned to the Southampton starting line-up and scored two stunning goals in a rare win for the Saints against Newcastle. The first was breathtaking with four touches and a half-volley. In their next game he scored two more when they lost 4-2 to Liverpool with Fowler collecting his first Premiership hat-trick. The month ended with Manchester United beating QPR 2-1 to stretch their lead to 11 points.

November

Tim Flowers became the world's most expensive goalkeeper when he followed Alan Shearer and moved from Southampton to Blackburn for £2m to take Kenny Dalglish's spending to more than £22m. He told *Focus*

Southampton's Matt Le Tissier is one of the finest players ever to have graced the Premiership stage. Although he was not a prolific scorer, he was a scorer of magnificent goals like the first of two in a 2-1 win against Newcastle at the Dell in October, for which he beat two defenders before half-volleying the ball into the back of the net.

that he had turned down the chance to move to Liverpool. 'The top line for me is that I'm going because I want to win a medal and I believe that Blackburn Rovers will do that.'

After 13 games Manchester United had 34 points, 11 ahead of their closest rivals Norwich and Bob Wilson noted that it was the biggest lead any club in the top division had ever had at the beginning of November.

Things weren't going too well for Glenn Hoddle at Chelsea and he saw them beaten for the fifth time in a row when Leeds put four past them in a 23-minute spell at Elland Road. By contrast, Southampton kept their first clean sheet in 14 games on the day that Ian Andrews replaced Flowers in goal. They beat Tottenham 1-0 as Blackburn lost by the same score at QPR.

Andy Cole's hat-trick for Newcastle against Liverpool took his tally to 16 for the season and, after 16 attempts, Swindon won a Premiership game for the first time when Keith Scott was the only scorer in their home match against QPR.

A 1-0 win at Coventry enabled Manchester United to stretch their lead to 14 points over Leeds who went second when they beat Swindon 3-0 with all the goals coming in the final ten minutes. Blackburn's progress stalled at Ipswich who managed their first win in a month thanks to a rare Eddie Youds' goal.

December

The season had reached the stage where managers were coming under pressure but Howard Kendall pre-empted the call from his chairman by resigning as Everton boss after their first home Premiership win in ten weeks when they beat Southampton 1-0. Jimmy Gabriel took over as caretaker as the club began an even worse run and failed to score in their next six league games.

At the top of the table Manchester United and Norwich drew 2-2 at Old Trafford to

leave the visitors with the bizarre statistic of having scored 24 away goals but just three at home. A few days later a confident and stylish United moved 15 points ahead after winning 3-0 at Bramall Lane against Sheffield United. Third-placed Blackburn continued to look strong and Alan Shearer was in inspirational form once again as they won 2-1 at Oldham. Despite having five defenders around him he still managed to prod in the first, Rick Holden equalised before half time but then Shearer's 14th goal of the season secured victory.

At the other end of the table Chelsea went second from bottom when they lost 3-1 to Southampton who had only scored three goals and taken three points from their previous seven games. The one small consolation was that Mark Stein scored his first goal for Chelsea following his £1.5m move from Stoke. Their fortune finally turned in their next match when Stein scored the only goal of the game against Newcastle. It was their first win in

The England squad at the turn of the year included (left to right) three million-pound-plus keepers in Blackburn's Tim Flowers (£2m), Arsenal's David Seaman (£1.3m) and Sheffield Wednesday's Chris Woods (£1.2m).

12 attempts. Swindon continued to leak goals when they lost 4-0 at home to Arsenal. Kevin Campbell hit a hat-trick and there was a stunning fourth from Ian Wright who spotted Fraser Digby off his line and chipped him from outside the box

January 1994

The New Year began with Manchester United on 56 points, an impressive 14 ahead of second-placed Blackburn. Leeds were a point back in third, Arsenal fourth with 40 and Newcastle fifth on 36. In contrast the bottom six clubs were only separated by five points: Manchester City were 17th with 20 from 22 games and below them came Oldham on 19, Chelsea, Southampton and Sheffield United all with 18 and, still propping up the table, Swindon who had clawed their way to 15 points.

Leeds managed to close the gap slightly when they held Manchester United to a 0-0 draw at Old Trafford in the first match of the year. The leaders' next game, however, was a candidate for match of the season. At one point they were three up against Liverpool through goals by Bruce, Giggs and Irwin, but the visitors fought back with three of their own in the second half to finish at 3-3. Nigel Clough scored twice and Neil Ruddock headed a third.

The first big row of the month came when Mike Walker resigned as Norwich manager to join Everton, who faced accusations of poaching. John Deehan replaced him at Carrow Road. Walker, who had taken Norwich to third place and secured a place in Europe the previous season, spoke to Ray Stubbs to explain why he resigned. 'I got pushed into a bit of a corner as there was no assurance of a contract on a personal note.

Pundit Gavin Peacock

Gavin Peacock captained Newcastle to promotion into the Premiership under Kevin Keegan and was then Glenn Hoddle's first major buy for Chelsea at the start of the 1993–94 season. He remained with the Blues for three years before moving to QPR.

'At Stamford Bridge I was fortunate to play with Gullit, Zola and Vialli, but as a pure and amazingly subtle player with the ability to get himself into a game Hoddle was one of, if not, the best. He was a maestro and in training it was as though he had a computer for a brain as he would scan all the options, spot the best one and then make the perfect play. You have to remember that it wasn't the side of today but Glenn was changing the face of Chelsea, the way we trained, our diet and our style.

The most memorable games of that first season for me were the two against Manchester United as we did the double over them and I scored the winner in both. They weren't the most spectacular goals but gave us crucial points against an amazing United side. After the first game Cantona described Hoddle as "like Mozart in a world of heavy metal".

The second one stands out as I scored it at Old Trafford in front of the Chelsea fans. Craig Burley picked the ball up and pinged it onto Mark Stein's head. I made my run and, as it bounced towards the goal, I saw Bruce and Schmeichel coming in. But I got to it first and clipped it over him. Schmeichel left stud marks all down my thigh that took two weeks to go and I reminded him of that when we first started working together at the BBC, but it was worth it just to get the satisfaction of that win.'

Radio Five Live

Radio Five Live has been the national home of Premiership football on the radio since the channel replaced its predecessor, Radio 5, in March 1994. The network devotes more than 20 hours a week to its Premier League coverage through Five Live Sport which runs on weekdays from 7 p.m. to 10 p.m. and at weekends from midday.

The main presenters are Mark Pougatch, Mark Saggers and Eleanor Oldroyd with Alan Green, Mike Ingham and John Murray among their leading match commentators. There are also reporters at every Premiership match and many other support shows including the famous fan phone-in, *606*, that runs on Wednesday, Saturday and Sunday evenings and whose presenters have included David Mellor, Richard Littlejohn, DJ Spoony, Adrian Chiles, Alan Green and Ray Stubbs.

Under the most recent contract deal with the Premier League there will be 224 matches broadcast on national radio for each of the three seasons starting in 2007–08. There are also matches on Five Live Sports Extra, a digital channel launched in 2002, and many other games are broadcast across the BBC's extensive local radio network.

I enjoyed my time there and left them with a bit of credibility in England and in Europe, but the bottom line is that there is a difference in ambition, that was my feeling.'

Four days later there was another managerial change, this time at Southampton when Ian Branfoot quit after two and a half years in charge. Alan Ball took over with former Saints boss Lawrie McMenemy returning as general manager.

Everton finally ended their seven-game run of six defeats and a draw when they beat Swindon 6-2 with Tony Cottee hitting his second Premiership hat-trick of the season. Their next match was at Old Trafford where the teams were led out by a piper in tribute to Sir Matt Busby, who had died that week aged 84. Manchester United extended their lead to 16 points when Ryan Giggs headed home Roy Keane's cross.

Another managerial change ended the month when Graeme Souness resigned from Liverpool after almost three years in charge. His assistant, Roy Evans, moved out of the famous Boot Room to succeed him. On *Match of the Day* Alan Hansen expressed surprise that Souness had gone as the team were fifth in the table at the time. However, in summing up the tough Scotsman's tenure in the hot seat at Anfield, Hansen concluded, 'He hasn't bought bad players but he hasn't bought great players, and there is no pace in the side.'

Meanwhile, in Manchester, former player Francis Lee took over as chairman of City from Peter Swales after buying his 29.9 per cent stake in the club. Jimmy Hill felt that he was very brave to do so. 'It's a hard life and I only hope that the torch he's holding up at the moment, with everyone's approval, won't burn his backside.'

February

Only two points separated the bottom five clubs after Swindon beat Coventry 3-1 with Jan-Aage Fjortoft hitting all three, while Blackburn narrowed the gap at the top to ten points with a game in hand when they beat Tottenham 2-0 at White Hart Lane. Shearer's goal meant that he had scored in 15 of their last 19 league games.

Alan Ball was still in his honeymoon period on the south coast and his first home match saw Southampton beat Liverpool 4-2. Matt Le Tissier's hat-trick included two penalties and moved the Saints out of the bottom three. Blackburn cut Manchester United's lead back to six points when they beat Newcastle 1-0 and then drew 2-2 at Norwich.

Newcastle moved into third spot when Andy Cole hit a second-half hat-trick against Coventry as part of their 4-0 win and there was yet another stunning strike from Le Tissier when Southampton beat Wimbledon 1-0 to improve their chances of survival. He was passed the ball from a free kick, chipped it up and casually volleyed it into the top corner. The Guernsey-based striker scored 25 of the club's 49 league goals during the season.

Blackburn's title hopes were damaged when Kevin Gallagher, who had scored seven league goals, fractured his leg and looked to be out for the season as they went down 1-0 at Arsenal while Manchester United drew 2-2 against West Ham at Upton Park.

March

Gavin Peacock's goal for Chelsea at Old Trafford on 5 March meant that both he and the club had scored an incredible league double over Manchester United, who had been unbeaten in 22 games since last succumbing to a Peacock goal at Stamford Bridge in September. Blackburn took full advantage and beat Liverpool 2-0 to cut the gap to four points while third-placed Arsenal's 5-1 win at Ipswich included an Ian Wright hat-trick. John Lyall's Tractor Boys did manage to win their next match, 1-0 against Aston Villa, but that was their last victory of the campaign.

Newcastle didn't even need a goal from Andy Cole when they gave Swindon their biggest hiding of the season, 7-1 at St James' Park, but Eric Cantona did contribute two of Manchester United's five against Sheffield Wednesday, a result that restored their seven-point lead.

In one of the biggest encounters of the season Arsenal and Manchester United

One bright point in a poor season for Swindon Town was the form of Norwegian striker Jan-Aage Fjortoft who scored 12 of the club's 47 goals. However, the real problems came at the other end as they became the first Premier League club to concede 100 goals in a season.

drew 2-2 at Highbury, a match which saw Eric Cantona sent off for the second time in four days having also been dismissed during their 2-2 draw at Swindon. Lee Sharpe, back after a three-month layoff with injury, got the first when David Seaman couldn't hold a Mark Hughes shot, but Paul Merson's free kick made it 1-1. Sharpe restored the lead after Nigel Winterburn deflected a Cantona shot into his path in front of goal and then Merson added his second with 12 minutes remaining. With nine games left to play Manchester United had 73 points, three in front of Blackburn with Newcastle on 60 and Arsenal with 58.

Chelsea recorded a fourth win in five games when their manager Glenn Hoddle came off the bench to score his first goal for the club during their 2–win over West Ham and, at the end of the month, Paul Ince scored the only goal of the match as Manchester United beat Liverpool to restore their six-point lead.

April

When Dalglish and Ferguson met head-on it was the younger of the two Scots who came out on top as Blackburn beat Manchester United 2-0 to move three points behind with seven games left. Inevitably both goals were scored by the deadly Alan Shearer. Having chased down a 16-point gap, Blackburn finally drew level with United on 79 points on 11 April when they beat Aston Villa 1-0, although their Manchester rivals still had a game in hand.

The points stayed the same as both teams lost their next games, Blackburn 3-1 at Southampton and United at 1–0 Wimbledon, while rivals Arsenal beat Chelsea 1-0. It was Seaman's 21st clean sheet in his 36th match and Ian Wright's 21st goal of the campaign. In a dramatic finish at Norwich Southampton recovered from 3-1 down to win 5-4 thanks to a last-minute winner by

Ken Monkou. Le Tissier had already scored a hat-trick in the highest scoring game of the season.

The next twist came when Eric Cantona scored twice on his return from suspension to win the Manchester derby and Blackburn could only draw at QPR to leave them two points behind with only three games left and United with a game in hand. Rovers kept their title hopes alive with a 2-1 victory at West Ham but Ferguson's men responded with a 2-0 win at Elland Road where Cantona was roundly booed all night.

Swindon's inevitable return straight to Division One was confirmed when Wimbledon beat them 4-2. The first goal was a stunning 13th minute long-range strike by John Fashanu who spotted Nicky Hammond off his line and chipped him. Wimbledon next damaged Oldham's survival chances with a 3-0 win at Selhurst Park as they moved up to sixth place.

When Newcastle beat Villa 5-1 Andy Cole notched up his 40th goal of the season in all competitions, a record for Newcastle, and Kevin Keegan spoke to *Focus* about their great first season in the Premiership. 'Sir John Hall used to be a multi- millionaire until I came here and I'm doing my best to just make him an ordinary one. We've bought some good players and within a few days they feel very much at home and that's why I think all the signings have come in and done well.'

With two weeks of the season left Manchester United had 85 points from 39 games, Blackburn were on 83 having played 40 and Newcastle were in third place a further nine points behind. A host of teams could still go down with Oldham, Sheffield United, Southampton, Everton, Ipswich, Tottenham and Manchester City all in the danger zone. Oldham had a game in hand over most of the sides but lost it 0-2 to Tottenham who ensured their own safety at the same time.

Above Alan Shearer leaps above Paul Parker to score one of his two goals against Manchester United in a 2-0 win at Ewood Park.

Opposite Chelsea's Gavin Peacock celebrates after scoring the winner against Manchester United at Old Trafford. It was the second time that he'd scored in two 1-0 wins for the Londoners as the Blues did the double over the Reds.

May

Manchester United beat Ipswich 2-1 at Portman road on May Day to go five points ahead with two games left. After Chris Kiwomya had given Ipswich the lead, Andre Kanchelskis crossed for Cantona to head level and Giggs scored the winner. A day later it was all over when Blackburn lost 2-1 at Coventry to give United the title. It was their ninth league title in all and, for the second year in a row, they were crowned without playing. As in the previous season they ran out in their final home game at Old Trafford as champions. This time they beat Southampton 2-0.

The final Saturday of the season began with five clubs still hoping to avoid finishing in the two remaining

Right Captain Steve Bruce and striker Mark Hughes show off the trophies that represented Manchester United's first-ever league and cup double. They were the fourth club to achieve this in the 20th century, emulating Tottenham Hotspur, Arsenal and Liverpool.

Awards

Footballer of the Year
Alan Shearer, Blackburn Rovers

PFA Player of the Year
Eric Cantona, Manchester United

PFA Young Player of the Year
Andy Cole, Newcastle United

Final League Table

Team	P	W	D	L	F	A	Pts
Manchester United	42	27	11	4	80	38	92
Blackburn Rovers	42	25	9	8	63	36	84
Newcastle United	42	23	8	11	82	41	77
Arsenal	42	18	17	7	53	28	71
Leeds United	42	18	16	8	65	39	70
Wimbledon	42	18	11	13	56	53	65
Sheffield Wednesday	42	16	16	10	76	54	64
Liverpool	42	17	9	16	59	55	60
QPR	42	16	12	14	62	61	60
Aston Villa	42	15	12	15	46	50	57
Coventry City	42	14	14	14	43	45	56
Norwich City	42	12	17	13	65	61	53
West Ham United	42	13	13	16	47	58	52
Chelsea	42	13	12	17	49	53	51
Tottenham Hotspur	42	11	12	19	54	59	45
Manchester City	42	9	18	15	38	49	45
Everton	42	12	8	22	42	63	44
Southampton	42	12	7	23	49	66	43
Ipswich Town	42	9	16	17	35	58	43
Sheffield United	42	8	18	16	42	60	42
Oldham Athletic	42	9	13	20	42	68	40
Swindon Town	42	5	15	22	47	100	30

Leading Goalscorers league only

Andy Cole	Newcastle United	34
Alan Shearer	Blackburn Rovers	31
Chris Sutton	Norwich City	25
Matthew Le Tissier	Southampton	25
Ian Wright	Arsenal	23
Peter Beardsley	Newcastle United	21
Mark Bright	Sheffield Wednesday	19
Eric Cantona	Manchester United	18
Dean Holdsworth	Wimbledon	17
Rod Wallace	Leeds United	17

relegation spots. Everton conceded two at home to Wimbledon but recovered to win 3-2 and stay up. Ipswich were saved by their goalless draw at Blackburn leaving them a point and a place above the drop and Southampton's 3–3 draw at West Ham was enough to keep their place in the Premiership for another year.

Swindon ended their adventure in the top flight with a 5–0 thrashing by Leeds and they were joined in Division One by Sheffield United, who lost 3-2 at Chelsea, and Oldham, who drew at Norwich.

Andy Cole and Peter Beardsley both scored against Arsenal to take their collective league tally to 55 for the campaign as Newcastle secured third place at the end of an incredible first Premiership season on Tyneside.

Honours List 1993–94

Champions Manchester United

Runners-up Blackburn Rovers

Relegated Sheffield United, Oldham Athletic, Swindon Town

Promoted Crystal Palace, Nottingham Forest, Leicester City

FA Cup Winners Manchester United

League Cup Winners Aston Villa

European Cup-Winners' Cup Winners Arsenal

League Cup
Aston Villa beat Manchester United 3-1 to end their treble hopes. Two goals from Dean Saunders and one by Dalian Atkinson gave Villa the trophy for the fourth time in the club's history.

FA Cup
Although they had beaten Manchester United in both their league encounters that season Chelsea could find no way through the United defence at Wembley and lost 4-0. Eric Cantona scored twice from the penalty spot with Mark Hughes and Brian McClair adding one apiece to give United the double and a record-equalling eighth FA Cup win.

European Cup-Winners' Cup
Arsenal beat Parma in Copenhagen to lift the European Cup-Winners' Cup after Alan Smith scored the game's only goal in the 19th minute.

FF 1994-95

Alan Shearer and Chris Sutton celebrate with the Premiership trophy on the pitch at Anfield. Despite losing 2-1 to Liverpool, Manchester United's failure to beat West Ham meant that Blackburn had won the title.

Programmes

The main *Grandstand* presenter, Steve Rider, took on the additional *Football Focus* duties when Bob Wilson left the BBC after the first show of the new season. Ray Stubbs also hosted on several occasions when Steve was based at an outside broadcast and Dougie Donnelly presented *Focus* when he was fronting *Grandstand*. Steve introduced the second edition with a tribute to his predecessor. 'The first thing that needs to be said at the start of today is that the transfer market has been pretty active this week, witness the empty chair alongside me filled for something like the past 20 years by Bob Wilson but now departed to our friends and rivals at ITV. They've got a good man and we've lost an excellent colleague.'

Presenter
Steve Rider

Pre-season

Chris Sutton became Kenny Dalglish's latest headline – grabbing name when he moved from Norwich to Blackburn in July for a new British record fee of £5m and Tottenham boss Ossie Ardiles also electrified the transfer market when he signed Germany's World Cup star Jurgen Klinsmann from Monaco for £2m.

Dalgish's former team-mate, Bruce Grobbelaar, ended a 13-year spell at Liverpool when he joined Southampton, John Fashanu switched from Wimbledon to Aston Villa for £1.35m and, having been at the club for 27 years, Billy Bonds was replaced as West Ham manager by his assistant Harry Redknapp.

It was to be a pivotal season for the Premiership as the league was being reduced from 22 to 20 clubs. This meant that four teams would be relegated and only two promoted in their place.

August 1994

The Premiership began with the defending champions Manchester United beating QPR 2-0 and there were debut goals for John Fashanu in Aston Villa's 2-2 draw at Everton and Dutch striker Brian Roy who had just joined newly promoted Nottingham Forest. His chip into the top left-hand corner of the net secured an opening-day win at Ipswich. Jurgen Klinsmann also scored on his debut as Tottenham won 4-3 at Sheffield Wednesday. Darren Anderton passed from the right and, with the defence too slow to pick him up, Klinsmann headed it home as though in a training ground practice match. He dived in celebration to try and refute the allegations that that was how he won his penalties. Klinsmann added to his tally with an overhead volley and a header on his home debut when Tottenham beat Everton 2-1.

Long-server Sol Campbell

Sol Campbell has made more than 439 league appearances for just three teams during his 15 seasons of Premiership football.

He made his debut for Tottenham in December 1992 but that was his only appearance of the season, although he established himself in the following years and captained them to success in the League Cup in 1999. In 2001 he made a headline-grabbing move to Arsenal where he won two FA Cups and two Premiership titles before joining Harry Redknapp at Portsmouth in August 2006. Campbell was also capped 69 times by England during his career.

New boys Crystal Palace had the toughest initiation losing 6-1 at home to Liverpool and in his first appearance for Southampton Bruce Grobbelaar saved a penalty from Alan Shearer, although the latter still scored the first of his 34 league goals in their 1-1 draw at The Dell. Chris Sutton opened his account in midweek when Blackburn beat Leicester 3-0. Shearer scored as well and their remarkable partnership was underway – at least one of them would score in 30 of the 42 league games this season.

This was the campaign that saw the emergence of a golden crop of Premiership goalscorers and many of them got off to a great start. Sutton hit his first hat-trick for his new team when they beat Coventry 4-0, Robbie Fowler scored three in five minutes in Liverpool's 3-0 win over Arsenal and Stan Collymore collected the ball from 40 yards out, turned, shrugged off two defenders, and drilled a shot into the bottom right-hand corner of Leicester's net as Forest won 1-0.

A 2-1 win at Everton in midweek gave Frank Clark's Forest ten points from their first four games and saw them briefly top the table, although they were soon replaced by Newcastle whose fourth straight win, 3-1 against West Ham at Upton Park, had produced their best start since 1908.

September

Coventry were involved in two big money transfers when Phil Babb left them to become the most expensive defender in British football, moving to Liverpool for £3.75m. They spent £2m of that on Dion Dublin who had only played 12 league games in his two years at Old Trafford, but he made an immediate impact, heading the equaliser on his debut in Coventry's 2-2 draw at QPR.

Forest's new hero, Bryan Roy, was one of the first of a new breed of international players who were now looking at the Premier League as the place to play their football. The Dutch striker was interviewed at his home in Nottingham and told Barry Davies that he had learnt from his mentor, Johan Cruyff, who was manager of Ajax when Roy made his debut aged just 17. He won the

October

At the start of the month Newcastle extended their lead to five points, winning 2-0 at Aston Villa through goals by Rob Lee and Andy Cole, and on the same day Blackburn's unbeaten run ended in match eight when they lost 2-1 at Norwich. Liverpool returned to form after three games without a win when Steve McManaman's brace helped them defeat Sheffield Wednesday 4-1. In the *Focus* round-up that week Clive Tyldesley described the 'exhilarating confidence oozing out of Steve McManaman since Roy Evans's decision to give him a roving commission'.

The blue half of the city ended the afternoon in deep despair, however, when their 2-0 loss against Manchester United left them three points adrift at the bottom with just three points from eight starts. Manager Mike Walker spoke to John Motson who pointed out that they had only won five out of 29 games since he arrived. 'I had to work with a team that was already there,' said Walker, 'but I've brought in Amokachi, Samways and Burrows and it is just a matter of time before it turns around. I signed a contract and I expect that to be honoured.'

Although a new television deal for Premier League rights meant that money was beginning to pour into the players' pockets, those pockets were all too often on dodgy outfits as Newcastle's Barry Venison proved when he joined Steve Rider as the studio guest on *Focus*. The immaculately dressed Rider looked at Venison in his loud checked outfit with the added value of a different check on the sleeves combined with a multi-coloured tie and a long blond mullet and remarked, 'I think Take That might make an offer for the jacket.'

Forest striker Bryan Roy (centre) formed a scintillating strike partnership with Stan Collymore. They scored 11 goals between them in an 11-match unbeaten run between August and October.

UEFA Cup with Ajax in 1992, went to Italy to play for Foggia and then flew with his wife to Nottingham for three days and fell in love with the countryside and the club. His manager, Frank Clark, was impressed. 'He has great pace, superb balance and great awareness.' He scored 13 league goals during the season.

Leicester, who had been promoted through the play-offs, finally won a match when they defeated Tottenham 3-1. Julian Joachim hit the first and third goals and set up David Lowe for the second. It was one of only six wins for Brian Little's side during the entire season, the worst record in all four divisions.

In contrast Newcastle's strong start continued when they collected their sixth successive three-point haul, winning 3-2 at Highbury and going four points clear at the top of the table. The lead was again narrowed to two points when Forest won 4-1 at White Hart Lane and Blackburn beat Aston Villa 3-1. After Sutton and Shearer had already scored, the third goal was simple and would

Sheffield Wednesday racked up only their second win of the season when a great ball from Chris Bart-Williams to an unmarked David Hirst set him up to put the ball past Peter Schmeichel as they beat Manchester United 1-0, and Newcastle's fifth straight away win was secured at Crystal Palace when Peter Beardsley scored in the 89th minute to restore their five-point lead at the summit.

Leicester pulled off one of the great comebacks of the season when they recovered from 3-0 down against Southampton with 12 minutes remaining to win 4-3, but that form was eluding Everton whose 1-0 loss at Palace was their fourth successive defeat and meant that, despite Walker's optimism, they had taken just three points from a possible 33.

After 11 games Newcastle were on 29 points, two ahead of Forest with Manchester United a further five back and Blackburn in fourth place on 21. Everton were in a desperate position on the bottom with Ipswich and QPR above them on seven points and Wimbledon and Leicester with nine. However, the Magpies' season turned in their final match of the month when they lost 2-0 at Manchester United. It was their first defeat but, with Andy Cole missing for a month with shin splints, they only won two out of their next 12 games.

November

There were several managerial changes at the beginning of the month as chairmen ran out of patience. Ardiles was sacked by Tottenham and replaced by QPR boss Gerry Francis, Joe Royle took on the Everton job when Mike Walker was fired and Ron Atkinson was dismissed from Villa as they had only won two of their first 14 games.

That number was luckier for Robbie Fowler who took his goal tally to 14 in 14 when he scored a brace against Chelsea as part of a 3-1 win that moved Liverpool into third place. Manchester United went second, two points behind Newcastle, when they demolished City 5-0, with Andrei Kanchelskis' hat-trick helping them to their biggest-ever derby win.

Newcastle were finally knocked off top spot when they lost 3-2 at Wimbledon and were overtaken by Manchester United, who beat Crystal Palace 3-0, and Blackburn, who beat Ipswich 3-1 at Portman Road. Leicester's fourth successive defeat, 1-0 against Manchester City, saw them second bottom with just nine points. Two places and four points above were managerless Aston Villa and, after several days of press speculation, Brian Little quit Leicester to take charge at Villa Park. 'I wasn't getting up in the morning and coming in with my usual zest and enthusiasm so it was time to do something different,' he said on *Focus*. His successor at Filbert Street was Mark McGhee.

Robbie Fowler's prolific season continued and his goals kept Liverpool in contention for the title as they headed into the New Year in third place.

Presenter Steve Rider

Steve Rider joined BBC Sport from ITV to front *Sportsnight* in 1985. He switched to *Grandstand* six years later and became the longest serving presenter of the show before moving back to ITV in 2005. Steve presented *Football Focus* for two years when Bob Wilson left the BBC after the first edition of the 1994–95 season.

'I didn't have any great football qualifications to present *Focus* but Bob had left rather suddenly and I was happy to take it on. It didn't really have a seperate identity at the time and was more a very long football opening to *Grandstand*, but it was the most challenging period of the show for me because for two seasons I had to be a contortionist in the presenter chair.

We would start with a fairly detailed football magazine and end with a comprehensive round-up whilst having several hours of rugby, racing and a host of other sports in between. It was a real examination of what we could do, not least because there was no autocue, but we tried to always make the five-hour show appear as seamless as possible.

They were exhilarating shows to present as I felt involved throughout and sat at the hub of things as *Grandstand* was still a studio-based programme and it was far more satisfying from my point of view than later years when everything became very fragmented.

That period did spawn a kind of *Focus* mania as cricket and athletics both gained their own editions and I remember once presenting the third round of The Open at Troon and being joined by Geoff Boycott to do a section of *Cricket Focus* in the middle of the golf!

I think that to have *Final Score* in *Grandstand* was a strength but although I enjoyed introducing it I was always an advocate of *Football Focus* being floated off as a separate football magazine show.'

Joe Royle made a winning start in the hot seat at Goodison as Everton beat Liverpool 2-0 to move off the bottom. Duncan Ferguson scored his first goal for the club and Paul Rideout added a second to secure the first of the three successive wins and two draws that lifted them to a safer position.

Four days later Arsenal's Paul Merson opened the public's eyes to another side of the game when he told the *Daily Mirror* about his cocaine, drink and gambling addictions. His club and the PFA offered support and Graham Kelly, the Chief Executive of the FA, told *Focus* that 'the emphasis is on treatment and rehabilitation'.

Gary Lineker returned from Japan having retired from football after scoring 330 goals in 15 seasons and was set to resume his career as a regular pundit on *Football Focus*, while his successor in the England team, Alan Shearer, hit three when Blackburn beat QPR 4-0 to go top, a position they maintained for most of the rest of the season.

when they went down 4-1 at home against Sheffield Wednesday. Goals by Nick Barmby and Teddy Sheringham resulted in Norwich's first home defeat since April as Tottenham came away with a 2-0 win. Manchester United briefly held top spot after their 3-2 win at Chelsea but Blackburn's 3-1 victory at Manchester City in the evening gave them a two-point cushion with 46 in the bag after 20 games played. Newcastle were third with 39 followed by Liverpool and Nottingham Forest, both on 36.

There was another round of games two days later and Brian Little gained his first win in his seventh match in charge of Villa, beating Chelsea 3-0. Robbie Fowler hit a spectacular left-foot shot to score Liverpool's second and take them into third spot after Terry Phelan's own goal had put Manchester City behind and George Burley, the new Ipswich manager, saw his side lose 2-0 at home to Arsenal.

December

Stuck at the bottom of the table, Ipswich became the latest club to lose their boss when John Lyall, who had masterminded their promotion to the Premier League in 1992, resigned after four years at Portman Road. Paul Goddard and John Wark took temporary charge of the club before former defender George Burley became the new manager.

After seven wins in a row Blackburn were held to a 0-0 draw by Leicester but still led Manchester United by two points when they were beaten 2-1 at home by Nottingham Forest. Stan Collymore and Stuart Pearce scored the first league goals to be conceded at Old Trafford since 4 April.

Boxing Day threw up a mixed bag of results with four 0-0 draws, but Everton conceded their first league goals in eight games after a club record seven clean sheets

Stan Collymore scores Nottingham Forest's first goal in a 2-1 win over Manchester United. It was the first league goal that United had conceded at Old Trafford since 4 April.

January 1995

Alan Shearer began the new year with a hat-trick in Blackburn's 4-2 win over West Ham, taking him to 20 league goals and his team to a six-point lead, although the gap was narrowed again the next day when Manchester United beat Coventry 2-0.

A week later Alex Ferguson pulled off the transfer coup of the season when he signed Andy Cole from Newcastle for £7m, a new British record that was made up by £6m in cash plus Keith Gillespie. On *Focus* Steve Rider remarked that, "The deal and secrecy were astonishing and have set a new benchmark for British football. Cole, the hero of St. James' Park, now at Old Trafford.' Newcastle's chairman Sir John Hall claimed that the sale was to allow the manager to reinvest in the squad, not to give money to the bank, and Kevin Keegan agreed. 'It's not a gamble from our point of view as I'm looking to improve the club and I think it

was an offer we couldn't refuse bearing in mind where we want to go.'

Twenty-nine-year-old Tony Cottee was in great form in his second spell at West Ham with six goals in his last five league games and, as he was known to have kept a close record and scrapbook of his own career, Clive Tyldesley interviewed him via a series of personalised questions as Cottee sat in the famous *Mastermind* chair. Cottee had been the leading goalscorer for West Ham in four of his five full seasons at Upton Park and had also been the top marksman in five of his six seasons at Everton, scoring 99 goals for them in total. He once again topped the chart for the Hammers with 13 Premiership goals in this campaign.

Liverpool suffered a surprise defeat at home to Ipswich when 21-year-old Adam Tanner, who was making only his third appearance, gave the Suffolk club their first ever win at Anfield. The joy was short-

Premiership-winning manager Kenny Dalglish

Kenny Dalglish is the only Premiership-winning manager to have had an outstanding playing career as well and is the third man, after Herbert Chapman and Brian Clough, to have led two different clubs to the English League title.

Born on 4 March 1951 in Glasgow he won nine major trophies with Celtic before moving to Liverpool in 1977 for a then British record fee of £440,000. In eight seasons as a player he added three European Cups, four League Cups and another five League Championships to his collection as well as becoming the first player to score 100 goals in both the English and Scottish leagues.

Dalglish became Liverpool's player-manager in 1985 at the age of 34 and led them

to the double in his first season. The club won two more titles and another FA Cup under his management before his sudden resignation in February 1991.

He was back in the game eight months later, this time as manager of Blackburn, taking them into the Premier League and spending Jack Walker's millions wisely to create a Premiership-winning side in the 1994–95 season, but left the club the following year.

The Scot was back in the top flight in January 1997 at Newcastle and took them to second place in his first season. After finishing 13th the following year he was sacked and, since a brief spell in charge of Celtic in 2000, Dalglish has enjoyed an extended break from the game.

lived though as they lost 14 of their next 18 games.

After 23 matches, Blackburn led the table with 55 points with Manchester United on 49 and Liverpool and Forest, who had each played a game more, on 45 and 42. West Ham, Everton, Ipswich and Leicester were in the relegation places.

On 15 January Ray Stubbs presented *Focus* from White Hart Lane ahead of Tottenham's home fixture against Manchester City. The programme started with Gary Lineker wandering around the ground to the inevitable strains of the Peters and Lee song 'Welcome Home'. Gary was already a busy man: as well as *Focus* he was also joining *Match of the Day* as a pundit and fronting *Sunday Sport* on Radio Five Live.

Despite the return from Japan of English football's favourite son it was a Frenchman who dominated the front and back page headlines for the rest of the month. Eric Cantona scored the game's only goal when the top two met at Old Trafford to reduce the gap to two points. And in their next game, a 1-1 draw at Crystal Palace, he provided the defining moment of the season. Having been sent off for kicking Richard Shaw, Cantona then launched a two-footed attack on an allegedly abusive spectator, before United's kit man, Norman Davies, pulled him away. The club suspended him for the rest of the season and he lost the French captaincy and was barred from the national team. The FA later suspended him until 30 September.

Meanwhile over at Ewood Park the leaders simply carried on winning with Shearer collecting his third hat-trick of the season in their 4-1 thrashing of Ipswich.

February

Manchester United closed the gap to two points once again by beating Aston Villa, courtesy of Andy Cole's first goal for the club. Then sixth-placed Tottenham inflicted

a 3-1 defeat on Blackburn to leave them looking suddenly vulnerable. Jurgen Klinsmann put the first through Bobby Mimms' legs after 18 minutes and Darren Anderton's shot left the keeper rooted when it took a deflection off defender Colin Hendry. Steve Sherwood pulled one back in the second half before a spectacular diving header by Nick Barmby wrapped up the points for Tottenham.

Coventry, who were having an otherwise anonymous season, sacked manager Phil Neal after 15 months at the helm and replaced him with Ron Atkinson whose former club, Aston Villa, produced their biggest win for 33 years when they beat

Below Beauty and the Beast. Eric Cantona scored the winner against top-of-the-table Blackburn to reduce their lead to two points. However, in United's next match, away at Crystal Palace, he attacked a spectator (bottom) who had hurled abuse at the Frenchman as he left the pitch having been sent off.

Liverpool's Jamie Redknapp gives his side the lead against Manchester United at Anfield with a left-foot drive. Steve McManaman added a second five minutes from time to secure the points.

March

Manchester United began the month by setting a new Premiership goalscoring record when they thrashed Ipswich 9-0. Andy Cole hit five goals, Mark Hughes two and Roy Keane and Paul Ince the others. United had started the day with a goal difference that was six worse than Blackburn's, but had wiped out the deficit in one game. However, their rivals beat Villa 1-0 on the same day to maintain a three-point lead at the top. With 11 games remaining, Kenny Dalglish's team had 69 points from 31 games. In the relegation zone Leicester were bottom with 21, two points below Ipswich with West Ham on 29 and Palace on 30.

Blackburn moved six points clear again when they beat Chelsea 2-1. Brian Stein put the Londoners ahead but Shearer and Sherwood scored to clinch the win and Manchester United blew three points when they lost 2-0 to Liverpool. Jamie Redknapp's left foot shot gave Roy Evans' side the lead and they sealed it with five minutes remaining when McManaman's effort was deflected off Steve Bruce's left leg.

Three days later United recovered their form to beat Arsenal 3-0. Alex Ferguson had used his programme notes to question whether the team still had the hunger for the championship. Mark Hughes, Lee Sharpe and Andrei Kanchelskis got the goals that proved they did. Southampton went 1-0 down against Newcastle but scored three in the final five minutes to secure the points, although they stayed in the drop zone. It was the start of a spell that saw them win six, draw three and lose two of their final 11 games to finish tenth as Alan Ball managed to re-motivate them. Neil Heaney levelled, new signing Gordon Watson tapped in his first for the club when Pavel Srnicek dropped the ball and then, when he failed to gather cleanly, the Czech keeper was punished again, this time by Neil Shipperley.

Wimbledon 7-1. Also out of work was Arsenal's most successful-ever manager, George Graham, who won six trophies in his nine seasons in charge at Highbury. He was sacked by the club following the Premier League Commission's investigation into allegations that he had received 'bungs'. Rick Parry, the Premier League Chief Executive, confirmed that Graham had received £425,500 from football agent Rune Hauge as part of several transfer deals he had conducted, although the money had now been returned to the club along with £40,000 in interest.

Gary Lineker felt that 'with George Graham the evidence was quite damning but to think that he is the only one takes some imagination. In the past, with some managers, it's almost been seen as an accepted perk.' He suggested a central clearing house for transfers. Stewart Houston took temporary charge at Highbury for the remainder of the season.

April

Sheffield Wednesday suffered their worst ever home defeat when Forest beat them 7-1 with Bryan Roy and Stan Collymore scoring two apiece while Chris Sutton's 67th-minute goal at QPR meant that Blackburn's lead was extended to eight points with six games remaining. Alan Shearer told *Focus*, 'We'd rather be eight points clear than eight behind as we were always chasing Man Utd last season and now it's the other way round. I'd rather be in our position.'

Grand National Saturday saw a brief edition of *Focus* presented from Aintree by Des Lynam with Gary Lineker. They profiled Gerry Francis, who was reviving Tottenham's fortunes, and included some surprising footage of a young Gerry on a 1964 BBC TV Show called *Open House* where he was judging a pigeon competition.

Arsenal continued their wretched form when they lost their sixth game in seven, 1-0 at home to Liverpool, and dropped to 13th in the league, just two points off the relegation zone with only five games left.

On 13 April Leicester became the first team to be relegated when West Ham beat Wimbledon 3-0 to continue an unbeaten run of five games. Cottee scored the third and felt that this was 'probably the best

This was a familiar sight at Premier League grounds around the country during the 1994–95 season as Blackburn's Alan Shearer topped the scoring charts with 34 league goals in his club's championship-winning season.

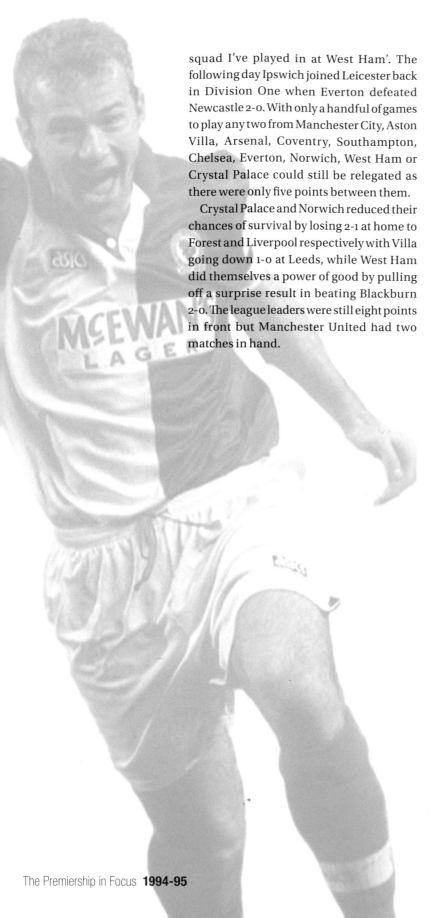

squad I've played in at West Ham'. The following day Ipswich joined Leicester back in Division One when Everton defeated Newcastle 2-0. With only a handful of games to play any two from Manchester City, Aston Villa, Arsenal, Coventry, Southampton, Chelsea, Everton, Norwich, West Ham or Crystal Palace could still be relegated as there were only five points between them.

Crystal Palace and Norwich reduced their chances of survival by losing 2-1 at home to Forest and Liverpool respectively with Villa going down 1-0 at Leeds, while West Ham did themselves a power of good by pulling off a surprise result in beating Blackburn 2-0. The league leaders were still eight points in front but Manchester United had two matches in hand.

May

Norwich finally lost their relegation battle after losing 2-1 at Leeds, their seventh successive defeat, while Coventry won 3-1 at Tottenham and Everton 1-0 at Ipswich to ensure their Premiership status for the following season. West Ham fans could also relax when their 3-0 victory over Liverpool made them safe. Meanwhile, at the top Manchester United had won both their games in hand and narrowed the gap on Blackburn to two points with one match to play.

On the final weekend of the Premiership Ray Stubbs asked, 'Has there ever been such a magnificent finale to the season?' and on *Match of the Day* Des Lynam opened by noting that 'Four hundred and fifty two games have been played and the championship had come down to the last day of the season.'

Blackburn, on 89 points, needed to win at Anfield to be sure of the title, but if they slipped and Manchester United won at West Ham then the Reds would be celebrating. Both managers spoke to *Focus* and Dalglish talked about how proud he was of his team whatever the outcome. Ferguson dismissed alleged rumours that Liverpool might not try. 'Everyone knows West Ham will run a million miles against us. All these rumours about Liverpool are an insult. For them not to try is unthinkable.' No mind games there then.

Shearer gave Blackburn the lead after 20 minutes but Liverpool captain John Barnes levelled the scores in the second half and, just before the final whistle, Jamie Redknapp's free kick flew into the top left-hand corner of the visitors' net for the winner. Blackburn look stunned but then the players started to hug each other and cheer and celebrate as news of Manchester United's 1-1 draw at West Ham filtered through. In the commentary box John Motson was amazed at the scenes he was describing. 'And Blackburn are suddenly celebrating. They must have heard something else from West Ham. I don't believe any of this, it's just too much like a fairy story. They are 2-1 down and they're celebrating!' An emotional club chairman, Jack Walker, watched from the stands as the trophy was presented to his team on the Anfield pitch. Blackburn Rovers were champions for the first time in 81 years.

Manager Dalglish, who had bought all 11 players who started the game, was ecstatic. 'I just had the feeling it was going to be our day. To win this is magnificent, as we've come from nowhere and we've done it.' The win also meant that Dalglish became only the third manager, after Herbert Chapman and Brian Clough, to win the title with two different clubs.

German striker Jurgen Klinsmann scored 20 goals in a never-to-be forgotten season at White Hart Lane before returning to Germany to play for Bayern Munich.

Final League Table

Team	P	W	D	L	F	A	Pts
Blackburn Rovers	42	27	8	7	80	39	89
Manchester United	42	26	10	6	77	28	88
Nottingham Forest	42	22	11	9	72	43	77
Liverpool	42	21	11	10	65	37	74
Leeds United	42	20	13	9	59	38	73
Newcastle United	42	20	12	10	67	47	72
Tottenham Hotspur	42	16	14	12	66	58	62
QPR	42	17	9	16	61	59	60
Wimbledon	42	15	11	16	48	65	56
Southampton	42	12	18	12	61	63	54
Chelsea	42	13	15	14	50	55	54
Arsenal	42	13	12	17	52	49	51
Sheffield Wednesday	42	13	12	17	49	57	51
West Ham United	42	13	11	18	44	48	50
Everton	42	11	17	14	44	51	50
Coventry City	42	12	14	16	44	62	50
Manchester City	42	12	13	17	53	64	49
Aston Villa	42	11	15	16	51	56	48
Crystal Palace	42	11	12	19	34	49	45
Norwich City	42	10	13	19	37	54	43
Leicester City	42	6	11	25	45	80	29
Ipswich Town	42	7	6	29	36	93	27

Awards

Footballer of the Year
Jurgen Klinsmann, Tottenham Hotspur

PFA Player of the Year
Alan Shearer, Blackburn Rovers

PFA Young Player of the Year
Robbie Fowler, Liverpool

Leading Goalscorers league only

Alan Shearer	Blackburn Rovers	34
Robbie Fowler	Liverpool	25
Les Ferdinand	QPR	24
Stan Collymore	Nottingham Forest	22
Andy Cole	Manchester United	21*
Jurgen Klinsmann	Tottenham Hotspur	20
Matt Le Tissier	Southampton	19
Ian Wright	Arsenal	18
Teddy Sheringham	Tottenham Hotspur	18

* including 9 for Newcastle

Blackburn Rovers take the applause of their own travelling fans as well as the Liverpool supporters at Anfield as they celebrate championship glory for the first time in 80 years.

Blackburn finished with 89 points, one ahead of Manchester United with Forest a further 11 back in third place. Alan Shearer had played in every match, hit three hat-tricks and scored 34 league goals. Liverpool and Leeds also qualified for Europe. At the other end of the table Crystal Palace completed the relegation group when they lost 3-2 at Newcastle and a few days later Alan Smith was sacked as their manager. Brian Horton became the 12th Premiership manager to be dismissed when Manchester City let him go after they finished 17th, just two places and four points above relegation. Trevor Francis also stepped down from the hot seat after a disappointing season at Sheffield Wednesday. Also leaving was Jurgen Klinsmann who ended his season as Tottenham's skipper for the day in their 1-1 draw with Leeds having contributed 20 league goals and helped them finish seventh in the table.

Honours List 1994–95

Champions Blackburn Rovers

Runners-up Manchester United

Relegated Crystal Palace, Norwich City, Leicester City, Ipswich Town

Promoted Middlesbrough, Bolton Wanderers

FA Cup Winners Everton

League Cup Winners Liverpool

League Cup
Steve McManaman scored twice in the Coca-Cola Cup final as Liverpool secured the first trophy of the season by beating Bolton Wanderers 2-1. Alan Thompson got Bolton's goal.

FA Cup
Since Everton had last won the FA Cup in 1984 they had lost five consecutive Wembley finals and, in a season of indifferent league form, the competition had become their main focus. The only goal in the final against Manchester United came after half an hour when Paul Rideout headed Everton into the lead. At the end of 90 minutes Dave Watson lifted the Cup leaving United without a major trophy for the first time in six years.

FF 1995–96

Stan Collymore looks delighted as he scores the winner for Liverpool against Newcastle in the dying seconds of one of the most exciting games in Premier-ship history. Liverpool's 4-3 victory signalled the end of Newcastle's title challenge.

Programmes

Steve Rider was still combining his duties as presenter of *Grandstand* and *Football Focus* although Ray Stubbs also fronted several editions when Steve was working on another major sporting event. Gary Lineker was the main pundit and was being groomed to take over in the presenter's chair and Jimmy Hill was also a regular studio guest during the season. The brand name was extended in 1995 when *Cricket Focus* appeared and ran for four summers on *Grandstand*. It was later followed by *Athletics Focus* but neither had the staying power of the original football version.

Below Len Martin (left) and Tim Gudgin, whose voices have become legendary from reading the football results. Len did the football and racing results on *Grandstand* from 1958 until he died in 1995. He was succeeded by Tim who added the football role to his existing duties reading the rugby results.

Presenter
Steve Rider

Pre-season

Changes in the dugout and on the pitch before the start of the new season included Kenny Dalglish moving upstairs to become director of football at Blackburn with Ray Harford as team manager. David Pleat moved from Luton to become the new boss of Sheffield Wednesday and Dave Merrington was promoted from coach to manager at Southampton when Alan Ball replaced Brian Horton at Manchester City. Roy McFarland was appointed manager of newly promoted Bolton who lost Bruce Rioch to Arsenal.

Rioch's first signings were David Platt from Sampdoria for £4.75m and Dennis Bergkamp for £7.5m from Inter Milan. The Italian club spent £7m of that on Manchester United's Paul Ince and also leaving Old Trafford was Mark Hughes, who moved to Chelsea for £1.5m, where he joined up with Dutch legend Ruud Gullit, an audacious Glenn Hoddle acquisition on a free transfer.

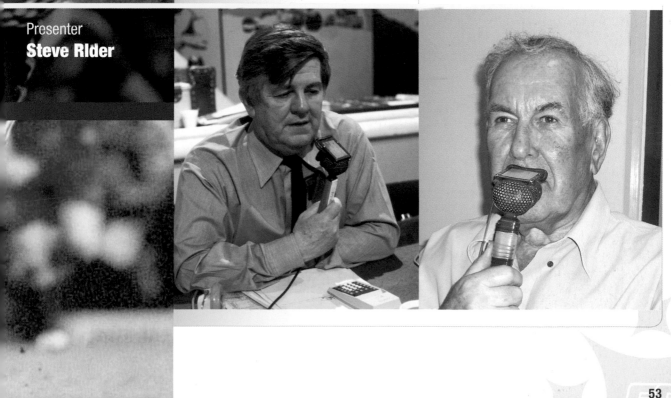

FF

Long-servers Ryan Giggs

Manchester United's left-winger is the only man to have played for the same team in every year of the Premiership and is second only to Sir Bobby Charlton in appearances for the club.

Giggs was born in Wales on 29 November 1973, made his debut at the age of 17 during the 1990–91 season and was famously protected from the media by Sir Alex Ferguson in his early seasons.

He has won nine Premiership winner's medals, four FA Cups, two League Cups and the Champions League and shares, with Bolton's Gary Speed, the distinction of being the only players to have scored in all 15 Premiership campaigns.

Liverpool paid a British record £8.5m to Nottingham Forest for Stan Collymore and Kevin Keegan made several major purchases to strengthen his Newcastle squad including David Ginola for £2.5m from Paris St Germain and QPR's 29-year-old striker Les Ferdinand for £6m

August 1995

As the new season began the bookies had Manchester United at 3-1, Blackburn 7-2, Newcastle 4-1, Liverpool 9-2 and Arsenal 6-1. Only Blackburn weren't in the top five at the end of a season which began in a heatwave on 19 August.

The champions opened with a 1-0 win against QPR but Aston Villa beat Manchester United 3-1 with United's only goal coming from 21-year-old David Beckham. When Alex Ferguson's side were discussed on *Match of the Day* that night Des Lynam remarked that 'United were scarcely recognizable from the team we've known over the past couple of seasons, what's going

on do you feel?' Alan Hansen replied, 'You can't win anything with kids... he's got to buy players, it's as simple as that.' He was almost accurate in his analysis. Apart from the small matter of Manchester United winning the double!

Les Ferdinand scored on his debut for Newcastle in their 3-0 win over Coventry and Matt Le Tissier hit a hat-trick at home for Southampton but still ended up on the losing side of a 4-3 result against Forest. Stan Collymore also scored in his first match for Liverpool, beating Sheffield Wednesday 1-0. He took the ball from John Barnes, made a little backheel, turned the defender and sent an inch-perfect curling left-foot shot to the top left-hand corner of the net.

One of the BBC's best-loved voices was silenced on 21 August when Len Martin died aged 76. He had been reading the football and racing results on *Grandstand* since 1958 and in the early years of televised sport had also voiced many hundreds of film reports. Tim Gudgin, who had been sitting alongside Len in the studio since the mid-1960s, added

Opposite top **Leeds striker Tony Yeboah** started the season in fine scoring form with explosive goals against Liverpool and Wimbledon.

Opposite bottom **Dennis Bergkamp** and **Ruud Gullit**, two of the extravagant European talents attracted to the Premier League in 1995.

Liverpool, Manchester United and Aston Villa all on nine. Manchester City were in bottom place with just one point so far. Newcastle lost their 100 per cent record but remained top despite losing 1-0 to a Jim Magilton goal at Southampton and Kevin Keegan was in an ebullient mood when he spoke with Gary on *Focus* the following week, live from St James' Park.

When asked if they could win games 1-0 he replied, 'We've got to look to be positive. We've got Beardsley, Ginola, Ferdinand, Gillespie, Fox, Sellers and Lee so it would be pointless to be spending hours and hours on defence, although we do work at it and we put a tremendous burden on the defenders, but the advantages of the way we play far outweigh the disadvantages.' In fact, only four clubs conceded fewer goals than Newcastle during the campaign.

The best spat of the season was undoubtedly between the Tottenham chairman Alan Sugar and his former striker Jurgen Klinsmann who had fallen out in a big way over the manner in which Klinsmann left White Hart Lane after just one year. Gary Lineker spoke to Klinsmann at his new club, Bayern Munich, where he explained that he wanted to stay at Tottenham and admired Gerry Francis but felt that Sugar wasn't going to invest in the team. The German striker was very upset that Sugar had publicly attacked him so gave a newspaper interview to explain that there was a clause in his contract allowing him to leave after one year and that the transfer fee was also stipulated in the contract at US$2m. Sugar had wanted more money for him despite the clause.

The chairman saw it differently and held up a shirt. 'Here's the last shirt he wore at the Leeds game, you see what he's written on there? Look... "To Alan with a very special thank you... I'm bloody sure it's a very special thank you, I'm the bloomin' mug who relaunched his career... well... I wouldn't wash my car with this shirt now.

the football role on Saturday afternoons to his existing rugby duties.

Tony Yeboah's stunning right-foot volley from 30 yards looped into the top right-hand corner of the Liverpool net past a leaping David James as Leeds won 1-0 at Elland Road, and there were two more for Ferdinand in Newcastle's 3-1 away win at Bolton. His second saw him run half the length of the pitch, through four defenders and past the keeper.

Sheffield Wednesday's 2-1 defeat of the champions started a wretched run for Blackburn who took just one point out of the next 15, but Dalgish's former club Liverpool were in better form at White Hart Lane a few days later beating Tottenham 3-1. The match included a wonderful John Barnes goal, his 100th for Liverpool. He shrugged off a defender and scored with a long-range toe poke into the top right-hand corner from outside the Tottenham box.

September

After four matches Newcastle led the table with 12 points, two ahead of Leeds with

Thousands of Middlesbrough fans turned up at the Riverside to help manager Bryan Robson welcome 22-year-old Juninho to Teeside on his arrival from Brazilian club São Paulo.

[threw shirt to reporter] You have it, you can auction it for a charity, obviously an appropriate one, if we can, a charity to get people to tell the truth in future or something like that.'

Then, on 20 September, the football transfer system was radically changed when the European Court of Justice produced the Bosman Ruling, named after the little-known Belgian footballer Jean-Marc Bosman, who had brought the case. As *Focus* explained, the essential facts were that when his contract expired a player would be free to move clubs without a transfer fee but that transfer fees would still exist if a player moved while under contract. There was also to be no limit on the number of foreign players in a team. Fulham chairman, Jimmy Hill, was very angry and worried that clubs would no longer develop youth teams as there was a loss of incentive. 'It's like growing an apple tree in your garden and letting the neighbours come in and take it for nothing. We have a healthy set-up in this country and for Europe to come in and disturb it in that way is abominable and as you may realise I'm not for it!'

Despite the controversy it proved to be a cracking weekend for strikers. Robbie Fowler hit four in Liverpool's 5-2 win against Bolton, Shearer's hat-trick helped Blackburn beat Coventry 5-1, Bergkamp got his first two goals for Arsenal as they overcame Southampton 4-2 and Ghanaian Tony Yeboah was in wonderful form for Leeds against Wimbledon. He scored three in their 4-2 win, the best being voted Goal of the Month when he took the ball on his chest, bounced it on his left knee, pulled it inside the defender and unleashed a powerful shot into the roof of the net off the underside of bar.

October

October was a relatively quiet month as there was a lot of European and international action although it began with a thrilling 2-2 draw between Manchester United and Liverpool, a match that also saw the return of Eric Cantona after his eight-month suspension. One fan had 'GOD' painted on her face and he certainly seemed to be smiling down favourably as, after just 67 seconds, the Frenchman crossed from the left for Nicky Butt to score. Robbie Fowler then scored twice, first with a turbocharged shot and then a wonderful chip but, just as it looked as though the comeback was going to be upstaged, Jamie Redknapp pulled down Ryan Giggs and with some 20 minutes remaining Cantona casually sent David James the wrong way to level the scores.

Aston Villa had moved into second place at the end of September by winning 3-0 at struggling neighbours Coventry and, after eight games, were level with Manchester United on 17 points, eight behind Newcastle.

Manchester City were featured on *Focus* as they had lost eight in a row and only scored three goals in nine games. With fans' favourite Francis Lee now installed as chairman and the popular Alan Ball as manager, it was their worst start for 30 years. Despite the dire situation Lee was still backing the manager, 'Alan Ball has got a three-year contract with Manchester City and I can't see any reason why he won't see it out.' He added that they were saddled with a huge wage bill so would have to sell before bringing in new players. They were relegated the following May having scored only 33 goals, the worst scoring record in the Premier League.

That afternoon Liverpool put six past hapless City with two goals each for Ian Rush and Robbie Fowler, while Les Ferdinand's three goals helped leaders Newcastle to a 6-1 win, their ninth in ten games, against Wimbledon. His two headers and a tap-in took his total to 13 in ten matches.

November

Middlesbrough's 22-year-old Brazilian Player of the Year, Juninho, made his debut amidst massive press interest in their 1-1 draw with Leeds and the £4.75m acquisition set up Jan-Aage Fjortoft to score after ten minutes. When Manchester City beat Bolton 1-0 it was their first win in 12 games and Nicky Summerbee's goal was only their fourth of the season. Everton added to Blackburn's problems beating them 1-0 with a Graham Stuart goal although it was their first win since August, and Forest condemned Wimbledon to a club record seventh successive defeat, beating them 4-1 to go third in the table.

The following week Blackburn also lost 1-0, this time to Newcastle, before the team responded in dramatic style to the criticism from the stands by demolishing Forest 7-0 to end their 25-game unbeaten run in the Premiership. Shearer hit three, Lars Bohinen two and Mike Newell and Graeme Le Saux scored the others on the day that Jack Walker opened a new stand at Ewood Park that bore his name.

Manchester United closed the gap at the top to six points when they beat Southampton 4-1. Ryan Giggs scored after just 16 seconds, the first of three goals in the opening nine minutes. Meanwhile United's former player, Andrei Kanchelskis, hit his first goals for Everton as they beat Liverpool 2-1 at Anfield with a 53rd-minute header and a powerful shot in the 70th.

The last Saturday of the month saw Coventry, reduced to nine men, come back from 3-1 down at home to draw with Wimbledon in the last few minutes thanks to goals by Dion Dublin and David Rennie. It was the second month without a league win for Wimbledon and the third for Coventry. Rob Lee and Peter Beardsley scored as the leaders Newcastle beat Leeds 2-1 after Brian Deane had put the Yorkshire team ahead in the first half. Swedish star

Tomas Brolin made his Premiership debut for Leeds having signed from Parma for £4.5m.

December

After 16 matches Newcastle were still top with 39 points, five ahead of Manchester United. Arsenal were third with 29 and Villa a point behind in fourth. Reigning champions Blackburn displayed their inconsistent side yet again when Coventry put five past them, although before Sky Blues fans were able to get too enthusiastic, they lost their Midlands derby with Aston Villa when a hat-trick by Savo Milosevic helped Villa to a 4-1 win.

In the Yorkshire derby Sheffield Wednesday beat Leeds 6-2 and in the North West a brace by Robbie Fowler saw Liverpool get the better of Manchester United. He followed that with a hat-trick in their 3-1 win over Arsenal to take his Premiership tally to 16 in 19 games. United

It's that man again – Alan Shearer celebrates scoring his 100th Premiership goal when Blackburn beat Tottenham 2-1 at Ewood Park on 30 December.

lost two in a row for the only time that season, also going down 3-1 at Leeds. Elsewhere, Keegan saw his side extend their lead to ten points with a 3-1 victory over Forest, Middlesbrough conceded four at Everton to start a sequence of eight successive defeats and Arsenal ended a run of five matches without a win by beating QPR 3-0.

The key match this month came right at the end when Manchester United began to close the gap by beating Newcastle 2-0 with goals by Andy Cole and Roy Keane. Gary Lineker felt that 'If United hadn't won it would have been pretty much all over but now it is thrown relatively wide open and I think that's good for everyone with the exception of Newcastle fans.' Newcastle still looked to be favourites though and had 45 points after 20 games with United on 38. Tottenham had quietly climbed into third place, three points behind with Liverpool and Arsenal both on 34.

Bolton were bottom, having taken ten points from a possible 30, Coventry were five above them in 19th place and Manchester City completed the relegation zone with 16 points. QPR and Wimbledon were above them on 18.

On 30 December Alan Shearer reached a new landmark when he became the first player to score 100 Premier League goals when Blackburn beat Tottenham 2-1 at Ewood Park.

Director Martin Webster

Martin Webster is one of the BBC's most experienced match directors having brought more than 150 Premiership games to the screen since 1992 as well directing many other FA Cup and international fixtures.

'The one thing that hasn't changed in the past 15 years is that we still try to give the viewers the best seat in the house but where we used to have four or five cameras a game there are now a minimum of eight with 13 or 14 for live matches.

We still produce the basic match coverage on three cameras but the extra ones allow us to cover a lot more off-the-ball incidents or offsides, and as there is so much more scrutiny and money at stake we try not to miss anything.

Viewers expect far more than in the pre-Premiership days and they want two or three angles to decide for themselves what happened so the expectations have definitely increased. The other big difference for us is the changing technology and the way that it has allowed us to improve coverage. Super slo-mo cameras give a stunning and totally different picture of the ball and we no longer have to wait for the old tape machines to rewind before we show a replay as the digital era means we can fire them in instantly.

On a matchday we normally get to the ground at around 11 a.m. and have a technical check late morning before covering the match in the afternoon. We probably have about 30 people on site to cover each game, including the director, camera and sound crews, riggers, production assistant and commentator, but the modernisation of the grounds has helped us to save time and costs as many of the grounds are now pre-cabled.

There is a really good camaraderie between directors although we all try to outdo each other and each have our own styles. Even after 22 years in the scanner it is still great fun to direct matches and get into the rhythm of the games.'

January 1996

Manchester United opened the New Year with a 4-1 at Tottenham but Alex Ferguson was to see his side lose only once more in the league during the season. David Ginola scored in the first minute and Les Ferdinand added a second soon after the break to launch Newcastle on a spell of five successive wins as they beat Arsenal 2-0 to restore their seven-point lead, having won all 11 matches at St. James' Park since the start of the campaign.

Bolton, with only two wins in 22 and eight points adrift at the bottom, sacked manager Roy McFarland and installed his assistant, Colin Todd. Newcastle raced nine points ahead yet again on 14 January with a 1-0 win at Coventry and then extended it to a seemingly unsurpassable 12 when they defeated Bolton 2-1 at home .

Liverpool beat Leeds 5-0 with two each from Neil Ruddock and Robbie Fowler plus one from Stan Collymore. Earlier that week Nigel Clough had moved from Anfield to Manchester City for £1.5 million.

Tottenham missed the chance to go second when they lost 2-1 at Aston Villa, a match which saw Paul McGrath hit his first goal in three years. Four minutes later Ruel Fox's shot deflected in off McGrath to give him membership of the small club of players who have scored in both Premiership nets in the same game and then, 11 minutes from the end, Dwight Yorke fired in a great winner from a tight angle.

Manchester United's win at West Ham was the first of 13 in 15 games and came courtesy of a goal by Eric Cantona, although their title hopes still seemed a long way off especially when Liverpool moved above them into second place, nine points behind Newcastle, when they beat Villa 2-0 in the Midlands.

February

On 3 February Kevin Keegan spoke to John Motson on *Focus* as he was four days away from celebrating his fourth anniversary at Newcastle. He was also waiting to clinch a deal for their latest striker, £7.5m Colombian Faustino Asprilla, who had been introduced to the fans a week before. The Tyneside supporters looked a lot happier than he did as they queued in the snow to meet him on a freezing day at St. James' Park.

Gavin Peacock hit three of Chelsea's five goals against Middlesbrough when they recorded their biggest win of the season, and Forest's 26-match unbeaten home run ended when Bergkamp scored the only goal of their game with Arsenal.

Football mourned another of its greatest names when the former Liverpool manager, Bob Paisley, died on Valentine's Day. *Focus* that week paid tribute to his incredible career with the memories of many former players. He had led the club to six league titles and three European Cups and the view was that his record would never be surpassed.

There was some rare joy for the fans of two of the relegation candidates, Bolton and QPR. Colin Todd saw his team register their first away win of the season when they beat Middlesbrough 4-1 while QPR stopped a run of seven straight league defeats with a 3-1 victory against Sheffield Wednesday at Hillsborough.

The gap at the top finally began to narrow when Giggs and Keane scored for Manchester United in their 2-0 win against Everton and Newcastle lost 2-0 at West Ham. In their next match Keegan's men had to come from behind three times to draw 3-3 at Manchester City. But two goals by Paul Scholes and others by Beckham, Bruce, Cole and Butt gave Manchester United their biggest away win for 36 years as they hammered Bolton 6-0. Their fifth win in a row took them to within four points of Newcastle, who had 61 points after 27 games, and five points clear of Liverpool in third place.

Opposite The highly creative Colombian international Tino Asprilla arrived at Newcastle from Italian club Parma in November. He fitted into the side immediately and kept the Magpies in contention for what the club hoped would be their first title since 1927.

March

Finally, on a Monday night, the fortress that was St James' Park was breached and United closed to within a point of Newcastle thanks to Eric Cantona's goal and several great saves by Peter Schmeichel in a 1-0 victory. Newcastle still had a game in hand but in Gary Lineker's view, 'This was the week that Man Utd blew the title race wide open although all three sides are playing wonderful football and great to watch.'

On 16 March United scored a massive psychological blow by drawing 1-1 at QPR to go top for the first time since 23 September, even though Newcastle had two games in hand. United had gone behind when Denis Irwin headed Danny Dichio's cross into his own net but Cantona got onto the end of a Giggs pass in the third minute of stoppage time to level the scores.

Alan Shearer scored an incredible fifth hat-trick of the season for Blackburn as the outgoing champions beat Tottenham 3-2 at White Hart Lane and then, in another flurry of activity, Newcastle returned to the top after beating West Ham 3-0 with goals by Albert, Asprilla and Ferdinand.

Two days later Eric Cantona produced one of his greatest goals for United when he chested the ball down and leapt at a half volley to send it looping over David Seaman and score the only goal of the game against Arsenal. The Gunners were again the catalyst when United returned to the top of the table thanks to a 2-0 win over Newcastle at Highbury.

At the opposite end of the table Bolton managed to lift themselves off the bottom for the first time in four months when they recorded a 2-1 victory against Sheffield Wednesday. It was a rare treat for Bolton's supporters as they only saw their team score 16 goals at Burnden Park all season.

When Manchester United beat Tottenham 1-0 on 24 March they drew three points clear of Newcastle and, even though Keegan's side had two games in hand, it looked as though Ferguson finally had the advantage.

April

Monday 3 April saw one of the most exciting matches in Premiership history when Liverpool beat Newcastle 4-3 in an astonishing encounter at Anfield. The home team were one up after 1 minute and 40 seconds when Robbie Fowler headed down a great cross from Stan Collymore. Les Ferdinand levelled but David Ginola then outpaced the Liverpool defence to give the visitors the lead on 14 minutes.

Fowler made it 2-2 in the second half when he got onto the end of a Steve McManaman cross, Faustino Asprilla put Newcastle back in the lead after he was put clear by a terrific pass from Rob Lee but Collymore cancelled that out when he rushed through the defence to collect a pass from Jason McAteer and crash the ball home. Then, in the dying seconds of the game, Collymore's left-foot drive hit the net to give Liverpool victory and condemn Newcastle to their fourth defeat in six matches, leaving them three points behind United with only one game in hand.

At the end of the match Keegan sat with his bowed head in his hands. 'We've lost control of our own destiny now', he said after the game. He later said that it was the best game that he had ever been part of, as player or manager.

Pundit Les Ferdinand

Les Ferdinand was one of the Premier League's most prolific strikers and retired with 149 goals to his name – the fifth highest total. He was the first man to score Premiership goals for six different clubs: QPR, Newcastle, Tottenham, West Ham, Leicester and Bolton.

'I have terrific memories of the 1992–93 season as I managed to scored three goals for QPR in the first week of the Premiership. We drew 1-1 with Manchester City in the first ever Monday night live televised game but had two more matches that week and I also scored against Southampton and Sheffield United.

Kevin Keegan warned me that I was going into a goldfish bowl at Newcastle as there is no privacy, everyone knows everything and everyone is into football. One day I remember going into a Post Office where there was a much older lady behind the counter, I got what I wanted and thought that it was great that I had finally found a place where I wasn't recognised. Then, just as I was about to leave she revealed her black and white striped coffee mug and asked for an autograph!

The most outstanding match that I ever played in was the 4-3 defeat to Liverpool in April 1996. I think that if we had won we'd have gone on to win the title. At one stage I was standing on the pitch while someone was getting treatment and just listened to the wonderful support from the Geordies. I remember the incredible noise and thinking that whoever was watching it was seeing an amazing game, but at the end we couldn't believe that we had scored three times and still lost the game.

Scoring the 10,000th Premiership goal in 2001 was also a special moment for me even though it was a little tap in for Tottenham against Fulham. There was lots of speculation that day about who would score. My goal came 20 minutes into the game and I assumed it had already been done but as I was running back they announced it over the tannoy.'

A week later, on Easter Monday, Cantona scored for the sixth game in a row as Manchester United beat Coventry. Newcastle continued to implode, dropping six points behind the leaders when losing 2-1 at Blackburn, conceding both to Graham Fenton inside the final five minutes.

In a bizarre incident at The Dell Alex Ferguson's team invited ridicule when they changed out of their grey shirts at half time having claimed that they couldn't see each other in the first half... the score was 3-0 to the Saints. Their new blue and white strip made no difference and they eventually lost 3-1. It was a crucial result for the home team, who stayed just out of the drop zone.

With the end of the season approaching and all results crucial, the psychological battle also cranked up. After United had beaten Leeds 1-0, and before Howard Wilkinson's team were due to play Newcastle, Alex Ferguson decided to criticise the Leeds players. 'They are cheating their manager. If they produced effort like that they would be in the top six

but, of course, you'd think for some of them it's more important to get a result against Manchester United than anyone else. Of course, when they come to Newcastle you wait and see the difference.' Manchester United were on 76 points with two matches remaining and three points ahead of Newcastle who had a game in hand. The gauntlet had been thrown down.

Alan Shearer's first goal for Blackburn against Wimbledon on 17 April was his 30th of the season. It was the third season in a row he had hit that mark, a record that had not been achieved in the top division since Jimmy Dunne of Sheffield United in the 1930s.

On 27 April the first two relegations were confirmed when Bolton lost 1-0 at Southampton, a result that also consigned QPR, despite a 3-0 home win over West Ham, to the drop. Manchester City and Coventry both won away from home meaning that the final spot was between them, Southampton and Sheffield Wednesday.

The following day United beat Forest 5-0 to stretch their lead to six points and then, in the aftermath of Newcastle's 1-0 win at Leeds on Monday, Kevin Keegan made an extraordinary outburst on Sky TV. He lost all composure and ranted about Manchester United, 'I tell you, honestly, I will love it if we beat them, love it.'

May

But the wheels had come off at St. James' Park and the Magpies could only manage a 1-1 draw at Forest which meant that Manchester United went into the last day of the season with a two-point advantage and their destiny in their own hands.

United duly clinched their third title in four seasons when David May, Andy Cole and Ryan Giggs scored at Middlesbrough to give them a 3-0 win and enable Steve Bruce to once again lift the Premiership trophy. Alex Ferguson was thrilled by his

Below Southampton's Ken Monkou rises to head his side into the lead against Manchester United at the Dell. United defender Steve Bruce is sporting the strip that was blamed for United's poor performance. Despite a change at half-time United still lost the game 3-1.

young players. 'I'm very proud of them. I think we always knew of their ability but what you don't know is how they can handle big game situations and their temperament, and they've acquitted themselves brilliantly.'

The other side of Manchester was left to deal with relegation following City's 2-2 draw with Liverpool at Maine Road when their manager Alan Ball mistakenly told them to keep possession when they needed to win to avoid the dreaded drop. They only managed 33 goals all season, the worst goals-for tally in the league, and finished on 38 points, the same total as Coventry and Southampton who stayed up by virtue of 0-0 draws with Leeds and Wimbledon. It meant that all three promoted teams had gone straight back down.

Below Brian Kidd (left) and Alex Ferguson celebrated United's third league title in four years.

Final League Table

Teams	P	W	D	L	F	A	Pts
Manchester United	38	25	7	6	73	35	82
Newcastle United	38	24	6	8	66	37	78
Liverpool	38	20	11	7	70	34	71
Aston Villa	38	18	9	11	52	35	63
Arsenal	38	17	12	9	49	32	63
Everton	38	17	10	11	64	44	61
Blackburn Rovers	38	18	7	13	61	47	61
Tottenham Hotspur	38	16	13	9	50	38	61
Nottingham Forest	38	15	13	10	50	54	58
West Ham United	38	14	9	15	43	52	51
Chelsea	38	12	14	12	46	44	50
Middlesbrough	38	11	10	17	35	50	43
Leeds United	38	12	7	19	40	57	43
Wimbledon	38	10	11	17	55	70	41
Sheffield Wednesday	38	10	10	18	48	61	40
Coventry City	38	8	14	16	42	60	38
Southampton	38	9	11	18	34	52	38
Manchester City	38	9	11	18	33	58	38
QPR	38	9	6	23	38	57	33
Bolton Wanderers	38	8	5	25	39	71	29

Leading Goalscorers league only

Alan Shearer	Blackburn Rovers	31
Robbie Fowler	Liverpool	28
Les Ferdinand	Newcastle United	25
Dwight Yorke	Aston Villa	17
Teddy Sheringham	Tottenham Hotspur	16
Andrei Kanchelskis	Everton	16
Ian Wright	Arsenal	15
Chris Armstrong	Tottenham Hotspur	15
Eric Cantona	Manchester United	14
Stan Collymore	Liverpool	14
Dion Dublin	Coventry City	14

Awards

Footballer of the Year
Eric Cantona, Manchester United

PFA Player of the Year
Les Ferdinand, Newcastle United

PFA Young Player of the Year
Robbie Fowler, Liverpool

Newcastle finished second, four points behind, having drawn 1-1 with Tottenham thanks to Les Ferdinand's 25th goal of the season. Liverpool were third, 11 points behind the leaders but eight ahead of Arsenal who were level on points with Aston Villa. The defending champions, Blackburn, were seventh on 61, the same as Everton and Tottenham.

At Chelsea the managerial merry-go-round started up again. Glenn Hoddle, popular with the fans despite an 11th place finish in the last two seasons, announced that he would accept the offer to replace Terry Venables as England manager. Blues fans, aware that George Graham was in the frame to replace Hoddle, spent much of the last match of the season, a 3-2 home defeat by Blackburn, chanting the name of their favoured replacement 'Rudi, Rudi'. Ruud Gullit was duly named as Hoddle's successor in the hot seat.

Honours List 1995–96

Champions Manchester United

Runners-up Newcastle United

Relegated Bolton Wanderers, Queens Park Rangers, Manchester City

Promoted Sunderland, Derby County, Leicester City

FA Cup Winners Manchester United

League Cup Winners Aston Villa

League Cup
Aston Villa won the League Cup for the second time in three years when they beat Leeds United 3-0 in the final. Savo Milosevic, Ian Taylor and Dwight Yorke were the scorers.

FA Cup
Manchester United reached the final for the third year in a row where they met Liverpool. Sadly, despite two star-studded sides, the cream Armani suits of the Liverpool team were more memorable than the game and it looked to be heading for extra time when Manchester United's captain, Eric Cantona, drove the ball into the Liverpool net for the only goal of the game. It gave them the Cup for a record ninth time.

FF 1996–97

Gianfranco Zola arrived at
Stamford Bridge from Lazio in
November. He adapted to the
Premiership immediately, putting
in some notable performances
and scoring some memorable
goals. His efforts were rewarded
when he was voted the Football
Writers' Player of the Year.

Programmes

Gary Lineker became the third full time presenter of *Football Focus* and found himself sitting inside a giant virtual football. In the studio he was actually surrounded by a big green backdrop but the latest technology meant that the viewers saw him and his guests in a large revolving ball with graphics and tables that flew out at different angles. In the early shows there was an unfortunate tendency for Gary and the pundits to look straight past them at a monitor placed out of shot, but once the producers got used to their new toys and extra sound effects it settled down. Ray Stubbs presented a number of programmes and the show's content was also beefed up with more stories, studio guests and features than in previous years.

Presenter
Gary Lineker

Premiership Top	pld	pts
1 Sheffield Wed	5	12
2 Chelsea	5	11
3 Liverpool	5	11
4 Aston Villa	5	10
5 Manchester Utd	5	9
6 Newcastle Utd	5	9
7 Middlesbrough	5	8
8 Arsenal	5	8
9 Leeds Utd	5	7
10 Sunderland	5	6

Pre-season

Having only escaped relegation the previous season by virtue of a better goal difference than Manchester City, Southampton sacked manager Dave Merrington and replaced him with Graeme Souness. Just before the season began Bruce Rioch was dismissed by Arsenal after just 61 weeks in charge. It was the briefest ever managerial reign at Highbury and press speculation suggested that his replacement was to be Frenchman Arsène Wenger.

In the transfer market an increasing number of European players were arriving to ply their trade in the Premiership. French star, Patrick Vieira, joined Arsenal from AC Milan for £3.5m while his compatriot Frank Leboeuf signed for Chelsea for £2.5m from Strasbourg. He was joined at Stamford Bridge by the Italian midfielder Roberto Di Matteo who moved from Lazio for a club record £4.9m. Having sold Lee Sharpe to Leeds for £4.5m Manchester United strengthened their squad with the Norwegian striker Ole Gunnar Solskjaer for £1.5m and Jordi Cruyff from Barcelona for £800,000.

Czech midfielder Patrik Berger moved to Liverpool for £3.25m from Borussia Dortmund and, in one of the biggest surprises, Bryan Robson added Juventus' Italian star Fabrizio Ravanelli at a cost of £7m and Brazilian midfielder Emerson to his Middlebrough squad.

Domestic moves included the Crystal Palace goalkeeper Nigel Martyn who switched to Leeds for £2.25m but the biggest headline came when Alan Shearer signed for Newcastle for a world record £15m. He chose to join Kevin Keegan at the club he had supported as a boy and received a rapturous greeting from the St James' Park faithful.

August 1996

Gary Lineker opened the first *Focus* of the new season on 17 August with the words, 'We've a new look for today as *Football Focus* boldly goes where no *Focus* has been before and the world's best players are choosing England as their footballing home.'

After a feature on the transfers the giant virtual ball slid round to show Bryan Robson for a live interview. 'We've got to compete with Premier League clubs in the marketplace. We needed more firepower and goals and I think that Emerson and Ravanelli will give us that,' said the Boro manager.

His buys seemed to pay off on the opening afternoon as Ravanelli hit a debut hat-trick in their 3-3 draw with Liverpool. The other newcomers, Sunderland and Leicester, drew 0-0. There was false hope for Nottingham Forest when Kevin Campbell also hit three as they won 3-0 at Coventry, but it was to be their only win in the first 17 league games of this season.

But the undoubted star of the opening day, in a moment that helped elevate him from promising youngster to the first rung of global superstardom, was David Beckham. Manchester United were already two up at Wimbledon when, in the 90th minute, the 21-year-old spotted keeper Neil Sullivan off his line and struck a perfect shot from the halfway line. A smiling Alex Ferguson told *Grandstand*, 'I've never seen it done. Pele in the 1970s and many others have tried it, but I've never seen it done. What a strike, absolutely phenomenal.'

David Pleat saw his Sheffield Wednesday team beat Leeds 2-0 at Elland Road to go top, Sunderland and Leicester both recorded opening wins, 4-1 at Forest and 2-1 against Southampton, and Alan Shearer scored his first league goal in black and white stripes on his home debut. In the 88th minute he struck a perfect free kick round the wall and into the top right-hand corner of the Wimbledon goal to complete a 2-0 win.

Kenny Dalglish surprised Blackburn's supporters when he left the club on 21 August, leaving Ray Harford in sole charge, and the following day Arsène Wenger, manager of the Japanese side Grampus Eight, was confirmed as the new Arsenal boss after much speculation and lots of leaks to the press.

September

After four wins in four games Wednesday were three points clear at the top from Aston Villa, who were followed by Chelsea and Liverpool, both on eight points. But the Owls' joy was brief as they won only two of their next 16 games.

Howard Wilkinson was sacked after eight years in charge of Leeds following a 4-0 defeat at home to Manchester United. He was replaced by George Graham in his first job back in football since the end of his 12-month suspension, while his former Arsenal skipper, Tony Adams, publicly confessed his alcoholism.

Blackburn went bottom when Shearer scored against his old club in Newcastle's 2-1 victory. Before the match he had told the show that he'd now achieved his dream by wearing the No. 9 shirt of his hometown club. He explained to Ray Stubbs that, 'Scoring goals is the greatest feeling in the

Below Four victories in a row, culminating in a 3-1 win against Southampton, saw Wimbledon (dark shirts) move up from bottom to sixth place in just three weeks.

Above Little known in England, Frenchman Arsène Wenger was appointed manager of Arsenal in August 1996 with Gunners stalwart Pat Rice (right) as his assistant.

off the foot of the left post after 23 minutes of their encounter with Manchester United and Arsène Wenger won his first match in charge of Arsenal when Ian Wright scored twice against Blackburn.

Arsenal briefly went top on goal difference following a 0-0 draw with Coventry and, astonishingly, Joe Kinnear was able to enjoy a dual celebration when he watched his Wimbledon side move into second place as a result of a 4-2 win at Chelsea, their seventh victory in a row.

In a period of constant change at the top, Newcastle went three points clear when they inflicted a 5-0 defeat on Manchester United, their biggest defeat for 12 years. Darren Peacock's header made it 1-0, a tremendous right-foot shot from the edge of the box by David Ginola doubled the score and Les Ferdinand struck a third when the ball looped over Peter Schmeichel, bounced off the bar, hit the post and went in. A flying Schmeichel saved shots from Peter Beardsley and Ferdinand before Shearer got through the Dane's defence to add a fourth, and the scoreline was completed by Philippe Albert's exquisite chip over the keeper from inside the box. It was the Magpies' seventh straight win.

If Alex Ferguson was unhappy with that performance then his infamous 'hairdryer' would have been on full power after United's next game when they lost 6-3 at Southampton. Egil Ostenstad's hat-trick and two from Eyal Berkovic were complemented by another classic goal by Matthew Le Tissier, who displayed wonderful close ball control and then chipped the keeper.

In the last week of the month Ray Harford left winless Blackburn and Tony Parkes took over as caretaker manager, Arsenal went back to the top with a 3-0 win over George Graham's Leeds and Nick Barmby moved from Middlesbrough to Everton for £5.75m.

whole world and when you hit the back of the net there isn't a better feeling. Don't play this will you, my wife might be watching!'

Manchester United took over top spot following their 4-1 victory over Forest and Liverpool were the next to take the lead after a 3-0 win at Leicester, a position they consolidated the following week by thrashing Chelsea 5-1.

There was a surprising reversal of fortunes for two clubs with radically different spending power. When Middlesbrough lost 2-0 at home to Arsenal it was the first in a run of only two wins in their next 20 games as they dropped from sixth to bottom, whereas Wimbledon's fourth successive win, 3-1 against Southampton, moved them up to sixth place having been in 20th spot three weeks earlier. Liverpool ended the month with 20 points, two ahead of Newcastle with Arsenal on 17 and Manchester United on 16.

October

Liverpool suffered their first defeat of the season when David Beckham's shot went in

November

As ever in television not everything went smoothly and the perils of working in a virtual set were demonstrated when Ray Stubbs sat in the *Focus* chair on the first Saturday in November with sparkle across his hair and shoulders, looking like the Ready Brek kid permanently materialising on the Star Trek transporter.

More tangible problems cropped up at Old Trafford where Alex Ferguson was preparing to celebrate ten years as manager. He was talking to Motty when the sprinklers came on and gave them a good spraying live on the show. There was still no joy for the champions as they lost a third successive match, 2-1 to Chelsea. It was their first home league defeat since December 1994.

Newcastle beat Middlesbrough 3-1 in the North-East derby to retake top spot and Blackburn beat Liverpool 3-0 to complete their first win of the season. Gordon Strachan replaced Ron Atkinson as manager of Coventry and Gianfranco Zola signed for fifth-placed Chelsea for £4.5m from Parma.

Champions Manchester United returned to form against Arsenal when David Seaman's howler led to a goal as he was out of position when Nigel Winterburn bundled Nicky Butt's cross into his own net. The goalkeeper then sustained two broken ribs to round off a miserable afternoon, an injury that caused him to miss the next eight league games.

Southampton demonstrated the fragile nature of form when they met Everton at Goodison Park just two matches after their epic win against the champions. A hat-trick from Gary Speed helped the home team to a 7-1 win. It was the start of a run of seven defeats in eight games for the Saints.

December

In a surprise move it was announced that the Chief Executive of the Premier League, Rick Parry, was to join Liverpool. The Reds celebrated by winning 2-0 at Tottenham which put them level on points with Arsenal but behind on goal difference. Michael Thomas scored the first but the second was a freak. Steve McManaman's weak shot was covered by a diving Ian Walker when it hit a divot and bounced over his body and into the net.

McManaman was profiled on *Focus* when he and Ray Stubbs sat playing video games in Robbie Fowler's bedroom as Robbie went and made them both tea. McManaman had started writing a weekly column for *The Times* in which he said he enjoyed being able to offer opinions and put his side of the story.

Patrick Vieira scored his first goal for Arsenal, a 90th-minute equaliser in a 2-2 draw with Derby, a goal that gave the Gunners a four-point cushion over Wimbledon who moved into second place by beating Sunderland 3-1. Liverpool, also on 31 points, were one point ahead of fourth-placed Aston Villa.

Newcastle's 0-0 at Forest was a remarkable result in that it was their first goalless draw for 73 games. Forest moved above Coventry into 19th place on goals scored and Newcastle went fourth.

The international stature of manager Ruud Gullit helped Chelsea lure stellar talent to Stamford Bridge, perhaps none greater than Italian midfielder Gianfranco Zola who would go on to delight crowds around the country with his magnificent talent and sporting attitude.

Presenter Gary Lineker

The most prolific club marksman of his era, Gary Lineker is also England's second highest scorer of all time with 48 goals, one fewer than the legendary Sir Bobby Charlton. Playing for Leicester City, Everton, Barcelona and Tottenham he collected winners' medals in the FA Cup, Spanish Cup and European Cup-Winners' Cup before ending his career in Japan with Grampus Eight. Having had spells as a pundit on *Football Focus* he fronted the lunchtime show for three seasons from 1996 before becoming the presenter of *Match of the Day.*

'Being able to work alongside Bob and Steve while still playing was a great experience as I was able to watch and learn from both. Actually, I didn't find punditry particularly difficult because being asked my opinions about the game wasn't especially demanding. Presenting was another story though. That was far more of a challenge.

I did some radio training which helped enormously, but suddenly on TV I had people talking in my ear, had to remember links, cope with looking at the right cameras and conduct interviews and that was a shock to the system.

I remember doing one pilot programme and then being pitched straight in at the deep end, fronting a high-profile show and trying to work out how to do autocue, deal with guests and the studio environment. It probably took me a year to become myself and begin to enjoy it.

I also had to cope with the experiment of a virtual reality set when I started. We were the guinea pigs and it was worth a try but I always seemed to have a shimmering halo effect around me and was relieved when it was gently put back into the TV history books.

I finished playing a year before the Premiership started and since then the game has got quicker, better and stronger. The training is more scientific, the players have unquestionably evolved physically and the levels of skills have improved over the years.

Another significant difference is the gulf between the big teams and the next group. There have always been a few who were ahead of the pack but the gap is bigger now and the elite are better, which is a positive, but it's not likely to be possible for a surprise team to come through or even a team like Leeds or Blackburn unless they get an Abramovich.

There have been lots of great players with the likes of Alan Shearer, Roy Keane, Dennis Bergkamp and Eric Cantona standing out but I love watching Thierry Henry play. He is not just a goalscorer but is also so graceful and a brilliant mover and entertainer.'

As Wimbledon were second in the Premiership, Garry Richardson went to visit their captain, the unconventional Vinnie Jones, down on his farm. He expressed some fairly forthright views. 'Images are created by the media and press,' he said. 'I play football in the only manner I know how and when I'm not in the arena you're surprised when you see what I'm like here. I was a yob when I came into football but I've changed and I've just been asked to do a film which they think is going to be a blast. Now if this goes well I could become a very rich lad. I play a debt collector.'

Jones was in his second spell with the Dons. 'I want to be remembered as a great captain and a leader. I'd prefer to be a legend and not a myth,' he said.

The run up to Christmas saw Liverpool storm into top spot with a couple of great performances. Robbie Fowler scored four, to take him past 100 for the club in just 165 games, one fewer than Ian Rush, as they beat Middlesbrough 5-1, and they then won 4-2 against Forest to establish a two-point lead over Arsenal. Collymore hit two against his old club who set a new Premiership record for the longest run without a win, 16 matches in all. As a result Frank Clark resigned as manager and Stuart Pearce took over as caretaker player-manager, and he had a dream start, inspiring them to a 2-1 win against Arsenal.

On 20 December Middlesbrough made a decision that was to have a catastrophic effect on their future. They announced that they were missing 23 players through illness or injury and cancelled their match with Blackburn. They were later docked three points as punishment. It was a punishment that had dire consequences come the end of the season.

There were five goal hauls for Manchester United and Aston Villa against Sunderland and Wimbledon though Newcastle went two better by demolishing Tottenham 7-1.

But it was in-form Liverpool who ended the year at the top of the table five points ahead of the rest after their 1-0 win at The Dell. John Barnes collected Dave Beasant's bad clearance and scored from 40 yards in the 76th minute.

January 1997

The month was dominated by one story, Kevin Keegan's shock resignation from Newcastle on 8 January. The city was stunned as their team was fourth in the Premiership and in the last eight of the UEFA Cup. Fans were angry, feeling that the manager had been forced out ahead of the club's planned stock market floatation. One dejected supporter was interviewed as she had her club tattoo removed. Although the club didn't collect any silverware under Keegan, his teams had produced some of the most exciting and entertaining football in Premiership history.

Pundit Alan Shearer

Alan Shearer is the most successful striker in the history of the Premiership with 260 goals from 441 appearances for Blackburn and Newcastle. Having been transferred from Southampton for a record £3.6m at the start of the first Premiership season he won the title under Kenny Dalglish in 1994–95 before joining Kevin Keegan on Tyneside a year later for a world record £15m. Twice Player of the Year he was three times the leading scorer in the Premier League.

'I used to watch *Football Focus* as a kid but it was hard to watch it when I started out in the Premiership as, 15 years ago, our pre-match meal was at midday. With all the dieticians and sports scientists on board now, the best time to eat is deemed to be 11.30 a.m. so I managed to catch it more often in recent years.

It was brilliant for a small club like Blackburn to take the big boys on and win the Premiership. With me, Chris Sutton and Mike Newell up front we complemented each other very well and also had great service from the wingers Stuart Ripley and Jason Wilcox.

Newcastle was my hometown club and I had dreamed of playing in the No. 9 shirt since I was a kid. So it was an astonishing experience when 20,000 or more supporters were there in the rain at St. James' Park when I signed, and they were great to me for ten years. The first goal in a black and white shirt was very special for me, as was the 201st, because Jackie Milburn was such a great player and it was an honour to break his club record.

Peter Schmeichel and David Seaman were easily the outstanding goalkeepers in the league and Tony Adams was the best defender I played against as we had very similar styles and approach. You could kick each other off the park during the match but shake hands at the end and say well done, which is how the game should be played in my opinion.

The managers I played under were very different. Kenny Dalglish placed more emphasis on tactics, as did Sir Bobby Robson, whereas Kevin Keegan just sent the players out to entertain and wanted them to express themselves. There were no hard or fast rules and he never changed his style.

Looking back over my 14 seasons in the Premiership the biggest differences are in the standard of stadiums, the players and football. There has been an overall rise in quality, especially with the mass influx of world-class players. It just used to be Italy and Spain who had them but the big TV money has helped bring the stars here, which makes it all more attractive.'

Opposite top **Robbie Fowler's four goals against Middlesbrough took him past the 100 mark for Liverpool.**

Opposite bottom **Dismayed Newcastle fans read the local paper in an attempt to understand why the iconic Kevin Keegan had resigned as manager at St James' Park.**

A few weeks later a relaxed Keegan told *Focus*, 'I had five great years and enjoyed it very much and I think people enjoyed the way we played. I think we won a lot of friends but unfortunately we didn't win the championship.'

The two favourites to succeed him were Kenny Dalglish and Bobby Robson, who was currently in Spain managing Barcelona. Barca were second in La Liga but Robson had taken a lot of criticism in the Spanish Press and the editor of *Focus*, Andrew Clement, thought that it might be worth going over to try and see if he would talk about the possibility of a move back to his native North-East. The story of the trip is told overleaf.

A few days later Kenny Dalglish was handed a three and a half year contract at Newcastle and found himself as Kevin Keegan's replacement for the second time in his career.

The making of a *Focus* report

As Martyn Smith happened to be in the *Grandstand* office on the Thursday evening he was asked to go to Spain the next day with Garry Richardson to see if they could get Barcelona manager Bobby Robson's thoughts on the vacancy at St James' Park. No interview was actually set up but a Spanish crew was organised and Garry and Martyn met at Heathrow the next morning to devise a plan. On the plane Garry mentioned that he'd worked with Robson before and predicted that he would first insist that he couldn't say anything and then talk non-stop.

'We were met at the airport by the Spanish crew, which was a tad larger than we were used to. Normal sport crews consist of two people, one to operate the camera and the other the sound. There were six in the team for this interview: camera, sound, driver, translator, boss and a man who said nothing but smoked a lot of roll-ups. Still, they seemed friendly and knew enough people at Barcelona's ground to help us gain access to the weekly press conference.

Eleanor Oldroyd was also there for Radio Five Live to conduct a previously arranged interview about Spanish football so we latched onto her contact in the club and after a lot of very polite chat and requests from Garry we were told that Bobby would indeed be happy to talk to us. We had the stunning experience of walking out of the players' tunnel and into that amazing stadium where we were met by Robson who immediately apologised but had nothing to say and really couldn't comment.

Once the shot had been set up, the crew were happy and the man who said nothing had gone off for a smoke, the interview began. After 30 minutes we had to change tape and after 45 we were able to wrap. Exactly as predicted, Bobby had opened his heart and we sped back to the airport and went straight to Television Centre where we edited the film, released some of the main quotes to the press in advance and finally handed the tape over for broadcast.

In the interview Robson said that he was very honoured and proud to be at Barcelona but, "I get a wonderful chance to go back home with the club of my choice really, where my head is and my heart is. It's come at the wrong time in a way, but that's life. Of course, the hearts strings are tugging towards Newcastle and nothing would have given me greater pressure than to go there at the right time but I'm honoured and proud to be at Barcelona."'

Opposite A hat-trick from Italian striker Fabrizio Ravanelli helped Middlesbrough to a 6-1 win over Derby County and gave the Teesside club a boost in their struggle to avoid relegation.

Below A goal on his home debut for Paul Kitson helped West Ham to a 4-3 win over Spurs and saw the East London club move out of the relegation zone.

February

Dalglish saw his team enhance their reputation for exciting football when Newcastle beat Leicester 4-3 at St James' Park. In a remarkable game the visitors scored three times in 14 second-half minutes to go 3-1 up, but Alan Shearer responded with a hat-trick in the last quarter of an hour. The first was a free kick through the wall, the second was a shot squeezed between defenders and the keeper, and the winner was a tap-in after Rob Lee's cross went straight across the goal in the final minute as the crowd erupted.

Derby took advantage of West Ham's poor form to register their first win since November when Aljosa Asanovic converted a 53rd-minute penalty. Arsenal suffered their first home league defeat of the season and dropped five points behind Manchester United when goals by Cole and Solskjaer gave them a fifth straight win, 2-1 at Highbury, and Liverpool beat Leeds 4-0 to stay second.

World Service

It was honours even at Stamford Bridge when Chelsea met Manchester United. Gianfranco Zola scored for the Londoners in the second minute and David Beckham replied in the 68th with a rasping volley off the underside of the crossbar to complete the scoring in a 1-1 draw.

In the final week Newcastle moved into third place behind Liverpool after a 1-0 win at Middlesbrough, their first away win for more than four months, while Ian Marshall hit a hat-trick for Leicester as they beat Derby 4-2. West Ham finally moved out of the relegation zone by beating Tottenham 4-3. Defender Julian Dicks added two more to his season's tally and there were headed goals from new signings John Hartson and Paul Kitson on their home debuts.

March

The managerial merry-go-round took another spin when Dave Bassett quit Crystal Palace to become general manager at Forest, Steve Coppell, who had briefly been in charge at Manchester City, rejoined Palace and Frank Clark, the Forest manager at the start of the season, was installed at Maine Road.

Manchester United beat Coventry 3-1 to go four points clear of Liverpool at the top of

the table but Wimbledon suffered a setback, losing 3-1 at home to a resurgent Leicester. The best of the Foxes' three goals was a bicycle kick by Mark Robbins from Emile Heskey's cross.

Under new management Forest pulled off a surprise 1-0 win at Tottenham. Dean Saunders was their sole front man and scored the club's first goal in four games when he turned sharply in the penalty area to beat Ian Walker. But that was to be their last win of the season as they drew seven and lost four of the remaining 11 scoring just seven times. They were in 17th place with 27 points, two ahead of West Ham with Southampton on 24 and Middlesbrough still bottom, five points further adrift. Steffen Iversen hit a hat-trick in Saints' 4-0 win at Sunderland to give them hope, his third a great strike from outside the box with an easy, casual, Le Tissier-like swing of the leg.

Another hat-trick man that day was Ravanelli when Middlesbrough beat Derby 6-1 to set off on a great run that saw them collect 20 points out of a possible 36 in their final 12 games. Neighbouring Sunderland regained form when they defeated Manchester United 2-1 to leave themselves in 15th place with a chance of survival.

Leeds also flattered to deceive when they beat Everton 1-0, but George Graham didn't see his team win any more of their remaining nine games and they only scored four more goals to end with a record low of just 28 goals for the season.

In an amazing repeat of the previous year Liverpool beat Newcastle 4-3 in a cracking game at Anfield. The visitors were 3-0 down but fought back with goals in the 71st, 87th and 88th minutes before Robbie Fowler broke Magpie hearts again with the winner in the 90th. Three points kept the Reds in second place, a point behind leaders Manchester United.

Sheffield Wednesday won their fourth game on the trot, 2-1 against Sunderland, and Chelsea made their biggest score of the season against the same club when they beat Peter Reid's men 6-2. Mark Hughes scored twice and there were also goals from Zola, Dan Petrescu, Roberto Di Matteo and Frank Sinclair. But United marched on with wins at home to Sheffield Wednesday and away at Everton while Liverpool could only pick up a point from a 1-1 draw at Forest.

Liverpool won 2-1 at Arsenal to leave them four points behind United and three points ahead of their hosts in a game best

Above Two headed goals from defender Gary Pallister in a 3-1 victory at Anfield effectively ended the Merseyside club's championship challenge and ensured that the trophy returned to Old Trafford for the third time in five years.

Right After hosting 99 years of football Sunderland's Roker Park saw its last match on 3 May when the home side beat Everton 3-0. But it was too little too late as Sunderland lost their final match of the season, 1-0 at Wimbledon, and were relegated.

The Premiership in Focus **1996–97**

remembered for Robbie Fowler's insistence that he hadn't been fouled by David Seaman when referee Gerald Ashby awarded a penalty to Liverpool. Fowler found himself a tabloid hero because of his spontaneous honesty. The following week he told *Focus* that he had jumped over the keeper, got up quickly and wasn't claiming a penalty. 'I was surprised, I said he hadn't touched me and apologised to Seaman. It was just the natural thing to do as he didn't touch me'.

Joe Royle became the latest managerial casualty on the other side of Stanley Park when he quit Everton after falling out with chairman Peter Johnson over transfer deals.

April

The title race opened up again briefly when Manchester United suffered a shock 3-2 home defeat against Derby. Costa Rican striker Paulo Wanchope scored on his debut when he picked up the ball in his own half and ran through four defenders to make it 2-0. Arsenal took full advantage by winning

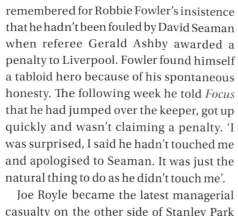

3-0 at Chelsea. With six matches remaining and a game in hand over Arsenal, Manchester United had 63 points, three ahead of both the Gunners and Liverpool, who had played one fewer than United. Newcastle were a further seven points back in fourth place.

Coventry and Southampton filled the bottom two spots, both with 30 points from 32 games. Forest had 31 from 34 and Middlesbrough 32 from 31. Liverpool were the next to falter and suffered their second home defeat of the season, losing 2-1 to Coventry. Gordon Strachan's side gained a crucial three points when Dion Dublin tapped in the winner in the 90th minute after David James missed the ball at a corner.

They followed that by moving out of the drop zone following their 3-1 midweek win over Chelsea. Fellow strugglers Southampton also gave themselves a survival chance by beating West Ham 2-0 and moving up to fifth from bottom. Forest, Middlesbrough and Sunderland now filled the relegation places.

Liverpool won 2-1 at Sunderland but three days later missed their chance to go top by drawing 1-1 with Everton. Their third match in seven days was the one that effectively knocked them out of contention when they lost 3-1 at home to Manchester United. Gary Pallister headed two of the goals and David James had a bad day.

Arsenal slipped up as well, twice, drawing 1-1 with both Blackburn and Coventry to give Manchester United a four-point cushion with two games in hand.

May

Forest became the first side to be relegated when they could only draw 1-1 with Wimbledon on 3 May. Middlesbrough beat Villa 3-2 to cling on but Paul Kitson scored a hat-trick and John Hartson the other two as West Ham surged clear of problems with a 5-1 win against Sheffield Wednesday.

Sunderland beat Everton 3-0 in their last ever game at Roker Park, their home for 99 years, and Southampton gave themselves a further chance of survival by beating Blackburn 2-0. They had been bottom a month before but four wins and three draws had seen them move up the table.

In an anti-climactic finish Manchester United won their fourth Premiership title but it was the third time that they had been crowned champions on a day that they weren't actually playing when Newcastle could only draw 0-0 with West Ham and Liverpool lost 2-1 at Wimbledon. The match at Selhurst Park was also significant because a teenager called Michael Owen scored his first league goal on his league debut for the Reds.

On the final day of the season United celebrated their championship by beating West Ham 2-0 at home to end on 75 points, having won more and lost fewer games than any other team. Newcastle beat Forest 5-0 to go second on goal difference from Arsenal and Liverpool who all finished with 68. Villa were fifth with 61 and Chelsea sixth on 59.

At the other end of the table Sunderland lost 1-0 thanks to an 85th minute goal by Jason Euell at Wimbledon and were relegated. Middlesbrough drew 1-1 at Leeds and ended the season with 42 points – one more than both Coventry and Southampton – but, because the three-point penalty was then applied, they were relegated. To compound an incredibly frustrating season for Boro fans, they also lost both cup finals.

It took Chelsea's Roberto Di Matteo just 42 seconds to open the scoring in the Blues' 2-0 FA Cup final victory over Middlesbrough.

Final League Table

Team	P	W	D	L	F	A	Pts
Manchester United	38	21	12	5	76	44	75
Newcastle United	38	19	11	8	73	40	68
Arsenal	38	19	11	8	62	32	68
Liverpool	38	19	11	8	62	37	68
Aston Villa	38	17	10	11	47	34	61
Chelsea	38	16	11	11	58	55	59
Sheffield Wednesday	38	14	15	9	50	51	57
Wimbledon	38	15	11	12	49	46	56
Leicester City	38	12	11	15	46	54	47
Tottenham Hotspur	38	13	7	18	44	51	46
Leeds United	38	11	13	14	28	38	46
Derby County	38	11	13	14	45	58	46
Blackburn Rovers	38	9	15	14	42	43	42
West Ham United	38	10	12	16	39	48	42
Everton	38	10	12	16	44	57	42
Southampton	38	10	11	17	50	56	41
Coventry City	38	9	14	15	38	54	41
Sunderland	38	10	10	18	35	53	40
Middlesbrough	38	10	12	16	51	60	39*
Nottingham Forest	38	6	16	16	31	59	34

* Middlesbrough had 3 points deducted for failing to fulfill a fixture

Leading Goalscorers league only

Alan Shearer	Newcastle United	25
Ian Wright	Arsenal	23
Robbie Fowler	Liverpool	18
Ole Gunnar Solskjaer	Manchester United	18
Dwight Yorke	Aston Villa	17
Fabrizio Ravanelli	Middlesbrough	16
Les Ferdinand	Newcastle United	16
Matthew Le Tissier	Southampton	13
Dion Dublin	Coventry City	13

Awards

Footballer of the Year
Gianfranco Zola, Chelsea

PFA Player of the Year
Alan Shearer, Newcastle United

PFA Young Player of the Year
David Beckham, Manchester United

Opposite Ole Gunnar Solskjaer, David Beckham and Phil Neville celebrate with the Premiership trophy on the pitch at Old Trafford on the final day of the season.

Honours List 1996–97

Champions Manchester United

Runners-up Newcastle United

Relegated Nottingham Forest, Middlesbrough, Sunderland

Promoted Bolton Wanderers, Barnsley, Crystal Palace

FA Cup Winners Chelsea

League Cup Winners Leicester City

League Cup
Leicester City beat Middlesbrough 1-0 in a replay having drawn the first match 1-1. Steve Claridge hit the winning goal in the 10th minute of extra time.

FA Cup
Middlesbrough had already suffered the heartbreak of losing the League Cup final and had also been relegated just six days before they walked out to face Chelsea at Wembley. They couldn't have got off to a worse start when Roberto Di Matteo scored the fastest FA Cup final goal at Wembley after just 42 seconds. Eight minutes from the end Eddie Newton added a second and Dennis Wise lifted the cup to celebrate Chelsea's first win in the competition for 27 years.

FF 1997–98

It was a season to remember for the Reds in North London as Arsène Wenger won not only his first Premiership title but the FA Cup as well, as the Gunners repeated their double success for the first time since 1971.

Programmes

Gary Lineker was still presenting *Football Focus* from inside the virtual football but he had a wider variety of guests this season including Trevor Brooking, Peter Beardsley and Graeme Le Saux. The former Liverpool defender Mark Lawrenson made his first appearance alongside Gary on 30 August and made increasingly regular contributions throughout the following months. He seemed to enjoy the Saturday sofa routine and a decade and three presenters on is still there, albeit without the moustache. Ray Stubbs also presented several editions of the show as well as conducting many interviews including, in February, a rare chat with David Beckham who was still being kept on a tight leash by Alex Ferguson. It was in the 'curtain' phase of the Beckham locks.

Presenter
Gary Lineker

Pre-season

Manchester United's talisman, Eric Cantona, stunned fans by announcing his retirement from football just before his 31st birthday. Further changes at Old Trafford saw Roy Keane made captain and Teddy Sheringham join from Tottenham for £3.5m.

Other major transfers included Marc Overmars moving from Ajax to Arsenal for £7m, Stan Collymore joining Aston Villa for the same fee and Paul Ince signing for Liverpool from Inter Milan for £4.2m. Middlesbrough's transactions included selling Juninho to Atlético Madrid for £12m and buying Paul Merson for £5m.

Newcastle were left looking vulnerable up front when they sold David Ginola and Les Ferdinand to Tottenham for £2.5m and £6m respectively, especially when Alan Shearer injured ankle ligaments in a pre-season friendly at Goodison Park, had an operation the next day and was out for several months. Another major casualty was Liverpool's Robbie Fowler who also missed much of the season when he badly injured his knee in a friendly in Oslo.

Early management changes saw Southampton appoint Stockport's Dave Jones to the hot seat after Graeme Souness' falling out with chairman Rupert Lowe, and at Everton where Howard Kendall returned for his third spell as manager.

August 1997

The opening games of the season were played in very hot weather and Manchester United made a good start to their title defence, beating Tottenham 2-0 at White Hart Lane. The returning Sheringham was on the end of a lot of stick, especially when he missed a penalty. Dion Dublin's hat-trick enabled Coventry to start the new campaign with a 3-2 win over Chelsea, but they only won two of their next 16.

Faustino Asprilla scored twice and celebrated with a spectacular somersault as Newcastle beat Sheffield Wednesday although the Owls' goal, by Benito Carbone, was the most spectacular. He took the ball on his chest, chipped it up and fired an overhead volley into the net. New boys Crystal Palace and Bolton won 2-1 at Everton and 1-0 at Southampton respectively but Barnsley lost 2-1 at home to West Ham. In sharp contrast to the previous season Blackburn, under new manager Roy Hodgson, went top after Chris Sutton scored a hat-trick in their 4-0 win at Villa Park.

Derby County had moved to a new home at Pride Park and *Focus* told the story of the building of their new £23m stadium of 'gleaming glass and concrete' which was opened by the Queen. More than 25,000 fans turned up to see the first match against Wimbledon, but 11 minutes into the second half the lights failed and the match was abandoned. Sunderland also had a new home, the Stadium of Light. There wasn't any royalty at its opening but Status Quo arrived in a helicopter and played on the pitch.

West Ham had a perfect start, following their opening day victory in Yorkshire with a 2-1 win at home to Tottenham. Hammers manager Harry Redknapp appeared on *Focus* to talk about his rising star, 18-year-old defender Rio Ferdinand. 'He is an outstanding prospect and every club in the country would want to buy the kid, but he's not for sale. If West Ham want to start selling Rio and people like that then we shouldn't be in the Premier League and we're going nowhere except into the First Division.'

In a high scoring weekend towards the end of the month Gianluca Vialli scored four of Chelsea's six at Barnsley and Blackburn topped the table after beating Sheffield Wednesday 7-2. In a lively encounter, Wednesday's Carbone was sent off for a headbutt after scoring twice and

Rovers' keeper, John Filan, broke his arm. Chris Sutton and Kevin Gallagher scored two each for Rovers.

There was an amazing game between Arsenal and Leicester at Filbert Street when Denis Bergkamp put the visitors two up before Emile Heskey and Matt Elliott, in the 84th and 90th minutes, made it 2-2. Bergkamp put the Londoners back in front when he completed his hat-trick in injury time, but then Steve Walsh drew the home team level in the sixth minute of added time.

After the first four matches Blackburn and Manchester United were top with ten points each and Arsenal were third with eight points. Aston Villa sat at the foot of the table having lost all four of their opening games.

Derby striker Ashley Ward can't hide his disappointment as the police decide to abandon the match with Wimbledon, the first at the new Pride Park, because of floodlight failure.

September

Ray Stubbs presented *Focus* with Trevor Brooking and posed the question, which Premier League goalkeeper can throw the ball the furthest? He claimed that third was Aston Villa's Mark Bosnich who could throw the ball to (Dwight) Yorke, in second place was Ian Walker of Tottenham who could reach (Justin) Edinburgh with the winner being Steve Ogrizovic at Coventry who was able to get it as far as (Dion) Dublin. A debate then ensured as to whether Dublin or Edinburgh was furthest. It had clearly been a quiet week in the production office.

Southampton were struggling without the injured Matt Le Tissier and went down 1-0 at Coventry. They had taken just three points from six games and only scored four goals. That was a commodity in ready supply at Ewood Park when there were seven in the first 34 minutes of the game when Blackburn lost 4-3 at home to Leeds.

Leicester had made a strong start to the season and were in third place after winning 1-0 at Leeds. Their front line was led by 19-year-old Emile Heskey who was gaining a reputation for scoring spectacular goals. His father was interviewed and had no doubt that his son would go a long way in football. He had named him Emile William Ivanhoe: William after his grandfather and Ivanhoe because it was his favourite movie of all time.

Arsenal took top spot from Manchester United on goal difference when they beat West Ham 4-0 and Alex Ferguson saw his side suffer their first defeat, 1-0 at Leeds. David Wetherall's diving header in the 34th minute was the difference between the teams but more importantly for United, Roy Keane snapped a cruciate ligament, which kept him sidelined for the rest of the season.

Derby County were proving to be one of the successes of the early season and scored nine in two games to go eighth. They won 5-2 at Sheffield Wednesday and then beat Southampton 4-0. Jim Smith had put together an early example of the Premiership's foreign legion with players from Estonia, Denmark, Holland, Croatia, Italy, Jamaica, Costa Rica, the Republic of Ireland, Scotland and England.

October

After nine games Arsenal led with 19 points, one ahead of Manchester United and Leicester with Chelsea and Blackburn both on 16. Southampton were still bottom with four points out of a possible 27. Barnsley, Sheffield Wednesday, Bolton and Everton sat above them although Danny Wilson saw his Barnsley side drop to 20th place when they were on the wrong end of a 5-0 beating by Arsenal. They stayed in the bottom three for the remainder of the season, losing the most games, 23, and with the leakiest defence, conceding 82 goals.

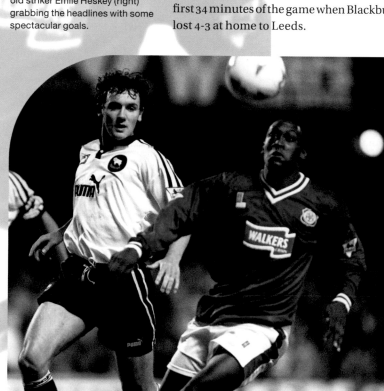

Premiership new boys Leicester City made a good start to the season with local-born 19-year-old striker Emile Heskey (right) grabbing the headlines with some spectacular goals.

Long-server Teddy Sheringham

Teddy Sheringham holds the Premier League records as the oldest scorer (he's got 147 so far) and outfield player and sits fifth in the all-time list of appearances.

Born in London on 2 April 1966 he began his career with Millwall in 1984 and, after a season with Nottingham Forest, signed for Tottenham in 1992, spending seven seasons with them in

two separate spells either side of a successful four-year period at Manchester United.

Sheringham was part of their treble-winning side in 1999 and won two other Premiership titles before returning to White Hart Lane on a free transfer. He spent a season with Portsmouth and then joined Championship side West Ham in 2005 and helped them win promotion back into the top flight.

Everton's Danny Cadamarteri scores Everton's first in a 2-0 victory in the Merseyside derby at Goodison Park on 18 October. But it was a false dawn for the Blue half of the city as they went bottom in early November, following a 2-1 defeat by Aston Villa.

Les Ferdinand and Ruel Fox missed the start of the second half of their 1-0 defeat at Newcastle when they were locked in a toilet. Some fans claimed that it was an appropriate place for them to be as Tottenham had scored just one goal in their last six matches. Also frustrated were Saints supporters and Southampton's 3-0 win against West Ham was only their second out of a possible ten, but it proved to be the start of a period of four wins in five as the returning Matt Le Tissier's influence turned things around.

Although Liverpool went into the first Merseyside derby of the season fresh from a 4-2 win over Chelsea, thanks to Patrick Berger's first hat-trick for the club, they were beaten 2-0 by Everton. Neil Ruddock turned in an own goal and 18-year-old Danny Cadamarteri scored with a terrific solo effort. He ran half the length of the pitch, turned the defender and calmly placed the ball in the bottom left-hand corner.

Leeds moved into sixth place after beating Newcastle 4-1 thanks to goals from new signing Bruno Ribeiro, Harry Kewell, David Weatherall and an own goal by John Beresford. It was a relief for the home crowd as they had only seen their team score twice in the previous five games at Elland Road. By contrast Frank Leboeuf's stunning 88th-minute drive for Chelsea against Leicester was their 25th goal in ten matches and only Manchester United scored more than their 71.

After six defeats in a row Ashley Ward and Neil Redfearn scored against Coventry to give Barnsley a rare win but they promptly lost their next match 7-0 to Manchester United. Andy Cole struck three, Ryan Giggs two and Paul Scholes and Karel Poborsky one each as they returned to the top of the table.

At the end of the month one of the worst Premiership signings, Tomas Brolin, left Leeds on a free transfer. He had cost £4.5m but in two years the Swede played just 27 games and scored four times.

November

United went four points clear when they beat second bottom Sheffield Wednesday 6-1 with two goals each from Sheringham, Cole and Solskjaer. Despite finishing seventh the previous May manager David Pleat was sacked and Ron Atkinson returned for a second spell in charge having left in 1991 to join Aston Villa. He agreed to stay until the end of the season to try and keep them up and, when interviewed by Gary on *Focus*, explained, 'I miss the buzz and the adrenalin flow.' He was a bit concerned about fans reaction but reminded viewers that he was still the only manager in the game to win major trophies with three different clubs.

Arsenal surrendered the last unbeaten record when Derby beat them 3-0 and struggling Everton lost all five games this month starting with a 2-0 defeat at home to Southampton. There were problems of a different sort at Upton Park where West Ham were 2-2 with Crystal Palace when the floodlights mysteriously failed in the 65th minute arousing match-fixing suspicions.

Liverpool's 4-0 win over Tottenham, which included Michael Owen's first goal at Anfield, added to the pressure on Gerry Francis. The club had slipped to 16th place and a few days later he quit after three years in charge as he felt he couldn't do any more with the team, although Alan Sugar had wanted him to stay. To the shock of most fans he was replaced by Christian Gross of Grasshoppers Zurich. Sugar told *Focus*, 'We feel that a continental approach to a Premier League club is needed for the future.'

Arsenal moved to within a point of the leaders when David Platt headed a late winner in their 3-2 win over Manchester United and Chelsea moved third, three points adrift but with a goal in hand, when they beat West Ham 2-1.

The 26,309 fans who went to Selhurst Park to watch Wimbledon take on Manchester

Announcer James Alexander Gordon

For any football fan who has tuned into the radio to hear the results at 5.00 p.m. on a Saturday afternoon when they are on the way back from a match, there is only one voice that they want to hear after the famous theme tune 'Out of the Blue' has been played – that of James Alexander Gordon.

His iconic and distinctive tones have been heard for almost 40 years on *Sports Report* from when it was on the BBC Third Programme, Radio 2 and now Radio Five Live. Born in 1935 the former actor drives into Television Centre every Saturday and makes his way to his booth before seamlessly reading the football scores and signing off with his trademark flourish and the pools news.

United had the ultimate experience of a game of two halves. Goalless after 45 minutes they saw seven goals after the break as the visitors won 5-2.

There were differing fortunes for the two new managers in their first home games. Atkinson's Wednesday won 2-0 against Arsenal but Tottenham lost 1-0 to Crystal Palace. It was Palace's last win for four months, a run that saw them drop from 12th to 20th place. Tottenham, however, recovered the following week with a 2-0 win at Goodison Park, a result that left Everton at the foot of the table on 12 points.

Chelsea beat Derby 4-0 to go level on 31 points with Manchester United at the top. Zola scored a hat-trick and Mark Hughes chipped in with a spectacular scissor kick. Blackburn were 3rd on 30 points followed by Leeds with 29 and Arsenal 27, although in the final games of the month United beat Blackburn 4-0 to move three clear again and Liverpool ended Arsenal's unbeaten home record when Steve McManaman scored the only goal in the 55th minute.

December

The good form of the leading pair continued when Manchester United won 3-1 at Liverpool and Chelsea inflicted the worst home defeat on Tottenham since 1935 when they won 6-1 with Norwegian striker Tore Andre Flo scoring a hat-trick. Blackburn moved back into second place after winning 3-1 at Highbury and Southampton ended a run of three defeats when they beat Leicester 2-1. Matt Le Tissier opened the scoring and then Francis Benali headed his first goal in 285 games.

Barnsley, Everton and Tottenham were in the three relegation places although Everton's 1-0 win at Leicester was their first away from home in the league for more than a year and their first in nine games.

Below A troubled season for Tottenham was made worse by a 6-1 thrashing at the hands of London rivals Chelsea for whom Norwegian striker Tore Andre Flo scored a hat-trick.

Right Ron Atkinson's reign as manager at Sheffield Wednesday began with a 2-0 home win over in-form Arsenal.

Three days before Christmas there came one of the biggest turnarounds in recent Premiership history when Alan Sugar welcomed Jurgen Kinsmann back to Tottenham on a six-month contract from Sampdoria. The move coincided with David Pleat's appointment as director of football at the club. But soon after the festive season there was more woe for Tottenham when Darren Anderton and Les Ferdinand were injured in their 1-1 draw with Arsenal. Their misery was compounded when Everton beat Bolton 3-2 courtesy of a hat-trick of headed goals from striker Duncan Ferguson and leapfrogged the Londoners, sending them into the New Year in 19th place.

January 1998

The Premiership didn't restart until 10 January and suddenly the title race seemed to be a foregone conclusion. Gary opened *Focus* by saying, 'After Chelsea 3 Manchester United 5 in the FA Cup third round, can anyone stop United in the league? Not on last weekend's evidence.' United added weight to the argument by beating Tottenham 2-0. It was billed as Sheringham versus Klinsmann, but it was Giggs who scored twice as they finished the day with a seven-point lead. He rifled in a volley for the first and headed the second.

West Ham remained in the top half after beating Barnsley 6-0, their biggest win of the season, and there was also a good start to the New Year for Arsenal. Marc Overmars scored both goals in their 2-1 win over Leeds to take them to fifth, 12 points off the lead.

Newcastle's troubles were the main talking point for Gary and Mark Lawrenson on *Focus* as Kenny Dalglish had been there a year but they had gone eight league games without a win, the worst run in a decade for the club. It was a shock for fans after the Keegan years especially with Ferdinand, Ginola, Beardsley and Asprilla all gone. Kevin Keegan was concerned that players were being sold as the club now had to satisfy the shareholders. The drought ended that afternoon when Alan Shearer returned after six months away injured, coming on as a sub towards the end of their 2-1 win over Bolton, but although he played in all Newcastle's remaining games, he only scored twice.

The following week Klinsmann scored his first goal since returning to Tottenham when they beat West Ham 1-0 and fellow strugglers Everton also pulled off a rare victory with a 3-1 result against Chelsea. They moved briefly up to 13th, but only won two of their remaining 15 matches as Kendall was unable to revive their fortunes.

Manchester United dropped six points in the last two weeks of the month when they lost 1-0 at Southampton, despite playing safe and turning out in white shirts this season, and suffered their first home defeat of the season, 1-0 to Leicester. Tony Cottee struck the winner in the 30th minute. It was his first of the season and his first ever at Old Trafford in 15 years of trying. Arsenal ended the month by putting three past Southampton, but were still eight points off the lead. The goals, from Dennis Bergkamp, Tony Adams and Nicolas Anelka, all came in a seven-minute spell in the second half.

February

Tottenham were in desperate trouble having lost five of their last nine in the league, gone out of the FA Cup early and seen Klinsmann injured but Christian Gross was convinced that good times would come. 'When I came the situation was already critical and still is but I have to do my best and believe I can do a good job for Tottenham.' Mark Lawrenson noted that although Gross had brought in a lot of strikers, including Nicola Berti and Klinsmann, they remained very weak defensively and were conceding two goals a game. After 24 matches they remained in 18th place with only 23 points, sandwiched between Bolton and Palace with Barnsley still last.

Manchester United drew 1-1 with Bolton at Old Trafford but still extended their lead because of the surprising results elsewhere. Blackburn lost 3-0 at home to Tottenham and Liverpool were shocked at Anfield when

Above The turning point? Arsenal's Marc Overmars strokes the ball past Manchester United keeper Peter Schmeichel at Old Trafford to secure three points, leaving the Londoners six points behind their title rivals but, crucially, with three games in hand.

Opposite Two first-half goals from Stephen Hughes were enough to secure a 2-0 victory for Arsenal against Chelsea at Highbury in early February.

Southampton won 3-2 with Egil Ostenstad and David Hirst scoring in the closing five minutes. Arsenal fared better, winning 2-0 against Chelsea, Stephen Hughes scoring both, to stay fifth with a game in hand but still six points behind the leaders. Chelsea chairman Ken Bates then stunned their fans by sacking manager Ruud Gullit despite the club being in second place. Even more surprising was the elevation of Gianluca Vialli to player-manager.

There was a blow for Arsène Wenger when he lost Ian Wright, who needed a cartilage operation having just recovered from a hamstring injury, and he missed the next 11 league games, but the Gunners still moved into second place with a 1-0 win over Palace, despite having 13 of their first-team squad unavailable through injury.

In yet another managerial change Brian Little surprisingly quit Aston Villa after four years, leaving them in the bottom half of the table. His replacement was the Wycombe boss John Gregory.

Phil Neville scored his first goal in senior football when he beat Chelsea's offside trap to secure the points in the top-of-the-table clash at Stamford Bridge and give Manchester United a seemingly unassailable 11-point cushion. They were so far ahead that one pessimistic Manchester bookmaker even paid out on them as champions. Chris Sutton's hat-trick steered Blackburn through a snow flurry and back into second spot with a 5-3 win over Leicester.

March

In a bottom of the table clash at White Hart Lane Tottenham beat Bolton 1-0 when Allan Nielsen scored in the 45th minute to secure a vital maximum points for the Londoners, and at the other end of the table Manchester United began to slip up, losing 2-0 at Sheffield Wednesday and then drawing 1-1 at West Ham.

Leeds went fifth when they beat Blackburn 4-0 and Chelsea recovered form to put six past crisis club Crystal Palace. Italian midfielder Attilio Lombardo was now in charge at Selhurst Park with Steve Coppell as general manager amid rumours that Terry Venables was about to take over.

The real turning point of the campaign took place on 14 March when Arsenal closed the gap to six points with three games in hand by beating Manchester United 1-0 at Old Trafford. Marc Overmars scored the only goal in the 79th minute, running onto Anelka's header before firing home through Schmeichel's legs. Despite this defeat United still looked like a safe bet for the title at that stage and Alex Ferguson remained confident. He told *Focus*, 'They'll have to win the games in hand and they'll find out how difficult that is. It makes it interesting doesn't it.'

Liverpool's 3-2 win at Barnsley ended in chaos with the home team down to eight players after three of them had been sent off. The match was suspended for a period when the referee, Gary Willard, left the pitch after angry Barnsley fans invaded the playing area. They were wrestled to the ground by players and officials before order was restored and the match restarted.

Meanwhile, Arsenal relentlessly narrowed the gap with 1-0 wins over Sheffield Wednesday and Bolton. Although Martin Keown was sent off in the match against Bolton at the Reebok, it proved to be a great day for Wenger's men when they secured victory through Chris Wreh's long-range shot in the 48th minute to keep a club and Premiership record eight consecutive clean sheets and move three points behind United, still with one game in hand.

April

It was Grand National day on 4 April so Tim Gudgin voiced the Premier League Relegation Hurdle odds. There were now five clubs who looked like candidates for the drop: *Focus* quoted them as Crystal Palace 33-1, Bolton 1-5, Barnsley 1-4, Everton 11-4 and Tottenham 11-4. The following weekend Bolton and Barnsley both won 2-1, Palace lost 3-0 at home to Leicester and Tottenham lost 2-0 at Chelsea. When the final whistles went Palace remained bottom with 26 points and looked doomed, but there were only four points between Barnsley, Bolton, Tottenham and Everton who had all played the same number of games.

On 13 April Arsenal played one of their two games in hand, against Blackburn, and were four up by half time, eventually winning 4-1 to close the gap to one point. After 34 games United had 67 points, Arsenal were on 66 from 32 with Liverpool eight points further back and Chelsea and Leeds level on 54.

A week later Manchester United were knocked off top spot for the first time in six

Premiership-winning manager Arsène Wenger

Arsenal's multilingual manager, Arsène Wenger, was born in Strasbourg on 22 October 1949.

He gained a Masters degree in economics before managing AS Monaco to the French Cup and league title. After an 18-month spell in charge of Japanese side Nagoya Grampus Eight, he arrived at Highbury as a relatively unknown figure on 1 October 1986.

Since then he has become the most successful manager in the club's history, winning the double in his second season, repeating that feat in 2002 and collecting three Premiership titles and four FA Cups in total. In 2004 his team became the first since 1888–89 to remain unbeaten for an entire league season. Arsenal's Premiership record is second only to that of their great rivals Manchester United. They have also come second on five occasions and also been runners-up in the 2000 UEFA Cup and the 2006 Champions League.

Widely credited with changing the training and dietary regimes in British football and renowned for his astute signings of overseas players, Wenger was also instrumental in the design of Arsenal's new Emirates Stadium and training ground and has now been in their dug out for more than 600 games.

Opposite top With the score at 2-2 referee Gary Willard gives Barnsley's Darren Sheridan his marching orders during their match against Liverpool at Oakwell in March. Already down to nine men following the dismissals of Darren Barnard and Chris Morgan, eight-man Barnsley conceded a last-minute goal to lose the match and, eventually, their place in the Premiership.

Opposite Arsenal striker Christopher Wreh sums up that winning feeling at Highbury after scoring in the Gunners 5-0 win over Wimbledon, a result that saw them move into top spot.

months when they could only draw 1-1 at home with Newcastle and Arsenal beat Wimbledon 5-0. The following week the Gunners beat Barnsley 2-0 and moved four points ahead knowing that all they had to do was win two of their remaining four matches to be champions.

There was a crucial win for Tottenham when headers by Klinsmann and Ferdinand secured a 2-0 win over Newcastle but bad news for Crystal Palace who were relegated when Manchester United beat them 3-0 at Selhurst Park.

Arsenal were looking good though and beat Derby 1-0 with a 34th-minute strike from Emmanuel Petit to leave them one match from glory with 75 points from 35 games, a lead of four and still having played a match fewer than United.

May

There was the possibility of a lifeline for Bolton when they beat Palace 5-2 and moved out of the bottom three for the first time since January. Colin Todd's team perfectly demonstrated the gulf between the Premiership and Division One as they were to score 41 goals this season compared to 100 when they were promoted the previous year.

Barnsley, however, went straight back down when they lost 1-0 at Leicester while Klinsmann scored four goals in 19 minutes to help Tottenham beat Wimbledon 6-2 at Selhurst Park and almost guarantee safety. Going into the last week of the season Everton were in the final relegation place with 39 points from 36 games. Bolton had played one game more and were a point above on 40.

On 3 May Arsenal beat Everton 4-0 to win their first Premiership title and their 11th top division championship overall. The match ended with their captain Tony Adams volleying home Steve Bould's pass having beaten the offside trap. Arsène Wenger became the first foreign manager to win the Premier League and the team set a new Premiership record with their tenth successive win. Ian Wright, who had missed much of the season through injury, came on as a late substitute, grinning broadly before a jubilant Adams received the trophy on the Highbury pitch in the spring sunshine.

Manchester United finished second a point behind the Londoners, but immediately signalled their intention to win back the crown by making Jaap Stam the world's most expensive defender when he signed for a club record £10.75m from Dutch club PSV Eindhoven.

The final relegation spot went to Bolton when they lost 2-0 at Chelsea and Everton drew 1-1 with Coventry. Both teams finished on 40 points but the Merseysiders narrowly survived as they had conceded fewer goals.

Having achieved his goal of keeping Sheffield Wednesday up, albeit in 16th place, Ron Atkinson left the club again after his short-term contract was not renewed.

Final League Table

Team	P	W	D	L	F	A	Pts
Arsenal	38	23	9	6	68	33	78
Manchester United	38	23	8	7	73	26	77
Liverpool	38	18	11	9	68	42	65
Chelsea	38	20	3	15	71	43	63
Leeds United	38	17	8	13	57	46	59
Blackburn Rovers	38	16	10	12	57	52	58
Aston Villa	38	17	6	15	49	48	57
West Ham United	38	16	8	14	56	57	56
Derby County	38	16	7	15	52	49	55
Leicester City	38	13	14	11	51	41	53
Coventry City	38	12	16	10	46	44	52
Southampton	38	14	6	18	50	55	48
Newcastle United	38	11	11	16	35	44	44
Tottenham Hotspur	38	11	11	16	44	56	44
Wimbledon	38	10	14	14	34	46	44
Sheffield Wednesday	38	12	8	18	52	67	44
Everton	38	9	13	16	41	56	40
Bolton Wanderers	38	9	13	16	41	61	40
Barnsley	38	10	5	23	37	82	35
Crystal Palace	38	8	9	21	37	71	32

Leading Goalscorers league only

Dion Dublin	Coventry City	18
Michael Owen	Liverpool	18
Chris Sutton	Blackburn Rovers	18
Dennis Bergkamp	Arsenal	16
J F Hasselbaink	Leeds United	16
Andy Cole	Manchester United	16
Kevin Gallagher	Blackburn Rovers	16
John Hartson	West Ham United	15
Darren Huckerby	Coventry City	14
Paulo Wanchope	Derby County	13

Awards

Footballer of the Year
Dennis Bergkamp, Arsenal

PFA Player of the Year
Dennis Bergkamp, Arsenal

PFA Young Player of the Year
Michael Owen, Liverpool

Opposite In a fitting end to the season Arsenal captain Tony Adams volleys the last goal in a 4-0 triumph over Everton which wrapped up the Gunners' first Premiership title in the last home game of the league season.

Below A jubilant Ian Wright celebrates in front of the Highbury hordes after coming on as a late substitute against Everton. Two weeks later there was further joy for north London when Arsenal beat Newcastle in the FA Cup final at Wembley to wrap up the double.

Honours List 1997–98

Champions Arsenal

Runners-up Manchester United

Relegated Bolton Wanderers, Barnsley, Crystal Palace

Promoted Nottingham Forest, Middlesbrough, Charlton Athletic

FA Cup Winners Arsenal

League Cup Winners Chelsea

League Cup

In a repeat of the previous year's FA Cup final, Chelsea beat Middlesbrough, also the previous year's League Cup runners-up, 2-0 in extra time with goals by Frank Sinclair in the 95th minute and Roberto Di Matteo in the 107th. It was the Blues' first win in the competition since 1965.

FA Cup

Newcastle United, chasing their first FA Cup victory since 1955, were to be disappointed once again as Arsenal emulated their 1971 double, winning the Wembley final 2-0. Marc Overmars scored the first after 23 minutes and in the second half Nicolas Anelka's shot secured the win to enable Tony Adams to lift the FA Cup for the second time in six seasons.

FF 1998—99

Aston Villa started the season well with new manager John Gregory singling out midfielder Ian Taylor for special praise as the Villans earned eight wins and four draws in their first 12 games.

Programmes

This was the season when Gary Lineker and Mark Lawrenson really began to develop their double act. Ray Stubbs also presented several shows and Damian Johnson joined the reporter roster. As well as the main presenters the role of the reporter has been crucial throughout the history of *Football Focus* as they generate ideas, carry extensive contact books, conduct the interviews, report on the programme's many weekly features and voice the goal packages.

When the Premiership began the commentators Clive Tyldesley and Jon Champion were two of the regular reporters alongside Tony Gubba and Gerald Sinstadt, but since then many have passed through the voice-over booths on a Friday afternoon. As well as those mentioned elsewhere in the book, Mark Pougatch, Steve May, Rebecca Lowe, Matt Smith, Ivan Gaskell, Ian Payne, and Juliette Ferrington have all had stints on the road each week visiting the Premiership grounds of England.

Presenter
Gary Lineker

Pre-season

Rangers boss Walter Smith crossed the border to become Everton's new manager as Howard Kendall had left the club for a third time, and Danny Wilson moved from relegated Barnsley to take charge at Sheffield Wednesday. A more unusual change took place at Anfield when Gérard Houllier, the former French national coach, became joint Liverpool manager with Roy Evans.

In the transfer market Chelsea signed Marcel Desailly for £4.6m from AC Milan. Several veterans were also on the move. Ian Wright joined West Ham, Mark Hughes switched from Chelsea to Southampton and Steve Staunton returned from Aston Villa to Liverpool.

August 1998

The opening day of the season wasn't a great one for TV viewers or studio editors as there were four 0-0 draws. Supporters of Newcastle and Charlton, Middlesbrough and Leeds, Everton and Villa and Blackburn and Derby failed to see a single goal between them, but there was one at Hillsborough where Ian Wright scored on his debut for West Ham against Sheffield Wednesday.

In the other matches with goals Wimbledon beat Tottenham 3-1, Chelsea lost 2-1 at Coventry and Manchester United drew 2-2 with Leicester. The following day there was instant success for the new managerial double act as Liverpool won 2-1 at Southampton and champions Arsenal began their defence of the Premiership with a 2-1 victory over Nottingham Forest.

On 20 August Alex Ferguson bolstered his squad still further signing Swedish international Jesper Blomqvist and Dwight Yorke from Aston Villa for a club record £12.6m. The Tobagan made his debut just a couple of days later in a goalless draw at West Ham.

It was 51 years since Charlton had played a top-flight match at the Valley and they celebrated by scoring five against Southampton. John Robinson scored the first after three minutes and Clive Mendonca hit a second-half hat-trick.

Just two weeks into the season and after 19 months in the job Kenny Dalglish was sacked as Newcastle manager and replaced by another star name in Ruud Gullit. He told *Focus* that he had empathy for Dalglish but felt that the club suited him and that he would do well there. Tottenham were also in trouble and the tabloids were gunning for manager Christian Gross. He was interviewed nine months to the day since his first game and looked under enormous stress following defeats in the club's opening two games.

With pressure mounting Tottenham registered their first win, 1-0 at Everton, when Les Ferdinand headed in from David Ginola's corner in the fifth minute. Gross had dropped their goalkeeper, Ian Walker, for Espen Baardsen and said afterwards, 'Our main targets were a clean sheet and a win. We got both and I'm pleased.'

Nottingham Forest inflicted a third defeat in a row on Southampton when they won 2-1 at the Dell. But it proved to be a rare highpoint for Dave Bassett's newly promoted side, as they didn't win again for five months.

September

Leeds topped the table after beating Southampton 3-0 – helped by an unusual opening goal when Jimmy Floyd Hasselbaink's shot was deflected in off Scott Marshall's backside – and Dwight Yorke scored twice on his Manchester United home debut when they beat Charlton 4-1. Paul Merson also scored in his first match for Aston Villa following his £6.75m move from Middlesbrough as they moved into first place with a 2-0 win against Wimbledon

The charismatic Ruud Gullit took his own brand of 'sexy' football to Tyneside when he was appointed Newcastle manager following the departure of Kenny Dalglish just two weeks into the season.

while his former club, Arsenal, spent £3m on Freddie Ljungberg, a 21-year-old Swede from Halmstad. David Pleat added the caretaker manager title to that of director of football at Tottenham when the luckless Christian Gross was sacked by Alan Sugar after just three matches of the new season.

One of the most exciting games of the year came when West Ham played Wimbledon at Upton Park. Having been three up in the first 27 minutes with two goals by Wright and one from John Hartson, the Hammers conceded four with Efan Ekoku heading the winner in the 81st minute.

Five games into the campaign Villa topped the table with 13 points, three ahead of Liverpool with Leeds a point further back in third. Southampton were having another wretched start, their worst ever, losing five in a row. It was to be a tough season for Saints' fans as only Forest scored fewer or

Tottenham's David Ginola shows Middlesbrough's Andy Townsend how it's done. However, Boro's 3-0 win was the Londoners' third defeat in their first four games.

after being sent off in Sheffield Wednesday's 1-0 win over Arsenal. Alcock went down as though he had been poleaxed. Di Canio was fined £10,000 and banned for 11 games.

Leeds chairman Peter Ridsdale joined Gary in the *Focus* studio at the end of the month amidst speculation that he was about to lose his manager, George Graham, to Tottenham. 'I believe George is happy, loyal to Leeds United and will still be here in the coming weeks.' One week later Graham took charge at White Hart Lane and his assistant, David O'Leary, succeeded him at Leeds.

October

Aston Villa's Ian Taylor scored twice in their 2-1 win at Coventry. It was their sixth win in eight games and left them top on 20 points, six clear of Manchester United who also won away, 3-0 at Southampton. Dwight Yorke scored from Andy Cole's cross in the 12th minute, Cole lifted the ball over the keeper on the hour and Jordi Cruyff volleyed a third with 15 minutes to go.

On 6 October, in an attempt to head off a breakaway European Super League by the dissatisfied top clubs, UEFA announced major restructuring changes to their European competitions. The Cup-Winners' Cup and the UEFA Cup were to be merged and the Champions League expanded to 32 teams.

Middlesbrough beat Blackburn 2-1 to go third while a resurgent Chelsea moved into fourth spot, a rise of 12 places in three games after their 2-1 win over Charlton. Southampton, in 20th place, had taken two points from a possible 27, Coventry sat above them with five and Forest and Blackburn each had eight.

Michael Owen scored four times in Liverpool's 5-1 win over Forest and in their tenth game Southampton finally collected three points beating Coventry 2-0. Villa drew 1-1 with Leicester to stay top and still unbeaten

conceded more goals, but they finally broke their duck by drawing 1-1 with Tottenham. Ruel Fox put Tottenham ahead but Matthew Le Tissier struck his 200th goal for the club in the 65th minute with an inevitably classy pull down and shot.

Robbie Fowler scored twice in his first Premiership start since February when Liverpool drew 3-3 with Charlton and there were also two from Alan Shearer in Newcastle's 5-1 win at Coventry. Jim Smith's Derby were having a terrific opening to the season and when they beat Leicester 2-0 moved into second place behind Villa, unbeaten in six games

Paolo di Canio became villain of the month when he pushed referee Paul Alcock

after ten games. It was their best league start since 1932 and eight of John Gregory's first-team squad were home grown.

In the battle of the strikers between Leicester and Liverpool, 33-year-old Tony Cottee, who's career had started when Michael Owen was only 3-years-old, came out on top when his 79th minute goal won the points for Leicester and marked the first of three consecutive defeats for the Merseysiders who dropped to mid-table.

November

Dion Dublin was on the move again, this time to Aston Villa for £5.75m. He told *Focus* that he felt Gordon Strachan and Coventry had made him a better player but he wanted to play for a bigger club and he scored twice on his debut in their 3-2 win over Tottenham.

There was a cracking game at The Dell where Middlesbrough were 2-1 up against Southampton with just eight minutes left on the clock although they'd had Robbie Mustoe and Phil Stamp sent off. Southampton hit two quick goals but Gianluca Festa scored the equaliser in injury time. A point kept Boro in fourth place, behind Villa, Manchester United and Arsenal. One place below them came Derby County who increased the pressure on Liverpool's managerial partnership by beating them 2-1 at Anfield. Speaking on that evening's *Match of the Day* Alan Hansen had reservations about its future. 'The situation is not ideal because in my experience you've got to have one man making decisions whether its substitutes, team selection or leaving people out.'

Five days later Roy Evans quit Liverpool after 33 years, leaving Houllier in sole charge. Evans said, 'I tried hard to make it work but if it's not working the bigger mistake would be to carry on.' On *Focus* Mark Lawrenson's view was that the problem was the players, 'Five or six are outstanding but the rest are interchangeable

and mediocre and Houllier's problems are just beginning. Some of the players need a kick up the backside but it's hard to do that now.' The new regime got off to a poor start as Liverpool dropped to 12th after losing 3-1 to Leeds at Anfield. One of the visitors' promising youngsters, 18-year-old substitute Alan Smith, scored on his debut.

A hat-trick from Dublin continued his dream start at Villa. His three goals in their 4-1 win at Southampton took his tally to five in two games and he added a couple more in the next match, despite finishing on the losing side, when Villa suffered their first defeat of the season against Liverpool.

Robbie Fowler contributed three goals in their eventful 4-2 win at Villa Park. Villa's Stan Collymore was sent off for putting his hands on Michael Owen's neck and pushing him to the ground and David James saved a penalty from Dublin. Villa stayed top and their manager John Gregory was able to smile after the game. 'It's been a bit of a silly day and I'm sure *Match of the Day*'s going to be very exciting tonight with lots of goals – and I won't be watching.'

Blackburn went bottom when they lost 2-0 at home to Southampton and 45 minutes later Roy Hodgson became the latest managerial casualty. It seemed to be a surprise to him as there hadn't been any hints in the post-match interviews. Tony Parkes was appointed caretaker for the fourth time in 12 seasons.

December

Brian Kidd agreed to take over at Blackburn after 20 years with Manchester United, most recently as assistant manager, and the move seemed to work as they ended their bad run of six defeats and a draw by beating fellow strugglers Charlton 1-0 after Jack Walker and Kidd had walked onto the pitch at the start with Rovers scarves draped around their shoulders.

Opposite Liverpool's Michael Owen scored four goals in the Reds' 5-1 thrashing of Nottingham Forest at the end of October.

Opposite A thrilling 3-3 draw between Southampton and Middlesbrough at The Dell saw old England pals Carlton Palmer (left) and Paul Gascoigne up against each other.

Online

The development of the Internet has revolutionised football coverage and now enables fans to have instant updates on all their club information as well as spawning numerous chat sites for supporters to swap gossip, share information and, of course, moan. Every club has its own website, the Premier League has a comprehensive site, there are betting pages, mobile downloads, podcasts, statistic sections, Wikipedia allows us to look up and adapt profiles on players and teams and Google features millions of sites devoted to the game.

The BBC's fledgling web presence began in April 1994 and BBC Online was launched four years later. BBC Sport's football pages now carry reports and photos of every Premiership match as well as extensive details of all the teams. Five million unique users a week were visiting bbc.co.uk/football at the beginning of 2007 with more than 20 million checking out the site during the 2006 World Cup.

The *Football Focus* homepage now also carries extended edits of the interviews and features that are broadcast each weekend, as well as a large number of classic features from the archives, along with blogs, competitions, information, feedback, predictions, webchats and news.

None of this was available or probably even conceivable when the league began 15 years ago but the new media revolution has been instrumental in the spread of the popularity of the Premiership.

The sudden appearance of YouTube in 2006 meant that goals and clips were being posted for people to instantly view anywhere in the world. This has raised a whole new series of questions about copyright infringements but has enabled a travelling fan to log onto their laptop at the top of a mountain or in the middle of desert and follow their team's activities.

Ray Stubbs met with David O'Leary at Leeds where they had lost just once in six games since he had taken charge. The club had won the FA Youth Cup in 1997 and O'Leary wanted to develop the club's young players together, keep them out of the spotlight and throw a Ferguson-style protective field around them. 'I'm a discipline person, it's important to have respect. Just because you're earning a lot of money doesn't make you a bigger man.' He then talked through the youngsters who he felt could bring the glory years back to Leeds: Harry Kewell, 20, Jonathan Woodgate 18, Alan Smith 18, Ian Harte 21, Stephen McPhail, 18, Lee Bowyer, 21, and Paul Robinson, 19. Some experience was also added to the Elland Road line up when David Batty returned from Newcastle for £4.4m.

Michael Owen had mixed fortunes on 13 December. He missed a penalty when Liverpool lost 1-0 at Wimbledon, but he was later voted BBC Sports Personality of the Year, becoming only the third footballer to collect the award. Bobby Moore had won it in 1966 for skippering England when they won the World Cup, and Paul Gascoigne won it in 1990 for crying when they didn't.

Late goals by Gus Poyet and Tore Andre Flo saw off Tottenham and enabled the King's Road to celebrate seeing Chelsea on top of the league for the first time in the 1990s. Middlesbrough fans were also happy having watched their team win 3-2 at Old Trafford, although that was Manchester United's last defeat of the season. Forest drew 2-2 with Blackburn but dropped to bottom and stayed there for the rest of the campaign.

Blackburn drew 1-1 at Leicester to complete an unbeaten month, two wins and three draws earned Brian Kidd the Manager of the Month award, and they began to pull clear of

Below Ray Parlour (left), dubbed the 'Romford Pele' by the Arsenal fans, was a consistent performer in the Gunners midfield and a major factor in their good form during the Chrismas season.

Long-server David James

trouble. Forest, Southampton and Charlton ended the year in the relegation positions. At the other end of the table Aston Villa were back in top spot having regained it with a 2-1 victory over Sheffield Wednesday. Ugo Ehiogu headed the winner after Benito Carbone's overhead bicycle kick had cancelled out Gareth Southgate's opener. They had 39 points from 20 games. Chelsea were two behind, Manchester United and Arsenal each had 35 and Leeds were fifth with 33.

January 1999

Despite having brought them into the Premiership as champions, Dave Bassett left Forest at the start of the New Year and Ron Atkinson took over until the end of the season. His first signing was veteran midfielder Carlton Palmer who moved from Southampton for £1.1m.

Wimbledon went sixth after beating Derby 2-1 but only collected three points once more in their remaining 17 games as they plummeted towards the danger zone. This was despite paying a club record £7m for 23-year-old John Hartson from West Ham.

The Londoners gave another of their rising stars, Joe Cole, aged just 17, his debut against Manchester United although he had to experience a 4-1 defeat. Harry Redknapp then signed Paolo Di Canio from Sheffield Wednesday for £1.7m and Camaroon international Marc-Vivien Foe from Lens at a cost of £4.2m. Arsenal also ventured into the transfer market and paid Inter Milan more than £4m for Nigerian striker Nwankwo Kanu.

There were a number of goal fests on 16 January. Liverpool beat Southampton 7-1 with Robbie Fowler collecting a hat-trick His third was a free header from Michael Owen's cross despite there being six Saints players in the area. Their keeper, Paul Jones, had a shocker and twice conceded goals when he couldn't hold on to the ball enabling Jamie Carragher and then David Thompson to pounce. Sheffield Wednesday beat West Ham 4-0, Coventry were defeated 2-1 at Chelsea and Leicester met a rampant Manchester United at Filbert Street and lost 6-2. Dwight Yorke scored three and their sixth goal was Dutch defender Jaap Stam's first for the club.

The following day Martin Pringle's last-minute goal earned Charlton an equaliser and a 2-2 draw with Newcastle to avoid the club holding an unwanted Premiership record of nine successive defeats. On the Monday evening Aston Villa beat Everton 3-0, but then suffered a dramatic loss of form losing seven and drawing three of their next ten games to drop out of contention for the title.

The last day of the month was also one of the most significant of the season. Dennis Bergkamp's 31st minute goal gave the home team a 1-0 win against Chelsea. It was almost eight hours since Arsenal had conceded a Premiership goal and it was Chelsea's first league defeat since the opening day of the season. South of the Thames, Dwight Yorke's 89th-minute goal at Charlton sent Manchester United top, where they stayed for most of the rest of the season.

February

Alex Ferguson could only comment, 'in that form we are devastating' after he had watched his team win 8-1 at Nottingham Forest. Andy Cole scored twice, Dwight Yorke's brace took his tally to eight in the last five matches but Ole Gunnar Solskjaer stole the headlines when he came on as a late substitute and scored four times in the final ten minutes.

When he put his fourth past a disgruntled Dave Beasant he was one of four Manchester United players queuing up for the ball. It was a record away score for the Premiership

England managers

Eight men have managed England since the Premiership began and many of them have subsequently returned to manage Premier League clubs.

Graham Taylor   *1990–93*   38 games
Terry Venables   *1994–96*   23 games
Glenn Hoddle   *1996–99*   28 games
Kevin Keegan   *1999–2000*   18 games
Howard Wilkinson   *1999 & 2000*   2 games
Peter Taylor   *2000*   1 game
Sven Goran Eriksson   *2000–2006*   67 games
Steve McClaren   *2006–*   11 games

Jimmy Floyd Hasselbaink scored both goals as Leeds won 2-1 at Villa Park. The on-form striker finished the season as joint top scorer with 18 league goals.

and the biggest in the history of *Match of the Day*. Ron Atkinson summed it up with his customary modest understatement in his post match interview, 'They absolutely battered us.'

United were now four points ahead of Chelsea who had a game in hand. Arsenal and Aston Villa were still within range and Derby moved quietly into sixth spot with a 2-1 win over Everton. Deon Burton struck scoring both goals in the second half.

Arsenal conceded their first league goal in seven outings when they drew 1-1 at Old Trafford and Chelsea's match against Blackburn ended with the same score. The match, at Stamford Bridge, was a tempestuous affair resulting in seven yellow and two red cards being shown with Chelsea's manager, Gianluca Vialli, one of those dismissed. Leeds won 2-1 at Aston Villa, both goals coming from Jimmy Floyd Hasselbaink, in the first of seven successive wins that established them in fourth place.

Despite Ron Atkinson's experience, with Forest languishing on 17 points their position seemed hopeless. It looked as though the other relegation places would go to two of the four teams above them: Southampton, Blackburn, Coventry or Charlton.

March

Joe Kinnear was taken ill just before Wimbledon's 2-1 win at Sheffield Wednesday and missed the remainder of the season. They missed his guidance and didn't win any of their remaining eleven games as they dropped down table with their coach, Dave Kemp, taking charge in Kinnear's absence.

Another manager suffering from a loss in his club's form was John Gregory and when he was Gary Lineker's studio guest he tried to rationalise what had gone wrong and why Villa, having been top at the beginning of the year, had only taken one of a possible 15 points. 'We've done remarkably well to get

that far in the first place but we can't buy a win at the moment and I still need to improve the squad and get a bigger one.'

One of the main problems was that his £7m striker, Stan Collymore, had been suffering from depression and hadn't been at his best. Gregory pulled no punches with his comments. 'Stan goes to counselling on Tuesday, Wednesday and Thursday, a situation I'm not happy with, but our medical people say that there is a genuine case there, that it could actually be something mentally wrong with him and he needs this counselling. But it's not an ideal situation that we have him on Friday and Saturday, he goes on the bench and comes on for 20 minutes a game. It might be that it would benefit both Stan and Villa if he moved on.'

Andy Cole scored twice on his latest return to Newcastle as Manchester won the battle of the Uniteds to leave Ferguson's side at just 13-1 to win an unprecedented treble. With nine games remaining they had reached the 60-point mark and were four in front of Arsenal. Chelsea had 53 and Leeds 51.

The following week West Ham overcame Newcastle 2-0 to move into fifth place and Blackburn registered a rare win, beating Wimbledon 3-1. It was their last day of hope, however, as they drew five and lost three of their final eight games. The relegation battle was getting tighter and with more teams now drawn into the fight. Coventry and Everton both had 31 points, Blackburn 30, Southampton 29, Charlton 28 and Forest just 20.

April

Robbie Fowler's imitation 'snorting' of the white line after scoring a penalty in Liverpool's 3-2 win over Everton led to widespread condemnation, large club and FA fines and a four-match ban. He also received a further two-game suspension for a gesture to Graeme Le Saux during a clash earlier in season.

Leeds seventh straight Premiership win equalled the club record set by Don Revie's team in 1973. The third goal in their 3-1 victory over Forest was a cracking Alan Smith volley from a Jonathan Woodgate header six minutes from the end.

The two leading clubs were also on great, unbeaten runs. Arsenal extended theirs to 17 games after a goalless draw at Southampton that left them four points behind Manchester United who hadn't lost in 19 games in all competitions when they finished 1-1 at Wimbledon. Meanwhile Chelsea missed the opportunity to head the table when they drew 0-0 at Middlesbrough. It was the first of three successive draws for the Blues which cost them the chance of the championship.

United, meanwhile, just kept winning and when they knocked Arsenal out of the FA Cup in their semi-final replay the crowd also witnessed one of the great solo goals of all time, by Ryan Giggs. He picked up the ball in his own half, charged forwards and beat four defenders to score.

The top three each had six games left and United were still four points clear of Arsenal and Chelsea. Wenger's team closed the gap with a 5-1 win over Wimbledon. The Gunners then produced their biggest away win for more than 40 years to go top for the first time that season when they won 6-1 at Middlesbrough with two goals each for Anelka and Kanu.

In the latest relegation twist Everton were safe after a 4-1 win against Charlton, but Blackburn were still in trouble when they lost 1-3 at home to Liverpool. Southampton's 0-0 draw at Derby gave them a crucial point and Wimbledon's spirits were raised with the appointment of Mick Harford as their new manager. Joe Kinnear's recovery from illness had persuaded him to delay his return to work and he eventually decided to look for another club.

Robbie Fowler's infamous line sniffing after his goal in Liverpool's 3-2 win over Everton at Anfield was made in response to taunts from the away fans. It remains one of the most famous incidents in Premiership history.

Reporter Damian Johnson

Damian Johnson began his career in commercial radio but made his name with the BBC on *Look North*. Based in Yorkshire he is one of BBC Sport's leading and most versatile reporters on *Football Focus*, *Final Score* and *Match of the Day*.

'I was working in regional TV during the 1998–99 season and keen to have a go at a *Focus* story so the editor, Andrew Clement, challenged me to come up with an idea that he could commission.

Benito Carbone was making an impact with Wednesday so, as I lived in Sheffield and had interviewed him a couple of times, I gave him a call to see if he would like to do a feature for the show. He was very helpful and suggested meeting at a favourite Italian restaurant. He arrived in a sporty Mercedes and we then drove around the Peak District on a beautiful day as we filmed a *Top Gear*-style feature.

It was one of those days where everything just fell into place, it gave me a leg up in the *Focus* team and I've been one of the reporters for the show ever since, although there has definitely been a dramatic change since then as interviews are a lot more controlled by press officers and clubs which can be very frustrating.

We often get greater access with smaller and newly promoted teams, which probably helps get them and their players featured more often. Sheffield United this season [2006–07] were a good example and their manager, Neil Warnock, was great value.

Gary Speed is one of the players I really admire as I've always found him to be a top quality bloke and a thorough professional on and off the pitch. I used to interview him years ago when he was at Leeds and I was on *Look North*, but I never imagined he would still be around today.'

May

The month began with the announcement of Sir Alf Ramsey's death, aged 79, and there was a minute's silence before all games that weekend in memory of the only man to have steered England to the World Cup.

The first team to have relegation confirmed were Nottingham Forest and with the pressure of uncertainty finally lifted they hit their best form of the season and won their remaining three games starting with a 2-0 victory against Sheffield Wednesday.

Southampton, Charlton and Blackburn were all on 32 points. Blackburn had been Premiership champions just four years before but despite four managers, a new stand, and a string of new players, Jack Walker's millions still couldn't guarantee success.

Southampton's 2-1 win over Leicester, their first of three in a row, lifted them from 19th to 17th to keep them up. James Beattie's crucial winner came in the 74th minute as he volleyed Francis Benali's free kick over Kasey Keller into the far side of the net from a seemingly impossible angle.

On Sunday 9 May, Dwight Yorke's 45th-minute header at Middlesbrough sent United back to the top after Nicky Butt had lofted the ball into the penalty area and Teddy Sheringham headed it on for Yorke to score. They were now level with Arsenal and with identical goal differences.

Two days later Leeds dented Arsenal's challenge by beating them 1-0 at Elland Road when Jimmy Floyd Hasselbaink's flying far post header ended the Londoners' 19-match unbeaten run.

The following night the sorcerer sank the apprentice when Ferguson's former assistant manager, Brian Kidd, saw his Blackburn team relegated following their goalless draw with Manchester United.

It left the Mancunians top with 76 points, one ahead of Arsenal with one game remaining. On the final day Arsenal beat Aston Villa 1-0 but it was out of their hands. Manchester United faced Tottenham at Old Trafford and, despite going behind to Les Ferdinand's first-half goal, managed to draw level just before the break through David Beckham before a brilliant solo effort by Andy Cole clinched the crucial three points and ensured that the Premiership trophy returned to Manchester for the fifth time.

Roy Keane lifted the trophy for the first time as captain and there was a special presentation to Peter Schmeichel who was leaving the club after 395 appearances in goal. He was replaced by Mark Bosnich who moved from Villa on a free transfer. After the match Ferguson declared that, 'This is without doubt the best ability of any team I've ever had.'

For the fourth time in six years Southampton's Premiership status was at stake on the last weekend of the season. They survived by beating Everton 2-0, but Charlton were relegated after they lost 1-0 at the Valley to Sheffield Wednesday. Alan Curbishley's team had rarely been thumped but were steadily outclassed throughout the season. Chelsea confirmed their best position for 29 years when their 2-1 win over Derby left them in third spot, Leeds were fourth and West Ham fifth.

Right Eleven days later the people of Manchester turned out in their thousands to welcome the United players home from Barcelona following their victory over Bayern Munich in the Champions League final – a triumph which completed an unprecedented and historic treble.

Final League Table

Team	P	W	D	L	F	A	Pts
Manchester United	38	22	13	3	80	37	79
Arsenal	38	22	12	4	59	17	78
Chelsea	38	20	15	3	57	30	75
Leeds United	38	18	13	7	62	34	67
West Ham United	38	16	9	13	46	53	57
Aston Villa	38	15	10	13	55	51	55
Liverpool	38	15	9	14	68	49	54
Derby County	38	13	13	12	40	45	52
Middlesbrough	38	12	15	11	48	54	51
Leicester City	38	12	13	13	40	46	49
Tottenham Hotspur	38	11	14	13	47	50	47
Sheffield Wednesday	38	13	7	18	41	42	46
Newcastle United	38	11	13	14	48	54	46
Everton	38	11	10	17	42	47	43
Coventry City	38	11	9	18	39	51	42
Wimbledon	38	10	12	16	40	63	42
Southampton	38	11	8	19	37	64	41
Charlton Athletic	38	8	12	18	41	56	36
Blackburn Rovers	38	7	14	17	38	52	35
Nottingham Forest	38	7	9	22	35	69	30

Leading Goalscorers league only

Dwight Yorke	Manchester United	18
Michael Owen	Liverpool	18
J F Hasselbaink	Leeds United	18
Andy Cole	Manchester United	17
Nicolas Anelka	Arsenal	17
Hamilton Ricard	Middlesbrough	15
Alan Shearer	Newcastle United	14
Robbie Fowler	Liverpool	14
Julian Joachim	Aston Villa	14
Dion Dublin	Aston Villa	14*

* including 3 for Coventry

Awards

Footballer of the Year
David Ginola, Tottenham Hotspur

PFA Player of the Year
David Ginola, Tottenham Hotspur

PFA Young Player of the Year
Nicolas Anelka, Arsenal

Left A sublime moment of skill from striker Andy Cole – who controlled a long pass from Gary Neville and then lifted the ball over Tottenham keeper Ian Walker for the winning goal – gave Manchester United the points they needed to clinch the Premiership title again.

Honours List 1998–99

Champions Manchester United

Runners-up Arsenal

Relegated Charlton Athletic, Blackburn Rovers, Nottingham Forest

Promoted Sunderland, Bradford City, Watford

FA Cup Winners Manchester United

League Cup Winners Tottenham Hotspur

Champions League Winners
Manchester United

League Cup
Tottenham picked up the trophy for the third time when Allan Nielsen scored the only goal of the match in the 90th minute of the final against last year's winners Leicester.

FA Cup
Having already secured the league title, the second part of Manchester United's historic treble came six days later when they met Newcastle United in the FA Cup final at Wembley. Their opponents had lost to Arsenal in the 1998 final and were determined not to suffer the same fate and manager Ruud Gullit led them onto the pitch convinced that this would be their day. It wasn't, however, and Manchester United lifted their fourth FA Cup of the decade. Teddy Sheringham scored in the first half and Paul Scholes in the second as they won 2-0 and completed the double for the third time in their history.

Champions League
Alex Ferguson finally achieved his dream of winning the European Cup when Manchester United met Bayern Munich in the final in Barcelona. United were 1-0 down at the end of 90 minutes but injury time goals by substitutes Ole Gunnar Solskjaer and Teddy Sheringham secured an astonishing 2-1 victory to complete the ultimate footballing treble.

FF 1999–2000

Having signed for Leeds in the summer from Sunderland Michael Bridges started the season with a hat-trick in a 3-0 win over Southampton. He ended the season as Leeds' top scorer with 19 Premiership goals.

Programmes

Just before the start of the season Desmond Lynam resigned from the BBC and switched to ITV to become their main football presenter. Having spent two years fronting the lunchtime show Gary Lineker took over *Match of the Day* and Ray Stubbs, who had already presented several editions, became its fourth full time presenter. There was also a new set as the virtual ball had been taken away and Ray and Mark Lawrenson now sat in front of the large computer-generated football ground. They were joined in the studio by a variety of footballing guests throughout the season including Peter Beardsley, Harry Redknapp, Dave Bassett, Carlton Palmer, Mark Bright and Garth Crooks.

Presenter
Ray Stubbs

Pre-season

At a cost of £4m Sander Westerveld became the most expensive goalkeeper in Britain when he replaced David James at Liverpool. James moved to Aston Villa for £1.7m and Paul Ince also left Anfield in a £1m switch to Middlesbrough.

Juventus' French World Cup-winning captain Didier Deschamps signed for Chelsea in a £3m transfer, and he was joined at Stamford Bridge by striker Chris Sutton, who cost £10m from relegated Blackburn.

Arsène Wenger was also busy at Highbury, selling Anelka to Real Madrid for £22.3m and spending £4m of that on the Brazilian left back Silvinho and paying a further £10m to Juventus for another French star, the 21-year-old Thierry Henry.

Having won an unprecedented treble in the previous season Manchester United began the new campaign with an additional honour after the knighthood conferred by the Queen on their manager in her birthday honours list and it was Sir Alex Ferguson who took his place on the bench for their opening game at Everton.

August 1999

The champions drew their opening match at Goodison Park 1-1, even though United players scored in both goals. Dwight Yorke hit their first of the season in the 7th minute but Jaap Stam headed into his own net just before the end to ensure that honours were even. Arsenal opened with a 2-1 win over Leicester, Alan Shearer was sent off for the first time as Newcastle lost 1-0 at home against Aston Villa and Liverpool made a better start this year by winning 2-1 at Sheffield Wednesday.

Bradford were the only promoted team to experience the winning feeling when they defeated Middlesbrough 1-0 at the Riverside. Watford lost 3-2 at home to Wimbledon, now under the new management regime of former Norway coach Egil Olsen, and Sunderland lost 4-0 at Chelsea.

Gus Poyet's head got to the ball before the keeper's hand in the 20th minute to score the first, Zola's flair beat Steve Bould's experience to put the ball past Thomas Sorensen for the second, a header from Tore Andre Flo's header made it 3-0 and a stunning volley from Poyet in the 79th minute ended the scoring and started the goal of the season debate.

The first home game at Old Trafford saw all three trophies paraded on the pitch before goals by Paul Scholes, Dwight Yorke, Andy Cole and Ole Gunnar Solskjaer gave Manchester United the first of six successive victories when they beat Sheffield Wednesday 4-0. Aston Villa's 3-0 win at Everton took them into an early lead in the table for the second year in a row, but manager John Gregory wasn't getting carried away and told *Focus*, 'It's a good start by us, a touch of déjà vu, but we've not had the hardest of games so far so don't read too much into it.'

Leicester's Steve Guppy was one of the first players featured on *Focus* this season. The 30-year-old was never a star name but he was the kind of player who makes up the bulk of most teams. He had played in every minute of every Premiership game in the previous season, scored four goals and, according to the official statistics, made 72 successful crosses. Only David Beckham, with 75, had made more.

Also featured that week was 19-year-old Robbie Keane who became British football's most expensive teenager when he moved from Wolves to Coventry for £6m, and *Focus* also reported on the exploits of another young striker, Manchester United's Andy Cole who was the latest player to try and set up a duel career in music. They played the video of his R&B track 'Outstanding' over a moody shot of him in a car. 'Tell the world my name, whose that? Andy. I play the scene, I scores the goals ...' Ray asked if it was, 'a hit, a miss or a maybe?' Mark Lawrenson wasn't feeling too charitable, 'I think its absolute toilet to be quite honest Ray. Andy, stick to scoring'.

Chelsea's Gus Poyet celebrates his goal in a 4-0 against Sunderland at Stamford Bridge on the opening day of the season.

Reporter Garry Richardson

Garry Richardson is one of the BBC's most persuasive, tenacious and respected sports reporters with an unrivalled contacts book, which he has used to great effect on many TV and radio shows including *Sportsweek*, *Today*, *Football Focus* and *Look Away Now*.

'My favourite *Football Focus* story came in 1999 when Bradford City had just been promoted to the Premier League and I went to interview their chairman, Geoffrey Richmond, ahead of their first match. I was looking for a place to film our chat and spotted a crane with a bucket that was part of the building site for their new stand at Valley Parade. Geoffrey

realised what I was thinking and said, 'I know what you are going to say. Absolutely not. No. No way.'

Twenty minutes later, after the health and safety advisors had given us the go ahead, we were winched up into the bucket wearing harnesses attached to the hook to ensure that if it dropped then we wouldn't go down with it.

Geoffrey was petrified but agreed to go along with the idea and, with the camera crew filming us from the ground, we ensured that *Football Focus* became the first show to interview a Premiership chairman while he was being dangled 130 feet above the ground. Somehow, I doubt that we'll repeat that idea with Roman Abramovich.'

A couple of days after he left Shearer on the bench when Sunderland beat Newcastle 2-1 at St James' Park, Ruud Gullit resigned as manager. They had only taken one point from the first five games and their football was a long way from being 'sexy'. Their supporters' agony was compounded in the next game when Andy Cole scored four as Manchester United won 5-1. Even their goal was an accident when Henning Berg turned it into his own net and Ryan Giggs chipped in the fifth with such ease from the edge of the six-yard box that he almost looked embarrassed.

September

At the age of 66 Bobby Robson finally became the new Newcastle manager saying, 'This is a great job for me, a massive job and one I'm going to relish,' although Frank Leboeuf ruined his debut by scoring Chelsea's winning goal when the teams met at Stamford Bridge. There was bad luck too for Jamie Carragher against Manchester United as he scored two own goals in the first half to help the visitors to a 3-2 win at Liverpool, and for Stuart Pearce who broke his left leg during West Ham's 1-0 victory against Watford. It marked a change in fortune for the Hammers. Having taken 13 points from a possible 15 they only added five more in their next eight games.

Garry Richardson interviewed the new Wimbledon manager Egil Olsen as he started his daily walk to work across Wimbledon Common to the training ground wearing his trademark wellington boots. He explained his style of play. 'I believe in zone defence which is different to the marking system in England.' Mark Lawrenson was concerned that his approach, which was very direct even by Wimbledon's old standards, had sent the team backwards.

Manchester United had a six-point lead after just seven matches although they had also played a couple of games more than Chelsea and West Ham who, with 13 points each, were immediately behind them. Sheffield Wednesday and Newcastle filled the bottom two places, each with one point from a possible 21.

Thierry Henry opened his account for Arsenal when he turned and shot from the edge of Southampton's penalty area to score the only goal of their encounter at The Dell and Kevin Phillips, who had hit 60 goals in 80 games for Sunderland before they were in the Premiership, proved that he could continue his scoring record at the highest level. He took his tally to eight in eight games with a hat-trick at Derby as Peter Reid's team won 5-0 to move into fifth spot. The following day their North-Eastern neighbours were also finally able to raise their glasses in celebration when Newcastle ended their winless run in spectacular style and put eight past Kevin Pressman in the Sheffield Wednesday goal. It was Bobby Robson's first home game and the club's biggest victory since 1946 (when they beat Newport 13-0). Alan Shearer scored five, including two penalties, and the others came from Aaron Hughes, Kieron Dyer and Gary Speed.

October

A fortnight later, and in their tenth game, Wednesday at last collected three points

Sunderland bounced back in the next few weeks thanks mainly to striker Kevin Phillips (right) who scored eight goals in the opening eight games.

themselves, beating Wimbledon 5-1, and Chelsea also managed to put five without reply past Manchester United. Gus Poyet scored after 27 seconds, Nicky Butt was sent off after 22 minutes, and goals by Chris Sutton, Poyet again, a Henning Berg own goal and Jody Morris completed the scoreline, which equalled United's worst defeat during Ferguson's time in charge.

There was bad news too for Patrick Vieira who received a six-match ban for spitting at Neil Ruddock after being sent off in Arsenal's 2-1 defeat at West Ham. But things were good at Elland Road where David O'Leary's faith in his young team continued to pay off and goals from Michael Bridges and Harry Kewell had fired them into top spot with a 2-1 win at Watford and 22 points from ten games, a point ahead of Manchester United. Sunderland were third with 20 and Chelsea, who had played two games fewer, were on 19.

There was a special *Focus* montage of the best of Matt Le Tissier's many spectacular strikes for Southampton as he had reached 99 Premiership goals for the club. It proved to be a curse for the player though as he only scored once more during the season, and that was a penalty on 1 April! However, for once the club were not yet in the relegation places. Those were still filled by Sheffield Wednesday and Newcastle with Bradford and Wimbledon just above them.

Leicester were enjoying a good season and went fifth after registering their fifth successive win, 2-1 against Southampton, while two more goals from Sunderland's Kevin Phillips were enough to wipe out Dion Dublin's strike for Villa, his seventh of the season, and move the Black Cats up to third place behind Manchester United and Leeds.

On the final weekend of the month Chelsea and Manchester United were on

Opposite David O'Leary's young Leeds side impressed during the early months of the season with plenty of goals from Alan Smith (seen here scoring in a 2-0 win over Sheffield Wednesday), Michael Bridges and Harry Kewell.

Pundit Carlton Palmer

When 33-year-old Carlton Palmer moved to Coventry he became the first player to appear for five different Premiership clubs following spells at Sheffield Wednesday, Leeds, Southampton and Nottingham Forest.

'Sheffield Wednesday was the best team I played for in terms of setup and among the players it was like a family. Ron Atkinson was there and he was fantastic, the best manager I played under, without doubt. He was brilliant with signings, got them right all the time and he moulded teams, which was a great art. He was tough on the players but they loved and respected him, and he knew how to get the best out of me and after that I was always searching for that atmosphere and team spirit, but never really found it again.'

Opposite Tempers flared in a explosive North London derby which saw Arsenal reduced to nine men when Freddie Ljungberg and Martin Keown were sent off during the Gunners 2-1 defeat.

the wrong end of surprising scorelines, although for different reasons. Vialli's side were two up at home against Arsenal with only 15 minutes left on the clock, when Kanu struck a rapid, and winning, hat-trick. While at White Hart Lane Tottenham beat United 3-1 – although United only lost one more of their remaining 26 league fixtures this season.

November

Manchester replaced Leeds in first place when the two Uniteds had differing fortunes at the start of the month. Sir Alex saw his side move back top with a 2-0 win over Leicester, but David O'Leary's team conceded twice and allowed Wimbledon to achieve their first clean sheet in 30 attempts.

Arsène Wenger witnessed his club's red card tally rise to 26 in just three years when Freddie Ljungberg and Martin Keown were both sent off at White Hart Lane as Tottenham beat Arsenal 2-1. The Gunners returned to form in their next match, however, thumping Middlesbrough 5-1 thanks to a hat-trick from Marc Overmars and a pair from Bergkamp.

Before their trip to West Ham, Danny Wilson's Sheffield Wednesday had only managed one away goal in the league all season. They scored three times in one game at Upton Park but still lost despite having been 3-2 up. Marc Vivien Foe equalised and Frank Lampard's left-foot shot in the 76th minute secured the points. Even though Elton John was watching them at home in the Premier League for first time, Watford went down 3-2 to Sunderland. Phillips scored another two to take his total to 15 in 16 games and move his club back into third place.

Alan Shearer wasn't far behind on 12 but didn't add to his tally when Newcastle racked up their fourth win under Bobby Robson, 2-1 against Tottenham, thanks to

goals from Steve Glass and Nikos Dabizas. Chris Armstrong was the Tottenham scorer that day but it had been the captain Sol Campbell who had been featured on *Focus* that morning. During his recovery from injury he had been monitored and filmed for a computer game. Mark Bright reported from a studio where Campbell was wearing a special suit and body sensors. The weird new world of Premiership players was already developing.

December

Leeds were leading once again with 35 points from 16 games, two ahead of Manchester United with Arsenal, Sunderland and Leicester close behind.

Peter Reid spoke to Barry Davies live on the show just ahead of his 200th game in charge of Sunderland, against Chelsea. 'I think Vialli's done a great job there. I just wish I could look as cool as him.' Coolness counted for nothing that afternoon though as Sunderland beat Chelsea 4-1 to give Reid a double celebration. Ole Gunnar Solskjaer scored the same number of goals on his own in Manchester United's 5-1 victory over Everton and Wimbledon also struck five, against Watford. Arsenal won 3-0 at Leicester, Liverpool came back from a goal down against Sheffield Wednesday to win 4-1

and Leeds remained two points clear when Ian Harte's stoppage-time penalty at Derby proved to be the only goal of the match.

One of the best games of the month came when Manchester United went to Upton Park. Dwight Yorke opened the scoring in the 9th minute, heading in a fine Beckham cross from the right, and Giggs added two more in the next ten minutes. Paolo di Canio responded with two goals of his own, the first was a volley in the 24th minute and then, with the entire defence appealing for offside, he carried on and rounded the keeper to score in the 53rd. Ten minutes later, however, Yorke put the ball through Shaka Hislop's legs to confirm the win.

The effect that the Premiership was having on the English game was demonstrated on Boxing Day when Chelsea began their match at Southampton without a single British player in their line-up. It was the first time it had ever happened and the team that day consisted of De Goey, Ferrer, Deschamps, Leboeuf, Petrescu, Poyet, Di Matteo, Flo, Babayaro, Ambrosetti and Emerson. It was, of course, the shape of things to come.

January 2000

At the beginning of the year Manchester United arrived in Rio de Janeiro to take part in the Club World Championship and thereby missed the third round of the FA Cup. The headlines were not flattering and accused United of devaluing the competition. They didn't win the competition but it gave them a break from the league and in their absence Leeds were unable to increase their lead at the top of the table, losing 2-1 at home to Villa.

In a surprise move the former World and European Player of the Year, George Weah, was added to the Chelsea squad, joining them on loan for six months from AC Milan and he scored an 87th-minute winner on his debut to give his new team a home win against Tottenham.

Sheffield Wednesday had taken only ten points from a possible 60 when their manager, Danny Wilson, found himself under attack from a collective group when four Sheffield MPs called for him to be sacked. It proved to be the perfect motivation for Danny and his boys as they immediately beat fellow strugglers Bradford 2-0.

Arsenal moved level on points with Manchester United after beating Sunderland 4-1 and Newcastle's revival continued as, helped by own goals from Southampton pair Richard Dryden and Gary Monk, they scored five times without reply. That left their visitors fourth from bottom and facing yet another relegation battle as only Bradford, Watford and Wednesday were below them, separated by just seven points.

Sheffield Wednesday moved off the bottom for the first time since August when they beat Tottenham 1-0 and Wimbledon also had a boost but their 2-0 defeat of Newcastle was almost their last real moment of hope during the season. They took just five out of the remaining 45 points available and ended the season with just seven wins. Bradford's Neil Redfearn was especially relieved when a 3-2 win over Watford gave them a lifeline as he had been relegated with Barnsley and Charlton in the previous two seasons and was desperately hoping to avoid a third successive drop.

After their unsuccessful trip to Brazil Manchester United's first Premiership match of the new century didn't come until 24 January when they drew 1-1 with Arsenal. This left the two clubs level on 44 points, three behind Leeds although United had two games in hand. Five days later, in front of a new record Premiership crowd of 61,267, referee Andy D'Urso gave a visiting team a penalty at Old Trafford for the first time in six years. After a great run from his own half, Middlesbrough's Juninho was brought down by Jaap Stam. A penalty was given, but United's players went ape and, led by their captain, Roy Keane, surrounded the referee in protest, but he held his ground. United keeper Mark Bosnich also held his and saved Juninho's spot kick. David Beckham scored the game's only goal when his shot went straight through Mark Schwarzer's hands, to send them back to the top.

February

Danny Wilson was awarded the Manager of the Month accolade and he celebrated in the usual way... by losing 1-0 to Manchester United at Hillsbrough leaving the Owls in 19th place, above Watford who seemed doomed for the drop, but five points behind Bradford. One place above them came Southampton who had a new caretaker manager in Glenn Hoddle who looked after things while Dave Jones was clearing his name in a court case.

United were now three points in front of Leeds with Arsenal a further three back on 44 and they doubled that lead by beating Coventry 3-2, although after the match Sir Alex said, 'What concerns me most now is complacency.' Arsenal were surprisingly beaten at Bradford when Dean Saunders nutmegged David Seaman to make it 2-1 in the 57th minute.

Sheffield Wednesday looked as though they would also pull off a shock win when they were 3-1 up at Derby after 90 minutes, but chaotic defending meant that Wilson had to watch in despair as they conceded two goals in time added on.

Stan Collymore was on the move again. This time he joined Leicester on an 18-month loan deal from Villa who would get £500,000 if he played 50 matches. Once Britain's most costly footballer he hoped that he had come through a bad time and was a better person for it. Mark Lawrenson was sceptical. 'He's always underachieved and everything has been a dream move that's turned into a nightmare.'

Long-server Nicky Butt

Although he only made one appearance in each of the first two Premiership seasons, Nicky Butt won six titles, two FA Cups and the Champions League with Manchester United before moving to Newcastle in 2004.

The tenacious midfielder spent a season on loan at St Andrews before returning to St James' Park in 2006. He also won 39 caps for England.

Right A run of poor results saw Sheffield Wednesday manager, Danny Wilson, come under pressure to resign from a group of local MPs. His team responded by beating Bradford 2-0 at Hillsborough.

The joint highest scoring game of the season took place at Upton Park where West Ham recovered from being 4-2 down to win 5-4 against Bradford City and there was drama after Chelsea's 3-1 defeat of Wimbledon as the police got involved during a players fight in the tunnel. There were more bad headlines when Leicester City players were sent home from a training break in La Manga after Collymore sprayed a fire extinguisher in the hotel bar. There had also been problems at Leeds and, at the end of a bad week for the game, four clubs and five individuals were charged with misconduct. In *Focus* Ray posed the question, 'Is football losing the plot or is it overpaid irresponsible footballers, indecisive governing bodies, incompetent match officials or does a hysterical insatiable media hype everything out of proportion?' More than seven years on and the jury is probably still looking for the answer.

On 20 February Andy Cole lobbed Leeds Nigel Martyn in the 52nd minute to register his 100th goal for Manchester United and seal the points. In a poor spell for Leeds it meant that they had lost to United, Liverpool, Villa and Arsenal in the last six games. Three days later football mourned the loss of another icon when Sir Stanley Matthews, the 'wizard of the dribble', died at the age of 85.

March

Chelsea moved third when Gus Poyet's header gave them victory at Newcastle and Stan Collymore struck a hat-trick in Leicester's 5-2 win over Sunderland. The first was a sensational volley from the edge of the box, the second a header and the third came when he got onto the end of Emile Heskey's cross. It had been 484 days since his last Premiership goal.

On 10 March 22-year-old Emile Heskey moved to Liverpool for £11m, the third most expensive transfer between Premiership clubs, having scored 40 league goals in 154 appearances. Two other strikers in form were Dwight Yorke and Steffen Iversen and both hit hat-tricks that weekend. Yorke's came as Manchester United began a remarkable run of 11 successive victories by beating Derby 3-1 and Iversen helped ruin Glenn Hoddle's return to Tottenham when the home side demolished Southampton 7-2.

With ten matches remaining Manchester United had 61 points, four ahead of Leeds with Liverpool and Chelsea both on 50. At the other end of things Danny Wilson's time finally ran

out and he was sacked by second to bottom Sheffield Wednesday. Peter Shreeves took charge for the final games. With Watford and Wednesday looking certain to be relegated the final position appeared to be between Bradford, Derby and Wimbledon.

When West Ham beat the Dons 2-1, Paolo di Canio scored one of the season's best goals. His leaping right-footed volley in the box to connect with Trevor Sinclair's cross had required him to adjust his feet in mid-air, but the result was a spectacular goal which was later judged Goal of the Season.

Arsenal scored three in the second half of their match against Coventry where they faced 42-year-old Steve Ogrizovic whose first appearance in goal for 18 months made him the second oldest player to play in the Premiership (after John Burridge who appeared for Manchester City in season 1994–95 aged 43).

Most of David O'Leary's Leeds United team were less than half Ogrizovic's age and their lack of experience was beginning to show. Their 2-1 defeat at Leicester was the start of a five-match run in which they won just one point and, after the match, O'Leary conceded that the title would be going back to Manchester.

April

The leaders notched up their biggest win of the season, 7-1 against West Ham, to go ten points clear as Leeds lost 1-0 at Chelsea. At the other end of the table Derby gave themselves a five-point cushion from the relegation group by beating Leicester 3-0, a match which saw Stan Collymore's season come to an early end when he broke his left leg slipping badly after making a pass.

Liverpool continued to chase for a European place and goals from Patrik Berger and Michael Owen secured a 2-0 win over Tottenham. Berger's goal was one of the Premiership's best ever when he turned

The first of 11 straight league wins in Manchester United's charge for the championship came thanks to a hat-trick from Dwight Yorke in a 3-1 win over Derby County.

Presenter Ray Stubbs

After playing football for Tranmere, Ray worked on the production teams of *A Question of Sport* and *On the Line* with BBC Manchester before becoming a presenter and reporter. He joined BBC Sport in 1990 and, having been the regular stand-in presenter of *Focus* for several seasons, took the role on full time for five years from 1999. Ray has also presented countless editions of *Match of the Day* and now fronts *Score* and *Final Score*. He demonstrated new talents in 2007 when he became the star performer on *Comic Relief Does Fame Academy*.

'As *Football Focus* started so did my career with Tranmere Rovers youth team and reserves but where I used to play there weren't any TVs, so it was some years before it became a regular part of my Saturdays.

Focus was incredibly exciting and daunting for me and I remember saying to myself that as a player I didn't take my opportunities so I set about trying to ensure I didn't waste this one. It was a thrill, week in week out, to make it entertaining, informative and as editorially current as possible.

It wasn't always easy during the 'virtual set' period when we appeared to be inside a giant football. The director, Martin Hopkins, would say, "Stubbsy look over there, left, stare there, that's where the league table is." As we looked at nothing but a big green background the viewers would see the table pop up out of the desk and I would stare in the general direction for a few seconds until they cut to it so that I could glance at a monitor and see what was actually on-screen.

From the first minute I really enjoyed working with Mark Lawrenson, whether it is discussing the burning issues in football or just the knockabout nonsense that he comes up with. He is fantastic at the job, a maverick super-pundit who, in any analysis of the programme is right at the very top. As TV analysis of football has changed dramatically Mark's huge strength has always been his bravery to have an opinion before a ball has been kicked that day, although it was usual for him to turn up on set just as the titles were running.

Alistair McGowan's appearance as Lawro remains one of my favourite moments in *Focus*. He really made an effort. He had taken two and a half hours to get made up and played it absolutely straight as a slightly eccentric pundit at the end of the programme. He was obviously very convincing as Motty phoned me after the show to said, "Lawro wasn't looking great today, was he?" which really made my day.

The toughest period was the three years when we lost the Premiership contract and couldn't show any action. The editor, Andrew Clement, and the production team during that time deserve real praise because their films became even more creative to compensate. We had a lot more guests and interviews but their professionalism coupled with Lawro's remarkable punditry and Andrew's exceptional editorial talents meant that we kept the show on the road.

Focus has been my football club really. We were serious when we felt it needed to be, but we wanted to have a spot of entertainment as well, although I was always mindful of the show's heritage and the importance of doing the job properly in the same way that Bob, Steve and Gary had done before me. after all, not many TV brands are still going strong after 33 years.'

and hit a left-footed half volley from the edge of the box. Heskey scored both when the Reds beat Wimbledon 2-1, but it was to be their last win of the season as a sudden slump in form meant that they only gathered two points from their remaining five games. Arsenal, however, were still maintaining a challenge and they moved ahead of Leeds after winning 4-0 at Elland Road.

Manchester United agreed to set a new British transfer record by bringing 23-year-old Ruud van Nistelrooy to the club for £18.5m from PSV Eindhoven but the move was called off when he failed a medical and the next day he collapsed and was ruled out for a year with a cruciate ligament injury. But the bad news turned good on 22 April when United were crowned Premiership champions for the sixth time in eight years after beating Southampton 3-1 at The Dell.

The following week United won 3-2 at Vicarage Road, a club-record ninth win in a row, and sent Watford down. Derby looked to be safe when they defeated the Saints 2-0, and John Dreyer's 60th-minute goal gave Bradford a surprise win at Sunderland after ten games without a victory. It left them still third from bottom but just two points behind Wimbledon with three games to play. At the end of the month they faced each other and Paul Jewell's Bradford secured an important 3-0 win, and Leeds' 3-0 defeat of Sheffield Wednesday left their Yorkshire neighbours facing the drop instead.

May

After an unsettled and unsuccessful 11 months Egil Olsen was sacked by Wimbledon and replaced by his assistant,

On 6 May after a routine victory at home to Tottenham, Manchester United were presented with the Premierhship trophy for the sixth time in eight years. It was the thirteenth championship in the club's 122-year history. The team had dominated the campaign from start to finish with the first choice midfield quartet of David Beckham (pictured), Roy Keane, Paul Scholes and Ryan Giggs at the heart of their fluent passing game.

Final League Table

Team	P	W	D	L	F	A	Pts
Manchester United	38	28	7	3	97	45	91
Arsenal	38	22	7	9	73	43	73
Leeds United	38	21	6	11	58	43	69
Liverpool	38	19	10	9	51	30	67
Chelsea	38	18	11	9	53	34	65
Aston Villa	38	15	13	10	46	35	58
Sunderland	38	16	10	12	57	56	58
Leicester City	38	16	7	15	55	55	55
West Ham United	38	15	10	13	52	53	55
Tottenham Hotspur	38	15	8	15	57	49	53
Newcastle United	38	14	10	14	63	54	52
Middlesbrough	38	14	10	14	46	52	52
Everton	38	12	14	12	59	49	50
Coventry City	38	12	8	18	47	54	44
Southampton	38	12	8	18	45	62	44
Derby County	38	9	11	18	44	57	38
Bradford City	38	9	9	20	38	68	36
Wimbledon	38	7	12	19	46	74	33
Sheffield Wednesday	38	8	7	23	38	70	31
Watford	38	6	6	26	35	77	24

Leading Goalscorers league only

Kevin Phillips	Sunderland	30
Alan Shearer	Newcastle United	23
Dwight Yorke	Manchester United	20
Andy Cole	Manchester United	19
Michael Bridges	Leeds United	19
Thierry Henry	Arsenal	17
Paulo Di Canio	West Ham United	16
Steffen Iversen	Tottenham Hotspur	14
Chris Armstrong	Tottenham Hotspur	14
Niall Quinn	Sunderland	14

Awards

Footballer of the Year
Roy Keane, Manchester United

PFA Player of the Year
Roy Keane, Manchester United

PFA Young Player of the Year
Harry Kewell, Leeds United

Terry Burton. But he wasn't able to save them and on the final day of the Premiership season they lost 2-0 at Southampton. After 14 years in the top division, 12 years to the day since they had won the FA Cup, they were relegated.

Bradford ended with a 1-0 win against Liverpool to cling on, amaze all the pundits and survive, finishing three points above the zone. Although Arsenal lost 4-2 at Newcastle they still came second but, with 73 points, were a massive 18 behind the champions. Alan Shearer's 22nd-minute goal was the 300th of his career, 200th in the league and 30th for Newcastle that season as they rallied to close in 11th place.

Leeds drew 0-0 at West Ham to clinch the third Champions League spot, finishing two points ahead of Liverpool on 69 in their highest position in the eight years of the Premier League. Chelsea were a further two behind in fifth place followed by Aston Villa, Sunderland, Leicester and West Ham.

Sir Alex's team ended with their 11th consecutive win, beating Aston Villa 1-0 at Villa Park. They had lost only three games during the season, beating the Busby Babes' total of 27 wins in a season and equalling the club and Premiership record, scoring 87 goals in the process.

Honours List 1999–2000

Champions Manchester United

Runners-up Arsenal

Relegated Watford, Sheffield Wednesday, Wimbledon

Promoted Charlton Athletic, Manchester City, Ipswich Town

FA Cup Winners Chelsea

League Cup Winners Leicester City

League Cup

Last season's runners-up Leicester City won the League Cup for the second time in four years when they beat Tranmere Rovers 2-1. David Kelly scored for Tranmere but Matt Elliott struck twice to take the trophy back to Filbert Street.

FA Cup

The 77th and last final to be played at Wembley before it was knocked down was between Chelsea and Aston Villa. It was a dull game with the only goal coming in the 72nd minute when Roberto Di Matteo scored to enable Dennis Wise to lift the trophy for the second time in four seasons.

FF 2000-01

Liverpool's Steven Gerrard and Danny Murphy combine to disposses Arsenal's Ray Parlour when the two sides met at Anfield in December. The Merseyside Reds won 4-0 on the day but Arsenal finished the season in second place one place ahead of their northern rivals.

Programmes

When the season began Ray and Mark Lawrenson were in another new set that resembled a multi-layered Meccano kit with replica trophies dotted around. They were joined regularly during the season by Mick McCarthy.

The BBC Sport Department was still reeling from the announcement in June 2000 that ITV had won the rights to show the Premiership highlights in a three-year deal that would begin in August 2001. It meant that *Match of the Day* would have an enforced break, apart from FA Cup weekends, and threw the future of *Football Focus* into doubt as well.

Presenter
Ray Stubbs

Pre-season

Having led France to the European Championship Didier Deschamps moved to Valencia from Chelsea, Dan Petrescu also left Stamford Bridge for Bradford for £1m and Chris Sutton switched to Celtic for £6m. Vialli's main imports were Jimmy Floyd Hasselbaink for £15m from Atlético Madrid and Croatian international Mario Stanic who joined for £5.6m.

Tottenham signed the Ukrainian striker Sergei Rebrov from Dynamo Kiev for a club record £11m but recouped a quarter of that when David Ginola went to Aston Villa. Arsène Wenger sold Marc Overmars and Emmanuel Petit to Barcelona for a combined fee of £30m and spent £6m each on Edu and Robert Pires.

Sir Alex Ferguson added the French goalkeeper Fabien Bartez to his squad. He cost United £7.8m when he exchanged Monaco for Manchester, and Robbie Keane moved from Coventry to Inter Milan for £13m doubling their investment in less than 12 months. Mark Viduka was another £6m acquisition, this time for Leeds from Celtic, and Nick Barmby became the first player to move from Everton to Liverpool in almost four decades.

The day before the start of the Premiership season Sir Jack Walker died aged 71. He had poured millions of pounds into Blackburn Rovers and seen them crowned champions in 1995.

August 2000

Ray opened the first *Football Focus* of the season standing outside the gates at Old Trafford. 'They've won six out of eight. Who can stop them making it seven out of nine?' No one was the answer as Manchester United simply carried on where they had left off the previous season by winning their opening game 2-0 against Newcastle.

Of the other pre-season favourites Arsenal lost 1-0 at Sunderland and had Patrick Vieira sent off for a fifth time in their colours, Leeds beat Everton 2-0 and Liverpool also made a solid start when Emile Heskey broke away from Bradford's defence to rifle in the only goal of the game.

The newly promoted teams had mixed fortunes. Ipswich provided encouragement for those who had backed them to go straight back down by losing 3-1 at Tottenham and Manchester City lost 4-0 at Charlton. John Motson had opened his commentary on that game by reflecting that, 'Weah and Wanchope are the strikers that Manchester City hope will give them Premiership class.' Unfortunately their main problems were at the other end of the pitch and when two of their defenders collided in the tenth minute, the previous season's top scorer, Andy Hunt, hit the first for Charlton and the pattern of Joe Royle's season was set.

Two days later Arsenal's 2-0 win over Liverpool was overshadowed by three sendings off, including a second red in consecutive games for Vieira, although he made headlines for the right reasons in their next match, scoring twice as they beat Charlton 5-3. A few days later Wenger spent another £13m when he added Sylvain Wiltord to his squad.

Bradford collected their only win in their first 15 matches courtesy of Dean Windass' climbing header and a swerving shot from Benito Carbone that deceived Ed De Goey in the Chelsea goal. Their 2-0 win was a rare event as they only won five games all season while also losing 22.

After Ipswich had drawn 1-1 with champions Manchester United, *Focus* compiled some statistics to demonstrate the gap between the two teams. The ground capacity of Portman Road was 22,700 compared to almost 69,000 for Manchester United. United's annual turnover was estimated at approximately £110 million with

Left On the opening day Sunderland beat Arsenal, one of the pre-season favourites, 1-0 at the Stadium of Light.

their squad worth twice that much. Ipswich's figures were £8 million and somewhere around £35 million. The final figures were left to the bookies who had United as 4-5 favourites to regain their title, while the Tractor Boys were quoted at 2000-1.

September

The month opened with a good weekend for Manchester. United thumped Bradford 6-0 and City produced a shock result at Leeds, winning 2-1. A Paulo Wanchope header was converted by Steve Howey and Gerard Wiekens volleyed the second with Lee Bowyer replying for Leeds.

Paul Gascoigne's return to White Hart Lane for his latest club, Everton, had looked to be going well when the Toffees took a 2-0 lead, but Tottenham rallied, Rebrov scored twice and Les Ferdinand touched in the winner on his first start for a year.

Newcastle went top for the first time in four years following their 2-0 win at Coventry, which included Alan Shearer's 200th league goal in 375 games. They had nine points from their first four matches

Right A point earned away at Sunderland on 1 October, the last of an eight-match unbeaten run, saw Leicester City in top spot for the first time since 1963.

Above Newcastle manager Bobby Robson was rewarded for his team's great start with the Manager of the Month award for August.

and were followed by Manchester United and Leicester, both on eight. At the equivalent week last year they had taken just one point from a possible 18. Bobby Robson told *Focus*, 'We've got a great squad of players who are motivated and proud to wear the black and white shirt and we've turned it round.'

Another manager doing well was Leicester's Peter Taylor and in most weeks the fact that they climbed to second spot after beating Southampton 1-0 would have been the lead story on *Football Focus*. But once again the spotlight was on Stamford Bridge and Chelsea's latest managerial change. Despite having won the European Cup-Winners' Cup, the League Cup and the FA Cup in his two and a half years in charge, Gianluca Vialli was sacked. He was replaced by another Italian, Claudio Ranieri, the relatively unknown coach of Atlético Madrid. Ranieri spoke very poor English and needed a translator at his press conferences. Things looked bleak in his first game in charge but the Blues rallied from 3-1 down to draw 3-3 at Old Trafford.

When David Seaman spoke to the show he gave viewers an insight into a couple of the Arsenal managers he had played under. 'The players used to call George Graham "Gadaffi" as he was so strict but Wenger is known as "Inspector Clouseau" since he's prone to have a few mishaps.'

October

On the opening day of the month Manchester United suffered their first league defeat since February when a spectacular goal by Thierry Henry gave Arsenal a 1-0 win. With his back to goal on the edge of the box he chipped it up, turned and volleyed the ball into the top right-hand corner.

Ranieri celebrated his first win when Chelsea put three past Liverpool, helped by the visiting goalkeeper, Sander Westerveld, who punched the ball into his own net. But the happiest manager was probably Peter Taylor when Leicester's goalless draw at Sunderland saw them take over at the Premiership's summit, a point ahead of Manchester United and Arsenal.

United were soon back on top, however, after beating Leicester 3-0 at Filbert Street and they remained there for the rest of the season. Arsenal regained second place after a 1-0 win over Villa. Henry was again the hero, nutmegging a defender to leave David James unsighted before tapping the ball in.

Chelsea's revival under Ranieri continued as they recorded their biggest win of the season, beating Coventry 6-1 with four goals by Hasselbaink, and there was also good news for Paul Gascoigne who helped Everton to a 1-0 win against Newcastle. It was the first time in 12 years that he had played a competitive match at St James' Park.

There was yet another drink in the last chance saloon for Stan Collymore who joined Bradford, his eighth footballing home. Their manager, Chris Hutchings, was under pressure after a poor start to the season and acknowledged that it was a gamble but they had only scored four goals in ten games with just Derby beneath them in the table. Club chairman, Geoffrey Richmond, told the programme, 'If we are going to go down we want to go with all guns blazing.' It was Collymore's fifth Premiership club after spells with Forest, Liverpool, Villa and Leicester. He made five starts, appeared twice as a sub and scored two goals. In true Stan style he struck a spectacular bicycle kick volley on his debut to help them draw 1-1 with Leeds, but then faded from the scene.

After ten games Manchester United and Arsenal filled the top two places with 21 points each, Liverpool were third on 18, followed by Newcastle and Leicester, both with 16, and two of the new sides, Ipswich and Charlton, who had 15 points apiece.

Ipswich were having a terrific first season back in the Premiership and were defying all expectations. Striker Marcus Stewart, who would score 19 goals in the league, said, 'We may not have many household names but we work hard for each other and hope to finish in the top half of the table this season.'

Both Manchester clubs were involved in five-goal thrillers at the end of the month, although they were looking at the results from different perspectives. Teddy Sheringham's hat-trick consisted of a chip, a side foot and a charge through the defence and Andy Cole added two more to give United a 5-0 win against Southampton. City, who had seen George Weah leave the club after just 11 weeks, conceded five at Arsenal.

November

Mark Viduka struck all Leeds' goals in their 4-3 win over Liverpool and James Beattie hit his first two of the season for Southampton as they beat Chelsea 3-2. It was the start of a great spell for him as he scored in eight of the next ten games. By contrast the brace from Alan

Long-server Ian Pearce

Ian Pearce is one of the select group of five who have played at least once in all 15 of the Premiership seasons although he only made one league appearance for Chelsea in the 1992–93 campaign before moving to Blackburn in December 1993.

Having played in their Premiership-winning side of 1994–95, Pearce was sold to West Ham in September 1997, but after 135 league starts in an injury-plagued career at Upton Park he switched to Fulham in 2004.

Shearer in Newcastle's 2-1 victory against Ipswich were his last goals of the season.

The Collymore signing wasn't enough to save Bradford manager Chris Hutchings and he was sacked after just 12 league games in charge, during which the club had taken only seven points. Stuart McCall took temporary control before Jim Jeffries was installed as their third boss of the year.

West Ham finally hit some form and won four in a row starting with a 4-1 win over Manchester City, which included a cheeky penalty by Paulo Di Canio who chipped the goalkeeper.

There were two big transfers this month. Tore Andre Flo doubled the Scottish record when he moved from Chelsea to Rangers for £12m and West Ham's 22-year-old, Rio Ferdinand, moved to Leeds for £18m to break the world record for a defender. His outgoing boss Harry Redknapp told *Focus*, 'He's got much more ability than Bobby Moore ever had, he's been here since he was a kid and it's not easy. He's special to us and it's a blow. He's a fantastic talent who can only get better and it will make my team weaker.'

The goals continued to come for Marcus Stewart and he scored twice in a 3-2 win at Manchester City to take his league tally to

Ipswich striker Marcus Stewart scored 19 league goals this season, including two at Maine Road in November.

Mark Viduka scores the first of his four goals in Leeds' 4-3 win over Liverpool in an astonishing match at Elland Road in early November.

nine. The points took Ipswich into third place, their highest position since the days of Sir Bobby Robson. Current manager, George Burley, was still cautious. 'If we get fourth bottom and stay in the Premier League that will be a good season for this club.'

When Tottenham beat Leicester 3-0 Les Ferdinand struck his first hat-trick in five years. He drove the first from the edge of the box, headed the second and collected his third with a left-foot shot after Darren Anderton's shot was parried.

December

After 15 games Manchester United were establishing their familiar lead, eight ahead of Arsenal with Ipswich and Leicester still tucked in behind. But it was mid-table Tottenham who featured on *Focus* on the first weekend of the month, or rather their in-form striker. His good friend Mark Bright opened the interview as the player sat facing him. 'Every now and then a striker's form is so good that we have to go and talk to them. We couldn't get Teddy Sheringham so here is Les Ferdinand.' Les hid his reaction well

as the interviewer collapsed in giggles before chatting about the seven-game goal free spell that he'd just ended. Mark later repeated the introduction on the Radio Five Live show that he fronted with Ian Wright, this time dropping in David Beckham's name, but Les got the last laugh and hung up until they apologised.

Leicester moved above Ipswich when they upset the Leeds debut of Les' cousin Rio with a 3-1 win and Ipswich failed to score for the first time during the season, losing 1-0 to Derby at Portman Road.

There was a bumper edition of *Match of the Day* on 9 December, which featured 31 goals. Bradford and Tottenham drew 3-3, as did Charlton and Manchester United although the home team had to pull back two in the final 11 minutes. Chelsea beat Derby 4-1, West Ham and Villa drew 1-1 and Beattie was on target again when Leeds lost 1-0 at Southampton. Middlesbrough's new coach, Terry Venables, who had joined up with Bryan Robson, saw his new team lose 1-0 to Sunderland at the Stadium of Light. Ray Parlour scored a hat-trick in Arsenal's 5-0 victory over Newcastle and

Manchester City pulled off their best result of the season, beating Everton by the same score. Having lost six on the bounce Walter Smith cancelled the team's Christmas party and made them watch a video of the game.

Everton's next match was a relatively dull 1-1 draw with West Ham but made the back pages when Paolo Di Canio became a fair-play hero for catching a goalmouth cross to stop play when he saw Paul Gerrard, the Everton keeper, apparently unconscious on the edge of the box.

Having taken only one point from their previous nine games, Venables' influence was apparent as Middlesbrough beat Chelsea 1-0. Bradford recorded their first win in 14, 2-0 against Coventry, and Manchester United suffered their first home league defeat for a year and 363 days when Danny Murphy's 43rd-minute free kick gave Liverpool victory at Old Trafford.

A few days before Christmas, after nine years as chairman of Tottenham, Alan Sugar announced that he was selling the majority of his shares to investment company ENIC. 'I'm not prepared to put up with all the abuse of fans,' he said. 'There are no rewards, thanks or recognition for all the work.' Future Tottenham striker Robbie Keane returned from a brief spell in Italy with Inter Milan to join Leeds.

Liverpool beat Arsenal 4-0, but the Gunners returned to form in their next match, Henry scoring three of their six against Leicester. Charlton were in a similar yo-yo spell of form, firstly losing 5-0 at West Ham and then ending the year with a resounding 4-1 win at Manchester City thanks mainly to a first half hat-trick from Jonatan Johansson.

January 2001

On New Years' Day, Charlton did Manchester United a favour by beating Arsenal 1-0, while Sir Alex's side defeated West Ham 3-1 at Old Trafford to extend their lead to 11 points. Debutant Robbie Keane scored Leeds' goal in their draw with Middlesbrough and

Left A free-kick from Danny Murphy (right) just before half time was enough to give Liverpool a rare win against Manchester United at Old Trafford.

Opposite New England coach Sven-Goran Eriksson was at Upton Park to see Sunderland beat West Ham 2-0. Stanislav Varga opened the scoring with this header just before half time and Don Hutchison scored the second just after the break.

Below Steven Gerrard also scored from a free-kick in the next match as the Reds demolished Arsenal 4-0 at Anfield two days before Christmas.

Sunderland's progress continued with a 4-1 win over in-form Ipswich.

On 10 January Sven-Goran Eriksson began his tenure as England's first foreign coach having resigned from Lazio the previous day. In the following weeks he became a permanent fixture in the stands at Premiership grounds as he began to plan his strategy for the national team. His first visit was to Upton Park where he saw Sunderland beat West Ham 2-0 to go second. It was to be the peak of their season as they only won three of their remaining 15 matches and finished in seventh for the second year in succession.

But Old Trafford continued to be the real focus of attention when Sir Alex Ferguson announced that he would retire the following year, although he planned to stay involved with United. There was another move away from the Theatre of Dreams when unsettled goalkeeper Mark Bosnich left for Chelsea after 18 unhappy months at a club where he had found it hard to step into Peter Schmeichel's considerable shoes. However, things were worse across the city at Maine Road where Joe Royle's team remained mired in the relegation places with Bradford and Coventry.

February

United's lead was extended to 15 points after their 1-0 win over Everton although their great form didn't win Ferguson the Manager of the Month accolade. Instead it was awarded for the first time to a non-manager, Terry Venables, for his work alongside Bryan Robson as coach at Middlesbrough.

Footballing finance was featured on *Focus* on 10 February. Manchester United were trying to market themselves in North America by linking up with the New York Yankees baseball team and other clubs knew that they had to take a fresh look at income streams if they were to compete. Colin Hutchinson, Chelsea's chief executive, explained his club's new approach, words which seem prophetic in light of the Abramovich years that lay ahead. 'The game is changing rapidly, particularly in the media field. We are sat now in our Chelsea studio that cost £500,000. We've got a joint venture with a broadcaster to exploit our internet and broadcasting rights in the years

to come and we all know that Manchester United won't go on for ever but that we've all got some catching up to do. We are working night and day to find the resources to compete with them because we need a competitive Premiership. It's not good for the English game if they get streets ahead.'

That afternoon Chelsea and United drew 1-1 at Stamford Bridge. It was the first dropped points of the year for the visitors and the challenge facing Sven to find the next generation of English World Cup winners was highlighted by the fact that there were 18 overseas players in the two squads. Andy Cole touched in from a Giggs cross on his 250th appearance for the club after Jimmy Floyd Hasselbaink had put Chelsea in front heading home when Paul Scholes failed to head back to his keeper.

Bradford lost 2-0 at Southampton and remained in 20th place without a goal in 510 minutes of football. They were to finish the season with their form confirmed by the stats: they won fewest matches (5), lost most (22), scored fewest goals (30) and conceded most (70).

The month ended with Arsenal licking their wounds as the gulf between the top two teams was demonstrated with ruthless efficiency when they were beaten 6-1 at Old Trafford. Dwight Yorke's hat-trick plus goals by Keane and Solskjaer had given Manchester United a 5-1 half time lead, and Sherringham added a sixth in the final minute as they surged 16 points clear of the chasing pack.

March

In-form Leicester beat Gerard Houllier's Liverpool 2-0 and moved up to fourth place on the same number of points as the Merseysiders, but it wasn't going to last. Ipswich leapfrogged them both after scoring three in the second half against Bradford. It was a good match for their Dutch player

Martijn Reuser who scored two and made the other.

There was more trouble in a troubled season at White Hart Lane where, days after winning a place in the FA Cup semi-final, George Graham was sacked. It was not immediately apparent why he had gone although the club's investors ENIC alleged a breach of contract. A few days later Tottenham appointed their sixth boss in eight years when Glenn Hoddle returned to the club that he had represented as a player for over a decade. 'It feels like I'm home and I feel instantly a part of the place,' he said. 'It's probably the only place I'd leave Southampton for.'

Leicester's fall from grace started a week later when their 2-0 defeat at Manchester United began a dreadful sequence of eight consecutive defeats, the worst in their 107-year history. In all they lost 14 out of the 19 matches that made up the second half of the season as they dropped from European contenders to 13th place at the end of the season. Their away form was a crucial factor as they only managed 11 goals on their travels. Their three points almost earned United the title.

Sunderland's travelling supporters, however, were in a more celebratory mood when they saw their side win at Stamford Bridge for the first time since 1957. Two goals from Don Hutchison as well as strikes by Gavin McCann and Kevin Phillips gave them a 4-2 win. On the last day of the month the leaders Manchester United lost for only the third time in the league this season when goals by Steven Gerrard and Robbie Fowler gave Liverpool a 2-0 win at Anfield.

April

Southampton had gone seven Premiership games without conceding a goal and were just one away from equalling their own club record that stretched back to 1922 when they

Leicester's season hit its peak with a 2-0 win over Liverpool, including this goal from Ade Akinbiyi. But nine defeats in the final ten matches of the season saw the Foxes finish in a disappointing 13th place.

faced Ipswich at The Dell. Unfortunately, Marcus Stewart had no regard for Saints' history and scored three times in a comfortable victory for the team from Suffolk. It was the first time that Paul Jones had picked the ball out of his own net since 1 January.

That win kept Ipswich in third place in the race for the final Champions League spot. They were on 52 points, two ahead of Leeds, with Liverpool on 49 and Sunderland on 48. Manchester United were still charging away having already reached the 70-point mark and Arsenal were 13 adrift in second.

With Bradford looking certainties for relegation the final two places appeared to be between Coventry, Manchester City and Middlesbrough, although the north-east side still had a four-point cushion. Their cause was helped by a surprise 3-0 win at Highbury, courtesy of own goals from Arsenal's Brazilians Edu and Silvinho.

On 14 April, in front of a post-war record crowd of 67,637 at Old Trafford, Manchester United secured their seventh title in nine seasons when they beat Coventry 4-2. They then relaxed and hit their worst form of the entire campaign taking just four points from their remaining five matches. But Alex Ferguson, always mindful of the future, finally signed Ruud van Nistelrooy from PSV Eindhoven for a new club record £19m.

Coventry managed to beat Sunderland in their next match to make it three wins out of four, but a single point from the last available 12 saw their slim survival hopes evaporate. Bradford's relegation was also confirmed. After surviving just two seasons in the Premiership they returned to Division One when they lost 2-1 at Everton on 28 April. The Toffees, who also struggled for most of the season, ended the season in 16th place.

At the end of the month it was announced that Barclaycard would become the new sponsors of the Premier League, replacing Carling, in a three-year deal worth £48m.

Below Southampton keeper Paul Jones (left) can't hide his disappointment as he concedes his first goal in eight Premiership games against Ipswich.

Reporter Mark Bright

Mark Bright's football career spanned 574 games with Port Vale, Leicester City, Crystal Palace, Sheffield Wednesday and Charlton Athletic. He scored 209 goals, including 48 in 132 Premiership matches for Sheffield Wednesday between 1992 and 1996.

'When I went to Sheffield Wednesday in 1992 Chris Waddle also joined from Marseille. He had an outstanding season, was one of the first stars of the new Premier League and the best player in the country that year. I played up front with David Hirst, another brilliant striker, and we had a great record together as we came seventh and reached both Cup finals.

It was a sensational time although at first we were not really conscious of the enormous changes that the Sky money was bringing about other than the introduction of the Sunday and Monday matches, which no one liked playing at first.

When TV became more involved and the media presence grew it was awesome to have the great stars joining English clubs and enhancing the league. I remember the excitement of Klinsmann making his debut against us and, with the likes of Bergkamp, Zola, Cantona, Asprilla and Ginola, it meant that we were all part of something big and special.

Because I played alongside many of them I was able to use my contacts to get interviews when I first became a reporter on *Football Focus*. I remember arranging features with Les Ferdinand, Paul Ince, Michael Owen, Dwight Yorke and many others, but it has become harder to get access with the increased interest in the league from around the world. There are now lots of foreign TV crews, which restricts the times that the players and managers are available. Arsène Wenger, for example, will do interviews in English, French and German.

Most clubs now have interpreters but it still challenges us as reporters as there are so many different nationalities and languages although many of them do speak good English. Names can be hard to pronounce but we have to get them right so we check with the press officers at the clubs as well as asking the BBC's pronunciation department to write them phonetically.'

Opposite Coventry fans can hardly bear to watch during a tense game at Villa Park on the penultimate weekend of the season. Two up at half time, they eventually lost 3-2 and their 34 years in the top-flight ended with relegation.

May

In the last few weeks Derby had also dropped into trouble but maximum points gained following their unexpected win at Old Trafford ensured Premiership safety when, despite being surrounded by red shirts, Malcolm Christie managed to turn and release a left-foot shot into the top corner of the United goal. Michael Owen struck all three in Liverpool's fifth straight win when they beat Newcastle, and Arsenal dented Leeds' challenge for third place, winning 2-1 at Highbury.

There was drama at Villa Park where Coventry had to win to give themselves a chance of staying up. They were 2-0 up after half an hour through Moroccan midfielder Mustapha Hadji, but it all went wrong after the interval when keeper Chris Kirkland failed to hold a cross in the 61st minute allowing Darius Vassell to tap in Villa's first. Juan Pablo Angel volleyed a second and then a cracking shot into the top right-hand corner by Paul Merson just five minutes from time ended 34 years in the top-flight for Gordon Strachan's team. Manchester City took the final relegation place when they lost 2-1 at Ipswich before finishing the season with another loss by the same scoreline against Chelsea.

In the final week of the season Harry Redknapp suddenly quit as West Ham's manager along with assistant Frank Lampard Senior. There were alleged disagreements over the money that would be available to improve the side who finished in 15th place after their last-day defeat at Middlesbrough. Boro too were looking for a new boss when Bryan Robson resigned a few weeks after the season ended. He had been in charge for seven turbulent years and was eventually replaced by Steve McClaren, Sir Alex's number two at Old Trafford.

Liverpool rounded off a strong league season by winning 4-0 at Charlton and pipping Leeds to the crucial third Champions League slot. They finished a point ahead of David O'Leary's side – who had also been semi-finalists in this season's European competition – and one behind Arsenal.

Manchester United's domination of the Premier League continued with their third title in a row. The hat-trick of championships had only ever been achieved in English football by three other teams: Huddersfield Town (1923–24–25–26), Arsenal (1932–33–34–35) and Liverpool (1981–82–83–84).

Final League Table

Team	P	W	D	L	F	A	Pts
Manchester United	38	24	8	6	79	31	80
Arsenal	38	20	10	8	63	38	70
Liverpool	38	20	9	9	71	39	69
Leeds United	38	20	8	10	64	43	68
Ipswich Town	38	20	6	12	57	42	66
Chelsea	38	17	10	11	68	45	61
Sunderland	38	15	12	11	46	41	57
Aston Villa	38	13	15	10	46	43	54
Charlton Athletic	38	14	10	14	50	57	52
Southampton	38	14	10	14	40	48	52
Newcastle United	38	14	9	15	44	50	51
Tottenham Hotspur	38	13	10	15	47	54	49
Leicester City	38	14	6	18	39	51	48
Middlesbrough	38	9	15	14	44	44	42
West Ham United	38	10	12	16	45	50	42
Everton	38	11	9	18	45	59	42
Derby County	38	10	12	16	37	59	42
Manchester City	38	8	10	20	41	65	34
Coventry City	38	8	10	20	36	63	34
Bradford City	38	5	11	22	30	70	26

Leading Goalscorers league only

J F Hasselbaink	Chelsea	23
Marcus Stewart	Ipswich Town	19
Thierry Henry	Arsenal	17
Mark Viduka	Leeds United	17
Michael Owen	Liverpool	16
Teddy Sheringham	Manchester United	15
Emile Heskey	Liverpool	14
Kevin Phillips	Sunderland	14
Alen Boksic	Middlesbrough	12

Awards

European Footballer of the Year
Michael Owen, Liverpool

Footballer of the Year
Teddy Sheringham, Manchester United

PFA Player of the Year
Teddy Sheringham, Manchester United

PFA Young Player of the Year
Steven Gerrard, Liverpool

Jimmy Floyd Haisselbank was the Premiership's leading scorer with 23 goals for Chelsea this season.

Ipswich drew 1-1 at Derby to clinch a well-deserved fifth and a UEFA Cup place, and there were a couple of emotional farewells elsewhere. Matt Le Tissier came on as a late substitute to score his only league goal of the season against Arsenal and it fittingly gave Southampton a 3-2 win. It was the last goal ever scored at The Dell before the club moved to their new St Mary's ground. It fell to Gary Lineker to utter the last words on a Premiership *Match of the Day* as ITV had now won the contract for a three-year spell. 'As for Saturday nights and the Premiership, well, thanks for watching and join us after the break – goodbye.'

Honours List 2000–01

Champions Manchester United

Runners-up Arsenal

Relegated Bradford City, Coventry City, Manchester City

Promoted Fulham, Blackburn Rovers, Bolton Wanderers

FA Cup Winners Liverpool

League Cup Winners Liverpool

UEFA Cup Winners Liverpool

League Cup
Liverpool beat Birmingham 5-4 on penalties after the match had finished 1-1. Sander Westerveld saved from Andrew Johnson to give the Merseyside club their first trophy for six years.

FA Cup
In the first FA Cup final to be held at the Millennium Stadium in Cardiff, Liverpool beat Arsenal 2-1. The Gunners had gone ahead in the 72nd minute when Freddie Ljungberg shot past Sander Westerveld. Michael Owen equalized 11 minutes later and then, with just two minutes left on the clock, he ran onto a long ball from Patrik Berger, evaded the Arsenal defence and put the ball just inside the far post. The Londoners were devastated but part two of Liverpool's treble was complete and they collected the famous trophy for the first time since 1992.

UEFA Cup
Liverpool's unique cup treble came when they beat Alaves 5-4 to win the UEFA Cup. It was their first European Trophy for 17 years and was won by a Golden Goal after the game finished 4-4 at the end of extra time. The climax came when Delfi Geli headed an own goal to end the final and start Liverpool's celebrations.

FF 2001–02

1   10

Liverpool's Michael Owen takes
on Chelsea's French defenders
William Gallas (left) and Marcel
Desailly on his return to the
Liverpool side after injury.
The Reds won 1-0 at the end of
March to keep up the pressure
on title rivals Manchester United
and Arsenal.

Programmes

Although the BBC had lost the rights to show Premiership football the decision was taken to keep *Football Focus* on the air so that it could still reflect the stories and personalities as well as cover the FA Cup and matches from Scotland.

For the first time it became a separate show, independent of *Grandstand*, and in a new set with a huge sweeping green sofa. There was a greater use of emails plus competitions and lots of fan interviews with facts popping up on-screen throughout the programme. Ray and Mark Lawrenson were regularly joined by Mick McCarthy and Bryan Robson with appearances by several of the other BBC pundits including Alan Hansen and Garth Crooks.

Saturday night highlights were now shown on ITV with *Match of the Day* reverting to an occasional show that concentrated on live FA Cup and England matches as well as some UEFA Cup games.

Presenter
Ray Stubbs

Pre-season

At the start of his supposed last season at Manchester United Sir Alex Ferguson paid Lazio £28m for Juan Sebastian Veron, and after four years, 31 Premiership goals and an impressive collection of winner's medals, Teddy Sheringham left United to rejoin Tottenham on a free transfer. As he arrived at White Hart Lane their captain, Sol Campbell, became the first high-profile player to make the move across North London to Arsenal since Pat Jennings in 1977.

Chelsea's chequebook was open again and their new recruits included Marseille defender William Gallas for £6m and the Barcelona pair of Emmanuel Petit and Boudewijn Zenden who cost almost £13m between them. West Ham's 23-year-old midfielder Frank Lampard went from being an Eastender to a West End boy when he also joined Claudio Ranieri's squad for £11m.

August 2001

Kevin Nolan scored the first Premier League goal of the season in the 15th minute of newly promoted Bolton's 5-0 win at Leicester, but their fellow newcomers both lost. Ruud van Nistelrooy scored twice on his league debut as Manchester United won 3-2 against Fulham and Fabrizio Ravanelli struck Derby's first in their 2-1 win against Blackburn and, although it was to be 11 games before they won again, the Italian striker had found the back of the net six times by the end of October.

The opening day of the season saw a harsh introduction for new Middlesbrough manager Steve McClaren when they lost 4-0 at home to Arsenal. Thierry Henry's opener in the 43rd minute was the first of 24 in the Premiership that would leave him as top scorer in May. Arsenal added three more in the final three minutes.

Pay-per-view arrived this season with the first of 40 televised matches coming on

19 August when Telewest, NTL, BSkyB and ONdigital broadcast Chelsea's 1-1 draw with Newcastle for a range of additional fees. Two days later Ipswich beat Derby County 2-1, but the team from Suffolk, last season's surprise package who'd defied all the odds to finish fifth, had a dreadful year and this was to be their only win in the first 17 games.

Fulham's first-ever Premiership victory came against Sunderland when Barry Hayles and Louis Saha scored in the second half. They had come up as champions having been in Division Two just three years ago. French striker Saha scored three times in their opening two fixtures but added only five more in his next 34 appearances.

After two matches Bolton were leading with six points and their manager Sam Allardyce told *Focus* that he had been advised to get the league table framed as they weren't likely to be there that long. The club hadn't been top since 1958 and in their previous two Premiership seasons had only won one of their first ten matches.

They remained there for another week after Dean Holdsworth's 30-yard shot in the last minute squeezed under Sander Westerveld in his only league appearance of the season to ensure maximum points in their 2-1 win over Liverpool. The visitors had signed Polish keeper Jerzy Dudek in the summer for just under £5m from Feyenoord and he played the remainder of the campaign.

Arsenal began an unbeaten eight-match run with a 4-0 win against Leicester, whose season's pattern already seemed set as they had conceded nine goals in their opening two games. Serial red card specialists, Patrick Vieira and Dennis Wise, were dismissed for squaring up during the game.

A surprise transfer came at the end of the month when Jaap Stam suddenly left Manchester United to join Lazio for £16.5m shortly after publishing a controversial autobiography. United replaced him with 35-year-old French international Laurent Blanc. Sir Alex felt he would play a specific role for him. 'Wes Brown, Phil Neville, Silvestre, even Ronny Johnsen are quiet lads and I just felt we needed someone who organised and talks. I know he's French and his English is limited but his communication's not a problem.'

September

Colin Cooper managed to score Middlesbrough's first goal of the season but they still ended the day with no points from their opening four matches, losing 4-1 at home to Newcastle. Alan Shearer scored twice as the Magpies collected maximum points for the first time in this campaign. Now in 19th place, Middlesbrough finally won their first points in the next match with a 2-0 win against West Ham, as did the bottom club Southampton who beat Bolton 1-0.

On 15 September the result of the day came at St James' Park where Bobby Robson celebrated his 100th match in charge with a terrific 4-3 victory over Manchester United. Ferguson's side came from behind three

times after Laurent Robert's powerful free kick beat Fabien Barthez in the fourth minute, Roy Keane was sent off for the ninth time in a red shirt and the winner came when Shearer's shot was deflected in by West Brown with eight minutes remaining. Robson was delighted, 'You need spills and thrills and goals at both ends and the game was on a knife edge. It was an absolute belter.'

Focus reported that Robert and Barthez were just two of a record 34 Frenchmen who were registered to play in the Premier League. The World and European champions provided the highest number of any nationality with only 22 Scots and 15 Welsh players in the competition.

After Manchester United had travelled south to beat Tottenham 5-3 at White Hart Lane, having been 3-0 behind at half time, Sir Alex said that it was the best away result of his career at the club. Tottenham's £8m debutant Dean Richards had scored the opener with Les Ferdinand and Christian Ziege adding further goals but after the break United brought on Mikael Silvestre and Ole

Gunnar Solskjaer and played three up front. The visitors immediately pulled back a goal with an Andy Cole header from David Beckham's cross and reduced the deficit to one when Blanc headed in Beckham's corner. Van Nistelrooy headed a third before Veron put United ahead and, with three minutes remaining, Beckham struck a terrific right-footed shot past Neil Sullivan from just inside the area to clinch a memorable win.

Everton ended a three-game losing streak by putting five past West Ham, Leeds took pole position after winning 2-1 at Ipswich and Leicester's Peter Taylor became the first manager to be sacked this season having seen his team win just five points in eight games. He was replaced by Dave Bassett.

October

Jim Smith was the next managerial casualty when he left Derby County after six years in charge. His assistant, Colin Todd, inherited a team who were second bottom having narrowly escaped relegation in the previous two seasons.

Unbeaten Leeds had a three-point lead over Arsenal at the other end of the table and maintained their record when drawing 1-1 at Liverpool. The main drama came just after half time when Gérard Houllier collapsed and spent many months recuperating from the subsequent emergency heart surgery. Phil Thompson took the managerial reins in his absence.

West Ham had managed only five points from a possible 18 and their crisis continued when they travelled to Ewood Park and were thrashed 7-1 by Blackburn. Garry Flitcroft headed the opener in the 18th minute and Craig Hignett wrapped it up in the 90th to give the club their biggest margin of victory since an 8-2 win over the same opponents back in 1963.

Bolton recorded a famous win over Manchester United at Old Trafford to give Sam

Allardyce a birthday present that he described as 'no better feeling apart from watching my children being born. It is my best result as a manager'. After Veron had given United the lead in the first half, Kevin Nolan struck a powerful volley past the diving Barthez and Michael Ricketts then lifted the ball over the keeper for an 84th-minute winner.

Arsenal returned to the top despite being held 3-3 by Blackburn at Highbury after David Dunn equalised with a 20-yard shot two minutes from the end, although they were in mourning the following week when the manager of their 1971 double-winning team, Bertie Mee, died at the age of 82.

It was all change at Southampton where former Coventry boss Gordon Strachan replaced Stuart Gray who had been sacked after just eight matches in charge. The club were happy at their new St Mary's ground but fans were complaining that they'd had four managers in five years and that Gray hadn't been given long enough.

Aston Villa led the table for the first time in three seasons following a 3-2 win against Bolton. They took over from Leeds who drew 1-1 at Manchester United and whose goalkeeper, Nigel Martyn, had been in superb form. It was only the fourth goal he had conceded in their opening ten games. In contrast, in Chelsea's 1-1 draw at Derby Jimmy Floyd Hasselbaink took his goalscoring tally to ten in ten.

November

A quarter of the way through the season and John Gregory's Aston Villa were leading the table with 21 points from ten games. Leeds were a point behind, Arsenal and Liverpool had 19 and they were followed by Manchester United, Newcastle, Tottenham, Chelsea and Bolton. Leicester were bottom having taken only six out of a possible 33 points with Southampton and Derby immediately above them on seven and Ipswich on eight.

Ravanelli scored on his return to Middlesbrough, but Derby conceded five. It was the only time that the home side scored more than twice in a Premiership game all season and represented one seventh of their total goals for the entire campaign.

One of their former players, Paul Gascoigne, scored his only goal of the season in Everton's 2-2 draw at Bolton. Liverpool went briefly to the top following their 3-1 win over Manchester United but they were overtaken the following day when Leeds defeated Tottenham 2-1. Aston Villa's 3-0 loss at Newcastle began a bad run for the Villans as they only won once in 11 games.

A surprise result at Highbury saw Arsenal concede four goals in 18 minutes either side of half time. Despite two goals from Thierry Henry, the Gunners went down 4-2 to Charlton. The Addicks were involved in another high scoring match a fortnight later, this time against fellow strugglers West Ham at the Valley.

In his first start for almost two years striker Paul Kitson put the visitors ahead in the third minute when he powered in a low shot from the edge of the area on his way to scoring what was only the second hat-trick in the Premiership that season. Following Kitson's second-half substitution with the score at 3-3, his replacement, Jermain Defoe, put the Hammers in the lead with a right-footed volley six minutes from the end but, with only seconds remaining, Jonatan Johansson scored his second of the match with a spectacular overhead kick to make the final score a breathless 4-4.

Liverpool's stand-in manager, Phil Thompson, was enjoying life at the top again when they took the lead from Leeds on goal difference. He was interviewed by his former team-mate, Alan Hansen. 'I've come full circle from standing on the Kop to coming back and leading the team out. It's boys' own stuff.' Another familiar Anfield face no longer seemed to fit at the club, despite having

Charlton's Jonatan Johansson scores with an overhead kick in the dying seconds as the Addicks share the points with West Ham in a 4-4 draw at the Valley.

scored 171 goals, and Robbie Fowler moved to their Elland Road rivals for £11m.

December

The month began with John Motson pointing out to *Focus* viewers that Arsenal were 5-1 for the championship, which he recommended as a great bet and was, as it turned out, very good advice. They moved into second place, three points behind Liverpool, after a 2-0 win at Ipswich. Leicester excited their fans with a rare away win of their own when they won at Villa by the same score. But it was to prove a mere flicker of form and their supporters had to wait four months before they won again.

Bolton were in a similar predicament and their 3-2 loss at Tottenham set them off on a period of 11 matches in which they gained only five points. Glenn Hoddle's side moved into fifth, five points behind leaders Liverpool. Following their 3-0 home defeat to Chelsea, Manchester United slipped back to eighth. This was their lowest ever position in the Premier League table and they had never previously lost five games by this stage in the season.

There was further woe for the reigning champions when they were beaten at Old

Blackburn midfielder David Dunn was in fine form during the early months of the season and scored twice in their 3-3 draw at Highbury in October.

ITV

Having paid £183m for the rights to show Premier League highlights, ITV's Saturday night programme was named *The Premiership* and ran for the three seasons that they had the contract from August 2001.

Although it began in an early evening slot at 7.00 p.m. it was soon moved back to a more familiar place later in the schedules at 10.30 p.m. when the ratings failed to match those of their more traditional light entertainment offerings. It was presented by the equally familiar Desmond Lynam who had switched from the BBC in 1999 and pundits included Terry Venables, Ally McCoist and Andy Townsend. ITV's lunchtime football show, *On The Ball*, was presented by Gabby Logan and Barry Venison during the same period but came to an end in 2004.

Trafford by West Ham. Defoe's 64th-minute goal gave the Hammers their first win in six, but Manchester United finally hit their stride a few days later when they put five past a woeful Derby defence and moved up to fifth place after the first of an eight-game winning run.

When Les Ferdinand scored the first of Tottenham's four against Fulham he wrote himself into the record books as it was the 10,000th goal to be scored in the Premier League. Brian Deane had scored the first for Sheffield Wednesday against Manchester United in 1992, the 1000th came from Mike Newell when Blackburn played Forest in April 1993 and the 5000th was by Villa's Andy Townsend in their match against Southampton in December 1996.

The most unlikely *Focus* report of the season came when Dylan Jones, editor of *GQ* magazine, explained that the sheepskin was the coat of the season. 'John Motson is a trendsetter,' he said. 'It has obviously taken him 30-odd years to achieve this but finally his dress has coincided with fashion so for the next three or four months he is the epitome of men's style in this country.'

Liverpool suffered their first defeat in 13 games when they conceded four at Chelsea which enabled Newcastle to move top when they finally overcame their London jinx at their 30th attempt, beating Arsenal 3-1 at Highbury.

The year ended with some high-scoring games. Having led 3-1, Leeds lost 4-3 at home to Newcastle, Ruud van Nistelrooy scored a hat-trick in Manchester United's 6-1 win over Southampton, Ipswich beat Sunderland 5-0, part of a run of seven wins in eight games, and Chelsea beat Bolton 5-1.

Arsenal began a 21-match unbeaten run with the first of 18 wins when they won 2-1 at Liverpool in the week before Christmas, and they repeated the score against Chelsea on Boxing Day. They ended 2001 as leaders, having achieved the same result against

Middlesbrough when Ashley Cole headed the winner from a Dennis Bergkamp cross in the 80th minute.

His namesake Andy moved from Manchester United to Blackburn for £8m after seven years, 122 goals, five titles, two FA Cups and a European Cup. 'They were the greatest club I ever played for and I enjoyed every minute of it,' he said of his time at Old Trafford.

January 2002

Manchester United went top for the first time this season when they beat Southampton 3-1. In their next game, a 2-1 win over Blackburn, Ruud van Nistelrooy became the first player to score in eight successive Premiership matches. The previous record of seven had been jointly held by Ian Wright, Mark Stein, Alan Shearer and Thierry Henry. Ferguson also strengthened his squad, buying Diego Forlan from Buenos Aires club Independiente for £7.5m.

Fourteen days into the New Year Colin Todd became the latest managerial casualty when he was sacked by Derby County after just 98 days and 11 defeats in 17 games. Billy McEwan stood in as their third manager of the season and immediately lost 3-1 at home to Ipswich. Former boss Jim Smith felt that the change hadn't been for the better saying, 'They've forgotten the word stability.' There was yet another twist when John Gregory resigned after four relatively successful years in charge of seventh-placed Aston Villa and a few weeks later picked up the reins at Derby who were one off the bottom.

There were two goals each for Jimmy Floyd Hasselbaink and Eidur Gudjohnsen when Chelsea beat West Ham 5-1, while Danny Murphy's 85th-minute goal gave Liverpool a 1-0 win at Manchester United to start a run in of 13 wins in their final 15 games, having not won for the previous five.

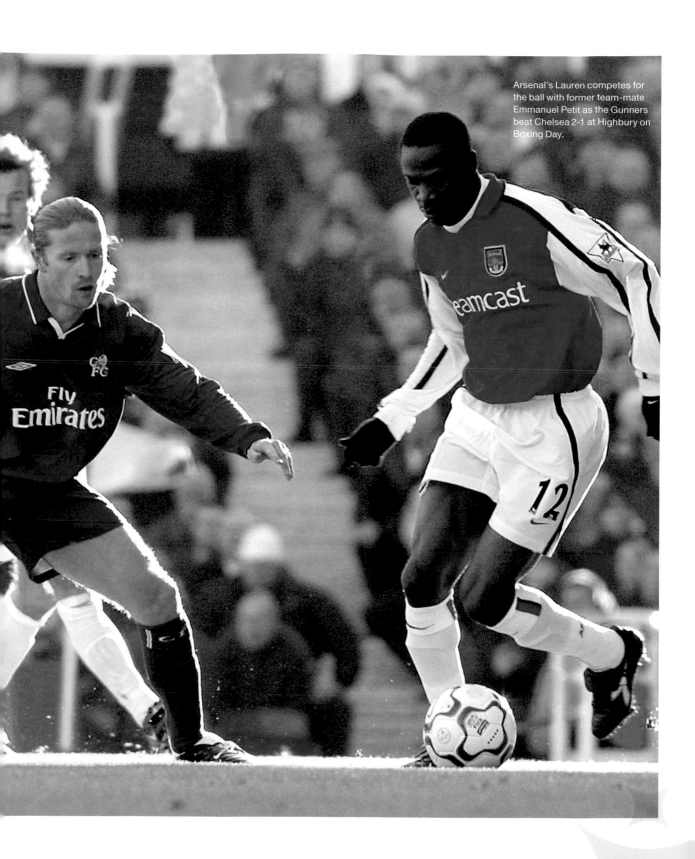

Arsenal's Lauren competes for the ball with former team-mate Emmanuel Petit as the Gunners beat Chelsea 2-1 at Highbury on Boxing Day.

February

Ipswich's fine form faltered after their 2-1 victory at Everton and, after almost making it into the top half of the table, they slid back towards the danger zone winning only one of their final 13 games.

Having spent almost £100m on new players pressure was mounting on David O'Leary to bring some silverware to Leeds, but that looked increasingly unlikely when Liverpool crushed them 4-0 at Elland Road. Rio Ferdinand turned Danny Murphy's free kick into his own net in the 16th minute, Emile Heskey added two more in three minutes in the second half and Michael Owen headed a fourth in injury time to leave the home team in sixth place while the visitors moved up to third.

Two managerial retirement decisions were reversed. After Manchester United's 4-1 thrashing of Sunderland the team sat two points clear at the top and then announced that Sir Alex had decided to sign a new contract and stay with the club. And Graham Taylor, who had moved into the boardroom at Villa Park, moved back into the dug out. 'The Premiership was founded when I was England manager and I haven't had the opportunity to have a big club at the top end,' he declared happily.

Newcastle sat in second place and strengthened their assault on the title by signing 18-year-old Jermaine Jenas from Forest for £5m, a new record for an English teenager. Liverpool added to the misery at Ipswich by sticking six past them at Portman Road with two more from Heskey and Owen as well as goals from Sami Hyypia and Portuguese defender Abel Xavier, his first for the club.

March

Football Focus introduced a fresh innovation on 2 March when a new text service was launched so that fans could get in touch with the show in addition to phoning or sending emails. At the end of the programme each week Ray and Mark would also take part in a special webcast to respond to viewers' thoughts and questions.

Newcastle's championship challenge was dented when they conceded two at home to Arsenal and they only picked up 16 points from their remaining ten games. Leeds, in a poor run having not won a game since they were top of the table on New Year's Day, finally turned things around when they beat Ipswich 2-0.

Arsenal won at home against relegation-haunted Derby thanks to Robert Pires' tenth goal of the season but the following day, on a windy Wednesday evening, Manchester United leapfrogged the Londoners to reclaim top spot after their 4-0 result against Tottenham with a brace each for Beckham and van Nistelrooy.

At the other end Everton were fifth from bottom when they sacked Walter Smith, who became the sixth Premiership manager to lose his job during the season. Preston's 38-year-old boss, David Moyes, replaced him after a compensation package of around a million pounds was agreed.

Robert Pires keeps his composure to crash home the winner against Derby at Highbury to take Arsenal back to the top of the table.

Pundit Mark Lawrenson

Mark Lawrenson formed a famous partnership with Alan Hansen at the heart of Liverpool's defence winning five League titles, the European Cup, FA Cup and three League Cups. He was forced into retirement by injury when he was just 30, but has been a regular guest and summariser on Radio Five Live, *Match of the Day* and *Football Focus* since 1997.

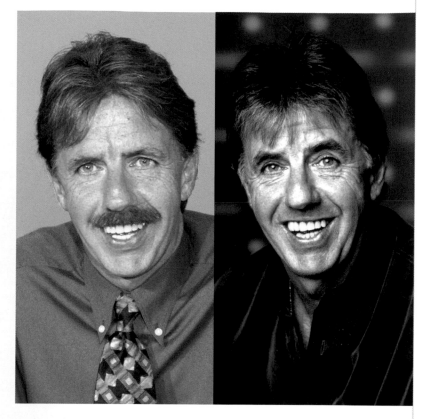

'I come to London from the North West on a Friday to do Radio Five Live and Irish Radio but the *Focus* producers always like to know that I'm down and ready to go the next day. The most important time of the day is when I walk into the office at 9.45 on a Saturday morning and have two well-done bacon butties and a cup of coffee. Then all is well with the world, I read the papers and see what the breaking football stories are.

Apart from analysis, I never ask what is going to be in the programme, never look at the script and don't rehearse. I think that if you are doing an opinion show then your first thought is usually the right one as it means I can react genuinely. The features and interviews are always fresh as it will be the first time I've seen them.

On Sundays I religiously go through all the papers to get the results, scorers, gates and teams in all the British leagues. I've always had a real interest in the lower leagues and I think that is important in being able to give an overall view of the game.

The three presenters have all been very easy to work with although they are all very different characters. Gary and I were both new to it and learning as we went along but he was always extremely laid back and could approach the job from his experience as a player at the highest level.

Ray is fantastic especially as he'll do all the worrying for you and he takes the side of the viewers, asking questions to which he thinks they want to know the answers. I didn't know Manish before we started and he's young enough to be my son and I'm very aware that he's from a completely different generation.

Stubbsy was the main instigator in getting rid of my moustache as he set it up with Bolton fans and suggested it to me live. It was one of the best things I ever did and looking back I wonder why none of my friends ever told me to do it, although, as moustaches go, it was very good, but it was from a different era.

Looking across the Premiership years I'd pick Thierry Henry as the greatest player. Even with Keane, Shearer, Zola and Bergkamp, he's the best and has been absolutely sensational. He scores and creates goals and success and is rarely injured.'

After 29 games Blackburn were 15th with 32 points, Everton, Ipswich and Bolton were all on 30, Derby 26 and Leicester a paltry 18.

Bolton's fighting spirit was epitomised by their unsung hero, Mike Whitlow. He'd won the league championship with Leeds, the League Cup with Leicester, been promoted four times, relegated twice and was very happy not to be especially famous. 'We've got nine games to go and a right good fight on our hands and the lads are determined,' he said. 'It was a nice start and we loved every minute of it but it would be an even better memory to have another crack next year.'

The fierce battle at the top continued. Leaders Manchester United went to Upton Park and clocked up their second 5-3 win of the season in London after West Ham had twice been ahead, but Liverpool replaced United yet again when Vladimir Smicer's last-minute volley gave them all three points against Chelsea and Sir Alex saw his side lose to 1-0 to Middlesbrough.

It was looking grim for the followers of Derby and Leicester after the results on the final weekend of the month. County went down 4-3 at home to Everton, the first of seven successive defeats, and they ended the season with 24 losses, the worst record of the Premier League. Everton too were deep in trouble after being thrashed 6-2 by Newcastle the following week. Leicester's fall had been extraordinary as their 2-0 defeat at Leeds meant they had only won four out of 41 Premiership games since being knocked out of the FA Cup by Wycombe a year ago when they had been in fifth place and pushing for Europe.

It left Liverpool on top with 68 points from 33, one point ahead of Manchester United with Arsenal, who had two games in hand, third on 66 and, on *Focus*, Mark now felt that 'Arsenal are now favourites, they have games in hand and their destiny is now in their own hands.'

Football said farewell to another of its iconic names when Kenneth Wolstenholme, the voice of football on the BBC throughout the 1950s and 1960s, passed away aged 81. He had commentated on 23 FA Cup finals and five World Cups including England's

1966 victory and been the first presenter of *Match of the Day* in 1964.

April

There was another change at Leicester as Dave Bassett was moved upstairs to take the role of director of football, and Micky Adams became the latest to take over the first team who were stuck in last place. Derby were next followed by Ipswich and Bolton who, with 36 points, were three above the drop zone. As Mark Lawrenson had been adamant that Bolton were for the drop a group of their fans challenged him to shave off his famous moustache if they survived in return for a £1,500 donation to charity. Having had the hair on his top lip for 25 years, he accepted the bet. The bristles

looked less secure when Bolton beat Ipswich 4-1 meaning that they had won three of their last four games.

At the top a relentless Arsenal continued their steady move towards the title with a 2-1 win over Tottenham, a match that featured two penalties in the last ten minutes, leaving them on 72 points with five matches remaining, two ahead of Manchester United who had played a game more. Liverpool were third with 68 points from 33. But Leicester became the first to have relegation confirmed when they lost 1-0 at home to Manchester United.

On 20 April Matthew Le Tissier was on the *Focus* couch alongside Ray and Mark having announced his retirement after 17 years at Southampton. He had scored 210 goals in 541 games, won eight England caps and

Editor Andrew Clement

Andrew Clement edited *Football Focus* for almost a decade from 1995 and was instrumental in steering the show through the three years without rights to show the Premiership. As well as editing football shows he is also one of the BBC's main match directors.

'I was very lucky on the first day of the Premier League as it coincided with my debut game as a director and I was there for the first ever Premiership goal by Brian Deane, although we only had a small, three-camera OB unit on that afternoon.

In the years without match action our challenge was to keep *Focus* on-air as it was still a successful brand that covered the national sport so we bought the rights to internationals, Spanish goals and the best of European football as well as concentrating more on Scotland and the FA Cup.

Of course, there was a lot more chat but what made a big difference was the double act of Ray and Mark as it gave us continuity and meant that we didn't have to book guests each week. Before Mark joined I used to dread having to make the late call to Trevor Brooking to ask if he could come in early when someone dropped out at the last minute. He was fantastic and always there as a permanent stand-by as was Garth.

We were also able to do longer pieces such as Gary's extended interviews with Klinsmann and Shearer, and Motty talked to the managers as many of them saw the value of being on the programme.

During that time we constantly outperformed *On The Ball*, which amazed me as it wasn't a bad programme and they had the action. But we were relieved as it showed a real loyalty to the programme, which was hugely satisfying to the whole team.'

produced several of the greatest strikes in the history of the Premiership. That afternoon Derby were relegated when they lost 2-0 at Liverpool as Michael Owen scored twice to put Liverpool back on the Premiership summit. His first came after 16 minutes and his second right on the final whistle when he latched on to Emile Heskey's pass, went round Andy Oakes and scored from a tight angle.

Alan Shearer became the first player to score 200 Premiership goals when his 89th-minute strike concluded Newcastle's 3-0 victory against Charlton. Arsenal finished the month strongly, comfortably beating Ipswich, West Ham and Bolton 2-0 to enter May five points clear of champions Manchester United and strong favourites to bring the trophy back to London.

May

It was all over on 8 May when, appropriately, Arsenal were crowned champions at Old Trafford after Sylvain Wiltord's goal secured a 1-0 win against rivals Manchester United, and with it the title and the first leg of another double. They had remained unbeaten away from home all season, a feat not achieved by any club since Preston North End in 1888–89, and had scored at least one goal in every single game.

Wenger was ecstatic at winning the club's 12th title. 'It was a job well done and we did it in style. We are a very young team and can get better.' They finished the season with a record 13th consecutive win in the Premier League, 4-3 against Everton.

Liverpool's 5-0 defeat of Ipswich secured them second place, with 80 points, seven

A new order? (From left to right) Ashley Cole, Patrick Vieira and Sol Campbell celebrate as Arsenal's 1-0 win at Old Trafford confirms the Gunners as champions on the way to their second double in five years.

Final League Table

Team	P	W	D	L	F	A	Pts
Arsenal	38	26	9	3	79	36	87
Liverpool	38	24	8	6	67	30	80
Manchester United	38	24	5	9	87	45	77
Newcastle United	38	21	8	9	74	52	71
Leeds United	38	18	12	8	53	37	66
Chelsea	38	17	13	8	66	38	64
West Ham United	38	15	8	15	48	57	53
Aston Villa	38	12	14	12	46	47	50
Tottenham Hotspur	38	14	8	16	49	53	50
Blackburn Rovers	38	12	10	16	55	51	46
Southampton	38	12	9	17	46	54	45
Middlesbrough	38	12	9	17	35	47	45
Fulham	38	10	14	14	36	44	44
Charlton Athletic	38	10	14	14	38	49	44
Everton	38	11	10	17	45	57	43
Bolton Wanderers	38	9	13	16	44	62	40
Sunderland	38	10	10	18	29	51	40
Ipswich Town	38	9	9	20	41	64	36
Derby County	38	8	6	24	33	63	30
Leicester City	38	5	13	20	30	64	28

Leading Goalscorers league only

Thierry Henry	Arsenal	24
R van Nistelrooy	Manchester United	23
J F Hasselbaink	Chelsea	23
Alan Shearer	Newcastle United	23
Michael Owen	Liverpool	19
Ole Gunnar Solskjaer	Manchester United	17
Robbie Fowler	Leeds United	15*
Eidur Gudjohnsen	Chelsea	14
Marian Pahars	Southampton	14

* including 3 for Liverpool

Awards

Footballer of the Year
Robert Pires, Arsenal

PFA Player of the Year
Ruud van Nistelrooy, Manchester United

PFA Young Player of the Year
Craig Bellamy, Newcastle United

behind Arsenal, and dispatched their opponents back into the First Division. Sunderland finished one place and four points above relegation, having been placed seventh in the previous two seasons.

Manchester United drew 0-0 with Charlton to finish third, Leeds achieved their fifth successive top-five finish when their 1-0 win over Middlesbrough took them above Chelsea, who lost 3-1 at home to Villa, but behind Newcastle. Shearer scored his 23rd of the season but his side lost 3-1 on the South coast as Gordon Strachan steered Southampton to a respectable 11th.

At the end of the season, Mark Lawrenson ended up with a naked top lip as Bolton remained in the Premiership for another season. It made him looks years younger and a Bolton hospice benefited to the tune of £1,750, although the really big money was elsewhere. Arsenal collected £8.8 million as champions while bottom-placed Leicester pocketed just £440,000.

Honours List 2001–02

Champions Arsenal

Runners-up Liverpool

Relegated Leicester City, Derby County, Ipswich Town

Promoted Manchester City, West Bromwich Albion, Birmingham City

FA Cup Winners Arsenal

League Cup Winners Blackburn Rovers

League Cup
Andy Cole added yet another winner's medal to his collection when he scored the vital second goal in Blackburn's 2-1 win over Tottenham in the League Cup final. It was the first time they had won the competition.

FA Cup
Ten different nationalities were represented by the 28 players who lined up for Arsenal and Chelsea on the pitch before the final. There were nine Englishmen, six from France, four Dutch players, two from each of Italy and Nigeria and one apiece from Denmark, Iceland, Sweden, Brazil and Cameroon. Ray Parlour gave Arsenal the lead after 70 minutes and Freddie Ljungberg added a second ten minutes later. Those goals were enough to give Arsenal their second FA Cup triumph in five seasons and their eighth in all.

FF 2002-03

Clinton Morrison's face says it all as he puts Birmingham in front in the derby against Aston Villa at St Andrews in September.

Programmes

Football Focus was still without Premiership highlights but expanded its coverage of Scottish and European football and had regular additional interactive shows so that Ray and the pundits could reply to viewers' questions.

Damian Johnson stood in for Ray on a couple of weekends and their regular studio guests included Mick McCarthy, Peter Reid, Garth Crooks, Bryan Robson, Gary Pallister and Lee Dixon. Mark Lawrenson, complete with a moustache-free top lip, was, as ever, present throughout.

Presenter
Ray Stubbs

Pre-season

Arsenal added another Frenchman to their title-winning squad when Pascal Cygan joined them for £5.5m from Lille along with Brazilian World Cup-winner Gilberto Silva whose move to Highbury cost £4.5m.

Denis Irwin left Manchester United for Wolves after winning seven titles in 12 years, but the biggest transfer of the summer was Rio Ferdinand's move from Leeds to Manchester for a staggering £30m – a new British record. His old team were left managerless when David O'Leary was sacked two days after saying that the defender should not be sold, and his office was occupied by the veteran Terry Venables, who joined a club in a very precarious financial state with a £60m debt.

Liverpool spent £15m on the Senegalese pair of El Hadji Diouf and Salif Diao and one of their former players, Nicolas Anelka, moved back to the Premier League when he joined Manchester City in a deal that netted PSV Eindhoven £13m.

The chequebooks were also open in the North East. Hugo Viana cost Newcastle £8.5m from Sporting Lisbon and Middlesbrough spent £14m on Juninho and Massimo Maccarone with George Boateng moving from Aston Villa for £5m.

August 2002

Arsenal began the defence of their title with a record 14th successive league win in the top flight when they beat newly promoted Birmingham City 2-0 leaving them unbeaten in the Premiership since 18 December 2001. In the ninth minute Thierry Henry – who else – scored the first, a low shot from a free kick on the edge of the box that crept in via Nico Vaesen's near post when the Belgian keeper failed to hold the ball. Sylvain Wiltord added the second 15 minutes later.

West Brom's first-ever Premiership match ended in a 1-0 defeat at Manchester United when Ole Gunnar Solskjaer scored his 100th goal for the club, and the third promoted side, Manchester City, took part in the first of several clashes between the five former England managers who were in charge of Premiership clubs this season. On this occasion Kevin Keegan's City lost 3-0 to Terry Venables' Leeds.

Having already won five Premiership titles with United, Peter Schmeichel was a surprise signing for Manchester City. 'I needed something extraordinary to keep me going and I think I've found it. I needed inspiration and a challenge and it took ten seconds in the presence of Kevin Keegan to know that he is the manager I want to play for.'

Everton celebrated becoming the first club to achieve 100 years in the top division with a 2-2 draw with Tottenham on the way to achieving their best position for seven seasons. Last season's top two continued their promising starts. Newcomer Diouf scored twice for Liverpool in their 3-0 win over Southampton, although he didn't reappear on the score sheet until March, and Arsenal beat West Brom 5-2. Ashley Cole scored the opening goal, one of only eight scored by English players out of Arsenal's league tally of 85 during the season.

Sunderland had narrowly avoided relegation last season after finishing in seventh place in the previous two years. They hadn't finished in the top half for 44 years before Peter Reid took over in March 1995 when they were 20th in Division One, but after their opening 0-0 draw with Blackburn, Reid was already under pressure. He was a regular interviewee on *Focus* and was still optimistic. 'We underachieved last year but there is no reason why we shouldn't have a dramatic improvement this year.' To underline his determination he bought Marcus Stewart from Ipswich and paid £8m to Rangers for Tore Andre Flo.

A subtle backheel from Harry Kewell set up Lee Bowyer to score the second of Leeds' three against West Brom as he struck a perfect right-foot shot into the top left-hand corner of the net as Venables saw his team win 3-1. But that week the great player clear-out at Elland Road continued. Robbie Keane was the latest to be sold, to Tottenham for £7m. The Londoners ended the month leading the Premiership with ten points from their first four games after Teddy Sheringham slotted home a last-minute penalty to give them a 2-1 result against Southampton.

September

Arsenal equalled Manchester City's 1937 record of having scored in 44 consecutive league matches when they beat them 2-1 to go top of the table after five games, ahead of Tottenham, Leeds, Liverpool and Chelsea. In contrast, rivals Manchester United were having their worst start to a Premiership season ever with just eight points from their first six matches. Their troubles were extended when a hip operation put Roy Keane out for three months.

Two 1-0 defeats had done nothing to please Sir Alex. Kevin Nolan gave Bolton maximum points at Old Trafford and Harry Kewell ran past three static defenders to head in Leeds' winner in the 67th minute of their match in Yorkshire. But that was to be the peak of Leeds' season as they lost eight of their next 11 games in the league.

Wiltord took his tally to six in six when he scored the second of Arsenal's three at Charlton. But the biggest drama of the month came when Birmingham met Aston Villa in the top flight for the first time in 17 years at St Andrews. Clinton Morrison's shot from seven yards on the half hour had given the home team the lead. On 77 minutes Villa defender Olof Mellberg took a throw in and hurled the ball back to his keeper Peter Enckelman. The Finn went to trap the ball

Below Aston Villa's Steve Staunton has to defend himself from a supporter during the disgraceful scenes that marred the Birmingham derby. Several fans were later banned from St Andrews for life for their behaviour.

Below New boys West Brom had a tough start to their campaign away at Old Trafford but only lost narrowly with United missing a host of chances like this header from Ruud van Nistelrooy.

Bottom Sixteen-year-old Wayne Rooney announced his arrival on the Premiership stage by scoring Everton's winner, a 30-yard curler, in the 90th minute to end Arsenal's record-breaking, 30-match unbeaten run.

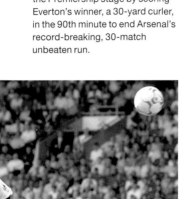

with his left foot, missed it and saw it roll slowly and agonisingly into his own net. Enckelman protested that the goal should not have been given, as he hadn't touched the ball, but referee David Elleray ruled that there had been contact and the goal stood. There was a disgraceful moment as one Birmingham fan ran onto the pitch and gestured at the hapless goalkeeper. Geoff Horsfield later made it 3-0.

Arsenal's keeper David Seaman celebrated his 39th birthday in the knowledge that his team had now gone ten months without suffering a Premiership defeat and when they won 4-1 at Leeds they stretched that run to 29 matches and established a new all-time record of scoring in 47 consecutive league games.

October

Having dropped to eighth Manchester United were returning to form and scored all the goals in the final five minutes of their 3-0 win against Everton but were still comfortably behind Arsenal who ended Peter Reid's reign at Sunderland when they beat them 3-1. After more than seven years in charge he was sacked and, in a surprise move, was replaced by Howard Wilkinson, the FA's technical director.

Reid became a regular pundit on *Focus* and was alongside Ray and Mark the following Saturday. 'When you get the sack it's not a nice thing but I'm quite philosophical about it although the timing was a little bit of a shock. They've got good players there but I didn't get the best out of them in the last year and a half.' He felt that he'd left them with a great stadium and training facilities and the players had thrown a big party for him in midweek.

Arsenal's unbeaten run finally came to an end at Goodison Park when they lost 2-1 to Everton. The Toffees' 90th-minute winner came from Wayne Rooney who, at 16 years and 360 days old, became the youngest ever Premiership scorer. It was a spectacular long-range shot. The ball came over his head, he brought it down, turned to make space and, from 25 yards out, fired it into the top left-hand corner past Seaman. It was the first of six consecutive league wins for the blue side of Merseyside.

At the other end of the striker age range, Alan Shearer scored his 300th goal, hitting both in Newcastle's 5-2 loss at Blackburn, for whom David Dunn and Martin Taylor each scored twice, and Liverpool went top when they beat Leeds 1-0 at Anfield in a midday start. The winner was an all-Senegalese affair when El-Hadji Diouf crossed from the left for Salif Diao to slide in his only league goal of the season and after ten games they led the Premiership with 24 points, one ahead of Arsenal. Leeds had slipped to tenth and Aston Villa, who had led the table at this stage last season, were 15th with Bolton, Sunderland and Manchester City in the bottom three.

Commentator Tony Gubba

Tony Gubba has been commentating on _Match of the Day_ for more than 30 years and is one of the BBC's most versatile voices as well as being the man behind the microphone for ITV's hit series _Dancing on Ice_.

'I've been watching football for about 50 years and there are only three instances when I have been mesmerised by a new player, someone who has something electrifying about him that marks him out.

The first was George Best's debut for Manchester United in 1963, the second was when Michael Owen came on as a sub for Liverpool against Wimbledon in 1997 and the third was when I first saw 16-year-old Wayne Rooney for Everton against Arsenal in 2002. It wasn't his debut but he had only played a few matches and he scored the goal that ended Arsenal's unbeaten run. I knew I was seeing something special and that he would go on to join Cantona and Henry as Premiership legends.

Managerially Fergie is obviously one of the greats in the Shankly and Busby mode. He is old fashioned, authoritarian, fierce, keeps the players on their toes and is not afraid to give out a severe rollicking. You could put him in almost any decade and he would be a success.

Of the newer breed Chris Coleman deserves great credit for what he did at Fulham as he didn't have a lot of resources but kept them in the Premiership, and what Steve Coppell is doing at Reading is also amazing.

The most memorable Premiership match that I've commentated on came at Old Trafford in March 1995 when I was covering Manchester United's 9-0 thrashing of Ipswich. Whatever they did it came off and every time United went forward it looked as though they would score. Andy Cole hit five, Ipswich wilted and by the end of the game they were chasing shadows. Ferguson's side were absolutely awesome that day.

A lot of clubs have new or bigger stadiums but whereas in the old days we used to commentate from a gondola under the roof at a lot of the new grounds we are at the back of the stand so can be several hundred yards from the action.

Blackburn is an exception as we still have to go to the back of the stand, up a ladder onto the roof, walk across and then go down another ladder. There's a great view but there's no loo and it's probably more suitable for a steeplejack.'

November

After two years in charge, Claudio Ranieri had steered Chelsea into third place, although their form was inconsistent. He told John Motson, 'The progress of the squad is like the progress of my English – getting better but slowly speaking.'

Ryan Giggs was profiled in *Focus* just ahead of his 29th birthday. He had just become the latest player to star in a video game. A jubilant Mark Bright managed to beat him at it before talking to him about his incredibly successful 12-year career with Manchester United. 'I've been lucky to play with so many great teams and players and just hope it stays that way,' said Giggs. 'With Manchester United you want to be winning trophies but the hunger just keeps getting more and more.'

On 16 November Arsenal beat Tottenham 3-0 in the North London derby to return to the top, a position they stayed in until April. The game's outstanding goal came in the 13th minute when Henry collected the ball deep in his own half and ran the full length of the pitch into the opposition penalty area before slotting it past Kasey Keller from ten yards with his left foot to open the scoring.

The same afternoon there was a change in fortune for Alan Curbishley and Charlton when they won 1-0 at Manchester City. They began the day close to the relegation zone but, with 11 minutes to go, Shaun Bartlett slid in Jonatan Johansson's cross to secure a crucial three points and set them on a run of ten wins and four draws in 15 games.

Bolton lifted themselves off the bottom the following day by winning 4-2 at Leeds thanks to two goals in the final two minutes. Michael Ricketts' penalty gave them the lead, after he had been brought down by Paul Robinson, and then Henrik Pedersen crashed in a volley from Stig Tofting's injury-time cross.

All three of Ruud van Nistelrooy's goals against Newcastle came from chances close to the Magpies' goal line when Manchester United beat Sir Bobby Robson's side 5-3 at Old Trafford, although Alan Shearer was able to celebrate scoring his 100th premiership goal for the Magpies. Olivier Barnard and Craig Bellamy also registered for the Toon.

When Dion Dublin climbed between goalkeeper and defender to head the third for Villa in their 4-1 win against West Ham it meant that he had become the tenth player to score 100 Premiership goals, joining the select group of Alan Shearer, Andy Cole,

Manchester United had already lost twice when they went down 3-1 in the Manchester derby on 9 November as Arsenal marched on. Stern words from Sir Alex Ferguson were said to be behind a return to form that saw them beat Newcastle, Liverpool at Anfield courtesy of two goals from Diego Forlan (below), and Arsenal in the run up to Christmas.

Les Ferdinand, Robbie Fowler, Teddy Sheringham, Ian Wright, Dwight Yorke and Matt Le Tissier.

December

Liverpool's keeper Jerzy Dudek had been in great form the previous year, but was having a poor spell and let the ball slip embarrassingly through his hands for Diego Forlan to score in the 65th minute. The Uruguayan immediately added a second as the Anfield crowd saw Manchester United win 2-1. United followed that with a 2-0 win over Arsenal as last season's champions, who were without Seaman, failed to score for first time in 56 matches. Veron struck his first league goal of the season when he ran onto a low Paul Scholes cross from the right and got to the ball just before the closing defenders, and then Scholes displayed some fine close control to collect and score as Ferguson's team closed the gap to three points.

Chelsea went second when they won 3-1 at Everton and after 17 games they were on 33 points, two behind Arsenal and one ahead of Manchester United. Liverpool were fourth on 31 and Everton fifth with 29.

Leeds, meanwhile, had sunk to 16th place, just three points off the relegation zone which was filled by West Ham, Sunderland and Bolton, although when West Brom lost 2-1 at Aston Villa they dropped into the bottom three and stayed there for the remainder of the season. Another team about to embark on a poor run were Sunderland. Although their fourth win of the season came thanks to a 2-1 victory against Liverpool, it was to be their last of the season as they lost 18 and drew two of their final 20 games, only scoring 11 more goals.

On Boxing Day Wayne Rooney was sent off for a lunging tackle on Steve Vickers of Birmingham in Everton's 1-1 draw at St Andrews and James Milner of Leeds took his crown as the Premier League's youngest scorer when he netted against Sunderland aged 16 years and 357 days. On the same day Manchester United lost in the league for the final time this season when Middlesbrough beat them 3-1 at the Riverside.

January 2003

Any supporters who left Highbury ten minutes early on 1 January would have missed four goals as Chelsea staged a late rally in their 3-2 defeat against Arsenal. It left the Gunners five ahead of Manchester United, who had also won, 2-1 against Sunderland, while Chelsea and Newcastle were both three points further back on 38.

Two more players exited Leeds in the first week of the New Year. Oliver Dacourt joined Roma and Lee Bowyer moved to West Ham, taking with him a six-match ban for stamping on an opponent's head during a UEFA match. Veteran striker Les Ferdinand also switched to Upton Park after more than five seasons with Tottenham.

One of the surprise teams of the season were Southampton and after their 1-0 win against Tottenham their manager, Gordon Strachan, told *Focus*, 'It's nice to say we're sixth but a couple of bad results and we'll be tenth or 11th. Is Europe in our thoughts? Yes, I'm going on holiday there.' Key to their success was the form of James Beattie who scored 15 goals in 14 games.

Robbie Keane scored three as Everton lost 4-3 at Tottenham and Wayne Rooney was able to celebrate a handsome pay rise later that week. Having turned 17 he signed his first professional contract with the club and saw his earnings rise from £90 to a reported £14,000 a week.

The BBC's football statistician, Albert Sewell, had a lot to update as the month witnessed several milestones. Alan Shearer scored the second fastest goal in Premiership history, just 10.4 seconds into their 2-0 win over Manchester City, Liverpool's 1-0 victory

The superb form of keeper Brad Friedel saw Blackburn Rovers winning six games out of seven in the early months of 2003.

Premiership-winning manager Sir Alex Ferguson

Sir Alex Ferguson is the most successful manager in the history of British football and remains the only man to have led sides to the English and Scottish titles.

Born in Glasgow on 31 December 1941 he was an apprentice toolworker on the shipyards of the Clyde before beginning a low-key playing career in Scotland. He turned to management in 1974 with East Stirling, joined St Mirren a few months later and then began an eight-year spell at Aberdeen, where he won three league titles, four Scottish Cups, the Scottish League Cup and the European Cup-Winners' Cup.

He was appointed manager of Manchester United in November 1986 when Ron Atkinson was sacked, and has since created several very different teams that have become dominant forces in the Premiership. To date he has won nine Premiership titles, five FA Cups, two League Cups, a European Cup-Winners' Cup, two doubles and a treble. In 1999 he added the Champions League trophy to the collection at Old Trafford. He was knighted that year but continues his quest for success and has been responsible for some of the best and most entertaining football in the 15 years of the Premiership.

at Southampton ended their worst league run for almost half a century and when Wayne Bridge was injured and was missing from the Saints' line-up for that match it was the first time he had been absent after playing a record 112 consecutive league games without being substituted.

After 9639 minutes of Premiership football Thierry Henry finally scored with a header as part of his hat-trick in Arsenal's 3-1 win against West Ham. And in one of the season's minor landmarks that passed most people by

the last team to be unbeaten at home lost to the last side without an away win when Aston Villa lifted some of the pressure off Graham Taylor by winning 5-2 at Middlesbrough.

February

The month began with yet more turmoil for Leeds with Jonathan Woodgate following Robbie Fowler out of the club. Fowler had joined Manchester City for £6m and Woodgate cost Newcastle £9m as the board desperately tried to reduce the crippling debts that had been run up during the previous few years. At a terse press conference Terry Venables sat alongside chairman Peter Ridsdale, but it was clear that their relationship was not looking good. Ridsdale admitted, 'As chairman of Leeds United I have a primary responsibility to the shareholders to make the right financial decisions. The manager didn't want Woodgate to go. I've made these decisions as the chairman of a public company and not as a fan of Leeds United football club.' His dream had gone horribly wrong. He admitted making mistakes and said he was now trying to rectify them, but in just over a year the club had lost its manager, was out of Europe, was fighting relegation from the top division and most of best players had left.

Charlton's travelling supporters would have enjoyed the game played at Sunderland. The home side found themselves bottom of the league after a seven-minute spell that saw them score three goals in a match for the

only time this season. Unfortunately, they were all own goals as Charlton returned to London with a 3-1 win. Stephen Wright deflected in Mark Fish's shot and Michael Proctor twice kicked the ball past his own goalkeeper, Thomas Sorensen, to leave the Black Cats in 20th place with 19 points, one fewer than West Ham and West Brom.

David Thompson scored Blackburn's winner against Southampton at the start of a strong period of revival for the club under Graeme Souness. The great form of their American goalkeeper, Brad Friedel, was instrumental in them winning six of the next seven games.

There was a double celebration on Tyneside when Sir Bobby Robson and Jermaine Jenas both had birthdays on 18 February. Robson's 70th was the subject of a BBC Sport documentary, while both he and his 20-year-old player were interviewed for *Focus*. The older man was clearly an admirer of the younger as he said, 'I wish I was your age and not my age. I hadn't played for England by the time I was 20. You must be better than me.'

March

The contrast at Old Trafford when Manchester United met Leeds was stark. United's 2-1 win marked the start of their title-winning run-in during which they picked up 28 of a possible 30 points, while it was only the goals of Mark Viduka, who scored against United, that kept Leeds in the Premiership at all, scoring 14 goals in their last ten games.

Sunderland, still bottom, had picked up only one point since Howard Wilkinson's appointment. He was axed and Mick McCarthy exchanged the comfort of the *Football Focus* sofa for the uncertainty of the Stadium of Light with only nine games left. A few days later a dejected Terry Venables parted company with Leeds and his replacement came once again from what was

Ruud van Nistelrooy finished as the season's top goalscorer, he scoring in each of the Manchester United's last eight games to finish the campaign with 25.

Reporter Gerald Sinstadt

Gerald Sinstadt made his name working for Anglia and Granada as a commentator and presenter before joining *Match of the Day* and *Football Focus* in the mid-1980s. As well as his match commentaries and reports Gerald is regarded by producers as the ultimate wordsmith and is renowned for his ability to always find the appropriate words and phrases for goal round-ups and obituaries.

'The round-ups have always been enjoyable to do, but when I started commentating we had to name every player who touched the ball and I came to the conclusion that that was counter-productive and overcomplicating things. So I set out to simplify the information for the viewer. I decided to allow room for the pictures to breathe by adding a bit of colour, humour and general background as the key was to hit the important name at the right moment rather than giving constant and often repetitive lists of names and statistics.

The Premiership has transformed the game but it remains to be seen whether it's for the better in terms of the growing numbers of non-British owners. They may turn out to be a good thing but I would like to know whether people are attracted for genuine investment opportunities, in which case we would hope that their skilled stewardship and business sense will be good for the clubs, or whether it is just the case that people with a lot of money now want to buy a football club. Has it become the latest acquisition for the man who has everything? Will it be a case of having a private jet, a yacht and now a football club? It is probably harmless, but it's too early to tell.

I don't subscribe to the view that the foreigners are keeping good young British players out of the game because if they are good enough then they'll make their own way. The very high quality of overseas players has raised the bar which is a good thing and even though not all have been value for money, that was the same in the days before the Premier League when British signings didn't always live up to their expensive billings.

On the downside, the Premiership has marginalised virtually all the rest of football. There's masses of newsprint to fill these days and yet on a Monday there will be a couple of decent reports on Championship games and the rest will be consigned to two or three paragraphs, whereas the lower leagues used to get a lot more coverage, but the glamour, money and celebrity are essentially confined to the Premiership now.'

Chris Coleman (left) became the Premiership's youngest manager, at 33, when he was appointed Fulham's new boss following Jean Tigana's departure in April. The young Welshman came out on top when Fulham beat Newcastle who were managed by the league's oldest boss, Sir Bobby Robson, who was still going strong at 70.

Arsenal contrived to spoil the party the following day by beating Everton 2-1 to retake top spot as the month ended.

April

But United seemed unstoppable. Ruud van Nistelrooy scored two more from the penalty spot when United beat Liverpool 4-0. It was United's biggest win over their Merseyside rivals for 50 years. Also in the goals, Paul Scholes struck a hat-trick in a 6-2 win against Newcastle at St James' Park to open a three-point lead over Arsène Wenger's men. In response Arsenal began to slip, drawing 1-1 at Aston Villa and then 2-2 in a top-of-the-table clash with United. The Gunners' only hope was that they had a game in hand.

There were contrasting fortunes for *Focus'* former pundits. Peter Reid achieved Leeds' best result of the season at Charlton when Mark Viduka's hat-trick formed part of their 6-1 win, but Mick McCarthy couldn't prevent Sunderland being relegated and their fate was confirmed on 12 April when they lost 2-0 at Birmingham. During the season they won and scored the fewest but lost and conceded the most, ending up with just 19 points, only one more than they had on Boxing Day.

Chris Coleman took temporary charge of Fulham when Jean Tigana left the club fighting for Premiership survival, and the Welshman inspired them to take ten points from their remaining five games. Peter Ridsdale severed all connections with Leeds, resigning from both the club and the PLC board, leaving them some £80m in debt, even after all the players had been sold. The pressure was also on West Ham as they continued to fight against the drop. Their manager, Glenn Roeder, collapsed with a minor stroke after their 1-0 win against Middlesbrough and Trevor Brooking stood in as caretaker for the last three games of the season.

fast becoming the most effective job centre in football, the *Focus* studio, as Peter Reid left Ray and Mark to try his luck in the north-west for the remainder of the season. Venables had been sacked after eight months in the job, with six defeats in his last eight games, but the writing had already been on the wall when he was appointed.

A record Premiership crowd of 67,706 saw Manchester United go top for the first time in the season when they beat Fulham 3-0 on 22 March. Van Nistelrooy scored all three, starting with a first-half penalty and completing his hat-trick in extra time, but his most spectacular goal was the second. He took the ball the entire length of the Fulham half, shrugged off several challenges and beat goalkeeper Maik Taylor to score one of the best goals of the season. However,

At the end of the month Manchester United were on 77 points with two matches remaining and Arsenal had 72 with three to play. Only two points separated Chelsea, Newcastle and Liverpool in the race for the two remaining Champions League places. West Brom had become the second team to be relegated, which left the final place between West Ham, Bolton, Fulham, Leeds and Aston Villa, although the Hammers were still favourites to go.

May

Manchester United moved to the brink of the title when their 4-1 win over Charlton included Van Nistelrooy's third league hat-trick of the season, and it was confirmed while Sir Alex was on the golf course on 4 May

when Arsenal lost 3-2 at home to Leeds. It was Ferguson's eighth title in 11 years. Ryan Giggs was especially happy. 'This ranks up there with the best because everyone was giving Arsenal the title before Christmas.'

On the final day of the season in what was billed as a £20m match Chelsea beat Liverpool 2-1 to claim the fourth Champions League place, joining Manchester United, Arsenal and Newcastle in Europe's premier cup competition. Bolton's 2-1 win over Middlesbrough sent West Ham into Division One when the Hammers could only draw 2-2 at Birmingham.

Elsewhere, Manchester City said farewell to Maine Road with a 1-0 defeat to Southampton, a result which lifted the visitors one place above them to their best ever Premier League position of eighth,

Right Chelsea's Jesper Gronkjaer ran the length of the pitch as his goal sealed the Blues' last day win over Liverpool and a place in the Champions League. It was a goal said to be worth £20m.

Below Manchester United players celebrate with the Premiership trophy after their 2-1 win over Everton at Goodison Park on the final day of the season.

Final League Table

Team	P	W	D	L	F	A	Pts
Manchester United	38	25	8	5	74	34	83
Arsenal	38	23	9	6	85	42	78
Newcastle United	38	21	6	11	63	48	69
Chelsea	38	19	10	9	68	38	67
Liverpool	38	18	10	10	61	41	64
Blackburn Rovers	38	16	12	10	52	43	60
Everton	38	17	8	13	48	49	59
Southampton	38	13	13	12	43	46	52
Manchester City	38	15	6	17	47	54	51
Tottenham Hotspur	38	14	8	16	51	62	50
Middlesbrough	38	13	10	15	48	44	49
Charlton Athletic	38	14	7	17	45	56	49
Birmingham City	38	13	9	16	41	49	48
Fulham	38	13	9	16	41	50	48
Leeds United	38	14	5	19	58	57	47
Aston Villa	38	12	9	17	42	47	45
Bolton Wanderers	38	10	14	14	41	51	44
West Ham United	38	10	12	16	42	59	42
West Bromwich Albion	38	6	8	24	29	65	26
Sunderland	38	4	7	27	21	65	19

Awards

Footballer of the Year
Thierry Henry, Arsenal

PFA Player of the Year
Thierry Henry, Arsenal

PFA Young Player of the Year
Jermaine Jenas, Newcastle United

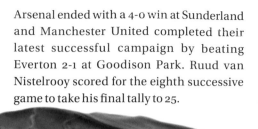

Arsenal ended with a 4-0 win at Sunderland and Manchester United completed their latest successful campaign by beating Everton 2-1 at Goodison Park. Ruud van Nistelrooy scored for the eighth successive game to take his final tally to 25.

United had won the most, lost the fewest and failed to score in only three games, but they lost one of their biggest names in the English game a few weeks after the end of the season when David Beckham joined Real Madrid for £25m.

Leading Goalscorers league only

R van Nistelrooy	Manchester United	25
Thierry Henry	Arsenal	24
James Beattie	Southampton	23
Mark Viduka	Leeds United	20
Michael Owen	Liverpool	19
Alan Shearer	Newcastle United	17
Gianfranco Zola	Chelsea	14
Paul Scholes	Manchester United	14
Robert Pires	Arsenal	14
Harry Kewell	Leeds United	14
Nicolas Anelka	Manchester City	14
Robbie Keane	Tottenham Hotspur	14

*including 1 for Leeds United

Honours List 2002–03

Champions Manchester United

Runners-up Arsenal

Relegated Sunderland, West Bromwich Albion, West Ham United

Promoted Portsmouth, Leicester City, Wolverhampton Wanderers

FA Cup Winners Arsenal

League Cup Winners Liverpool

League Cup
Liverpool beat Manchester United 2-0 to take the trophy back to Anfield for the second time in three years. Steven Gerrard opened the scoring in the 38th minute and Michael Owen sealed victory four minutes from the end.

FA Cup
The FA Cup Final between Arsenal and Southampton made history when it became the first to be played indoors. Bad weather meant that the roof over the Millennium Stadium in Cardiff was closed, creating a unique atmosphere for almost 74,000 fans inside. The match was settled by a 38th minute goal by Robert Pires and enabled Arsenal to become the first side to retain the trophy since Tottenham in 1982. The action was described by John Motson who was commentating on his 24th FA Cup final, one more than the previous record holder, the late Kenneth Wolstenholme.

FF 2003-04

In a season dominated from start to finish by Arsenal no one stood out more than the mercurial Thierry Henry.

Programmes

Once again Ray was joined throughout the series by Mark Lawrenson along with regular guest pundits Garth Crooks, Peter Schmeichel and Lee Dixon. Mark Pougatch and Manish Bhasin stood in as occasional presenters and BBC Sport launched a new *Score Interactive* service this season with the latest rolling scores, tables, a ticker and the vidiprinter. It ran throughout the afternoon on the Red Button and into *Final Score*.

In August 2003 the BBC had regained the rights to Premiership highlights, which meant that from the start of the 2004–05 season *Focus* would once again be able to show match action. The new deal also vindicated the decision to maintain *Football Focus* rather than take the show off the air. Sky retained the rights to live matches in a three-year deal that cost more than a billion pounds. The BBC's share was just over £100m. In October the BBC and Sky also signed a four-year contract to continue showing the FA Cup and England games.

Presenter
Ray Stubbs

Pre-season

Sir Alex Ferguson spent more than £12m on Sporting Lisbon's 18-year-old Portuguese star Cristiano Ronaldo, Harry Redknapp took Teddy Sheringham and Patrik Berger to newly promoted Portsmouth, Harry Kewell left Leeds for Liverpool and Arsène Wenger bought a new goalkeeper for £1.5m. It turned out to be a very shrewd buy as 33-year-old Jens Lehmann played every league game of the season and conceded only 26 goals.

David O'Leary returned to management at Aston Villa when Graham Taylor stood down again, Chris Coleman was confirmed as the Premiership's youngest manager at Fulham and Kevin Blackwell became the fifth Leeds boss in less than two years.

There was, however, only one real story in the close season and that was the purchase of Chelsea by the Russian billionaire Roman Abramovich. *Focus* reported that within six weeks of his £60m buyout from the club's chairman Ken Bates he had spent more than £250m on players as Claudio Ranieri went on the ultimate buying spree.

The 35-year-old Abramovich was listed by Forbes as the second richest man in Russia and the 49th wealthiest in the world, worth a reputed £3.8 billion. He seemed to be involved almost on a whim. 'I have always been interested in football as a fan but the idea of actually seriously buying a club has been in my head less than a year,' he claimed.

Chelsea's pre-season buys included Damien Duff (Blackburn £17 m), Adrian Mutu (Parma £15.8m), Geremi (Real Madrid £6.9m), Glen Johnson (West Ham £6m) Joe Cole (West Ham £6.6m), Wayne Bridge (Southampton £7m) and Juan Sebastian Veron (Manchester United £15m).

August 2003

A 25th-minute strike from inside the box by Veron got the new Chelsea underway at

Anfield, and although Michael Owen scored from a retaken penalty, Jimmy Floyd Hasselbaink slotted home the winner three minutes from time.

Manchester United opened their title defence by putting four goals into the Bolton net, Arsenal beat Everton 2-1 and Alan Shearer was on target twice, including a late equaliser, as Newcastle drew 2-2 at Leeds. Portsmouth's two experienced newcomers, Sheringham and Berger, both scored when they won their first ever Premiership match, 2-1 against Aston Villa.

Other veteran strikers on the scoresheet included Les Ferdinand who became Leicester's oldest ever debutant, at 36 years and 251 days, and celebrated by hitting their second in a 2-2 draw with Southampton. At Ewood Park Andy Cole's two late goals helped Blackburn to a 5-1 score against Wolves in their first match in the top flight for 19 years. It was a false dawn for Rovers, however, who only won one of their next ten matches.

Ruud van Nistelrooy set a new record at Newcastle the following week when he scored for the tenth consecutive Premiership match, taking his total in that time to 15, as Manchester United continued their good start with a 2-1 victory. Bolton conceded four for the second time in three games, this time at Portsmouth, where 37-year-old Sheringham scored the first hat-trick of the new campaign.

Having left Maine Road at the end of the previous season, Manchester City were in their new home at the City of Manchester Stadium, which had been used for the 2002 Commonwealth Games, and Kevin Keegan immediately began to add some more experience to his squad, buying David Seaman, who left Arsenal after 565 matches, and Steve McManaman who had twice won the Champions League with Real Madrid.

As former England players they were members of an increasingly endangered species in the Premier League, which was becoming more internationally dominated each year. *Focus* revealed that at the start of the first season in 1992–93 there were 49 foreign players registered in the Premiership. A decade on that figure had grown to 258 on the opening weekend of the season.

At the end of the month the table looked fairly normal. Arsenal and Manchester United were the early leaders, each having nine points from three games, and things seemed to be looking up for Leeds when Mark Viduka lobbed Mark Schwarzer in the 90th minute to give them a 3-2 win at Middlesbrough. It was his 50th goal in his 100th Premiership start. But the Leeds story had another twist to come before the end of the season, and it wasn't a happy ending, plus they lost eight of their next nine games.

September

The month began with two new additions to the Roman Empire when Chelsea bought Claude Makelele from Real Madrid for £13.9m and then persuaded Manchester United's Chief Executive, Peter Kenyon, to switch clubs.

Manchester City moved into third place behind Arsenal and United when Anelka scored a hat-trick in their 4-1 defeat of Aston Villa and two goals by Paul Dickov helped Leicester to their only win in the opening ten games as they demolished Leeds 4-0. Chelsea went top when they won 5-0 at Wolves, which included two strikes from Crespo, and a sixth-minute goal against Everton from Joseph-Desire Job was enough give Middlesbrough their opening win of the season.

Glenn Hoddle was the first managerial casualty of the season when his reign at Tottenham ended after their 3-1 home defeat to Southampton, the club he had deserted to return to White Hart Lane just a couple of years before. Yet another Tottenham dream had turned sour and they were third from bottom with four points from six matches. It

Teddy Sheringham began his career at Portsmouth in great style by scoring the first hat-trick of the season against Bolton in August.

Below The rivalry between Sir Alex Ferguson and Arsène Wenger was renewed during the Community Shield – the season's traditional curtain raiser – which United won on penalties after a 1-1 draw.

Editor Lance Hardy

Lance Hardy edited many editions of *Football Focus* between 1999 and 2004 and is now the editor of *Score* and *Final Score*.

'When we lost the rights to the Premiership it was a real challenge to keep the show on air but we decided to do more live interviews from outside grounds, increase the length of the films and encourage the producers to be more creative with them and think differently about how we used graphics and the growing interactive options. We still had access to the big names through our FA Cup and England contracts so we also tried to make use of that to get as many of them on as possible.

Things don't always go to plan though and I remember when Garry Richardson persuaded George Graham to give us his first interview after he was sacked by Arsenal. We had half an hour in his home and garden and it was a great interview by Garry, very passionate and open and emotional. We got outside, congratulated ourselves and were then told that the questions hadn't been recorded so Garry had to try to remember and repeat them while standing on the corner of a street as we were short on time and had to get back to the edit.'

Below But the heat was turned up when the teams met in anger at Old Trafford in September. First Patrick Vieira was sent off, then a penalty was awarded to United which Arsenal thought unfair. Ruud van Nistelrooy's spot kick cannoned off the bar and the player was then surrounded by celebrating Gunners. The match ended with no goals and a scuffle in the tunnel as the players left the field.

marked a change of fortunes for their visitors as well. Having risen to the dizzy heights of fourth place, they failed to score in seven of their next eight fixtures, winning just once.

The rivalry between two other managers, Arsène Wenger and Sir Alex Ferguson, was featured on *Focus* ahead of their top-of-the-table clash on 21 September. In the seven full seasons that they had gone head-to-head Manchester United had gained 561 points to Arsenal's 533, and had spent £167.14m on players, £52.74m more than the London club.

There were no goals in the match but no shortage of excitement and it became one of the most notorious matches of the season. Ray Parlour and Patrick Vieira were both sent off, Ruud van Nistelrooy was physically jostled and shoved by Arsenal players on the pitch after he missed a penalty that they thought was unfair and there was a scrap in the tunnel. All part of a normal day at the office, of course.

The events led to Arsenal and their players receiving a fine of £275,000 and four players being banned for a total of nine games, leaving Arsenal with 17 points, four ahead of Chelsea.

October

Wolves and Newcastle both registered their first wins of the season with 1-0 victories against Manchester City and Southampton, the latter including Shearer's 250th league goal.

One of the year's biggest stories came when Rio Ferdinand missed a drugs test in Manchester and was dropped from the England squad while the FA looked into the matter. It eventually resulted in a nine-month ban, which deprived United of his services for the final four months of the season.

But there was better news for United when Roy Keane's climbing header connected with Gary Neville's cross in the 81st minute for the only goal against Leeds at Elland Road. The points took United to the top on the same day that City beat Bolton 6-2. But it was to be a frustrating season for Kevin Keegan's team as only three teams would score more than their 55 goals but only the bottom three won fewer than their nine victories.

Liverpool found themselves in the bottom half of the table after losing to a Berger goal for Portsmouth. The match left a defiant Gérard Houllier pondering a third successive defeat and hostility from the press and phone-ins as they had collected only 11 points from a possible 27. 'I'm quite prepared to accept the criticism,' he said, clearly stung by the comments, 'but I'm not going to change the way I play.'

Bottom placed Wolves managed to double their goals tally for the season against Leicester when they pulled off a stunning victory at Molineux. Three down at half time, they fought back tenaciously and when Henri Camara scrambled in a fourth from just two yards out in the 86th minute it completed the most impressive comeback of the season and briefly lifted them clear of the bottom three.

Second placed Manchester United suffered a rare home defeat when Fulham, the surprise side so far, beat them 3-1 with goals from Lee Clark, Steed Malbranque and Junichi Inamoto, the first Japanese player to appear in the Premier League. It took them up to fifth place and they remained in the top half all season.

November

After ten games Leicester were in last place on five points, three below Leeds who, *Focus* reported, had published the worst-ever annual results by an English football club with a pre-tax loss of £49.5m and debts totalling £78m. This was despite selling Ferdinand, Keane, Bowyer, Woodgate, Fowler and others for more than £55m and was partly due to the way that they had purchased Mark Viduka and five other players through a complicated and expensive lease scheme.

Peter Reid was also under pressure on the field and, after losing successive games 3-1 to Liverpool, 4-1 against Arsenal and 6-1 at Portsmouth, he was sacked, the fifth boss to go in seven years. Eddie Gray, who had managed the side in the mid-1980s, assumed the caretaker role and within a few weeks Reid had rejoined Ray on the *Football Focus* sofa.

Having collected 13 points from five games, Newcastle caved in to Chelsea's relentless pressure and conceded five goals at Stamford Bridge, and Ryan Giggs scored twice at Anfield to give Manchester United a 2-1 win over Liverpool. Neighbouring City hit their worst run of the season and took only six of the next 42 available points after their surprise 3-0 home defeat to Leicester.

Since Peter Schmeichel left Manchester United, Sir Alex had used ten different goalkeepers including Tim Howard who had played in 19 of the 20 games in all competitions so far this season. The 24-year-old American had lived with Tourettes Syndrome from the age of ten. 'It affects me all the time and is something that you deal

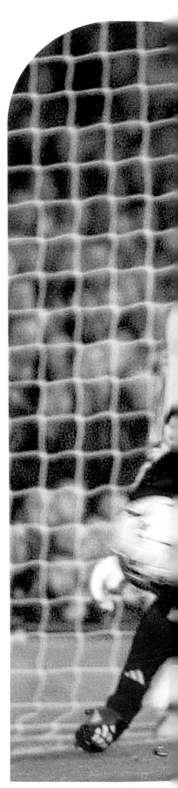

Hernan Crespo scores the second of Chelsea's five goals against in-form Newcastle at Stamford Bridge in November.

Manchester City's Shaun Wright-Phillips was earning rave reviews for his exhilarating form and was interviewed on *Focus* before the Manchester derby. He scored but City lost 3-1.

Above Veteran keeper David Seaman's career came to an end when he was injured playing for Manchester City against Portsmouth. The 40-year-old was playing in his 22nd season and walked out through a guard of honour at City's next home game against Blackburn in January to say farewell to the fans.

with on a 24-hour basis. It consists of involuntary verbal and physical tics and rapid movements in my eyes, hands and arms as well as speech. It changes month to month, but I just find a way to deal with it,' he explained in an exclusive *Focus* interview. Later that season he was to become the first American to collect an FA Cup winner's medal.

In a season of constant landmarks, Arsenal surpassed Liverpool's record of remaining unbeaten in the Premiership for the first 13 games, and led with 33 points. There were four London clubs in the top five with Chelsea second, Charlton fourth and Fulham fifth. Manchester United, in third place, were the only team from outside of the M25, and they suffered more indignity in the capital when Frank Lampard's 30th-minute penalty sent Chelsea top, the Blues having kept a fifth successive clean sheet.

December

Van Nistelrooy and Diego Forlan scored two apiece when Manchester United beat Aston Villa 4-0 at the start of a run of six straight wins, Blackburn won by the same score at Birmingham and Tottenham, who were still under their caretaker manager David Pleat, recorded their biggest win of the season by beating Wolves 5-2. Irish striker Robbie Keane struck a superb hat-trick but four successive defeats saw the Londoners drop back into relegation contention.

With almost a third of the season gone it was already clear that there were now effectively two divisions within the Premier League. Chelsea led with 36, Arsenal had 35 and Manchester United 34 but there was a nine-point gap to fourth-placed Fulham

Manchester City were tenth and, ahead of the Manchester derby, the Wright and Bright partnership was briefly revived when Mark met with Ian's 22-year-old son Shaun Wright-Phillips. 'Ian adopted me at 18

months and he's taught me everything I know,' explained Shaun. 'He played football with me in the house when I was young, since I could kick a ball, and just kept practicing with me. He used to say that if I didn't do so many kick ups I couldn't come inside the house!'

Although he managed to score that afternoon, City still lost 3-1. United returned top as Chelsea suffered their first home defeat of the season when John Terry put the ball in his own net in injury time to give Bolton a 2-1 win. Dennis Bergkamp's second goal of the season came the following day in a 1-0 win against Blackburn and was enough to end United's brief tenure and extend Arsenal's unbeaten run to 16 games.

January 2004

There were differing fortunes for the leading pack on the first day of action in 2004. Arsenal maintained their unbeaten record when they drew 1-1 at Everton, Manchester United won 2-1 at Bolton but Chelsea lost to Bruno Cheyrou's goal as Liverpool collected a win at Stamford Bridge. When Arsenal beat Middlesbrough 4-1 at Highbury a few days later they achieved the unusual distinction of claiming top spot by virtue of the alphabet as they and Manchester United were level on points, goal difference and goals scored. It was also the start of nine straight victories for the Gunners.

In the Midlands, Birmingham's 2-1 win over Southampton saw them embark on an eight-game unbeaten run and Bolton collected their first maximum in five when they won 4-3 at Blackburn. Kevin Nolan was the visitors' hero. He scored the fourth fastest goal in Premiership history, after just 14 seconds, and then struck the close-range winner in the 78th minute after Blackburn had twice taken the lead.

David Seaman retired at the age of 40 having been injured in Manchester City's 4-2 defeat at Portsmouth. He walked out through a guard of honour from both teams at City's next home game against Blackburn to say goodbye as Keegan swiftly moved to sign West Ham's David James as his replacement.

There were no goals when Newcastle travelled to Old Trafford but that point was enough to see Manchester United reclaim the lead in the title race with 50 points, one more than Arsenal after both had played 21 games. Chelsea were four points back but 11 ahead of fourth-placed Charlton. Wolves, Leeds and Leicester were in the relegation zone, just below Portsmouth, Blackburn and Manchester City.

The most surprising result of the season came on 17 January when bottom met top and Wolves managed to beat Manchester United. It was Ferdinand's last match before his ban started and the only goal came in the 67th minute when Kenny Miller took full advantage of Wes Brown's slip to accelerate away and place the ball neatly past Howard with a right-foot shot from the edge of the box.

It was Ferguson's fourth defeat of the season and he responded by bolstering his squad by signing French striker Louis Saha from Fulham. He made an instant impact, scoring on his debut in United's 3-2 victory against Southampton.

Arsenal had reclaimed top spot and also splashed out, signing 20-year-old Spanish strike José Antonio Reyes from Sevilla for 17.6m. Mark Lawrenson approved, 'He's a very good footballer who is going to turn into a world-class footballer.'

February

Charlton began the month in fourth place and a *Football Focus* report viewed them as a club that had defied the odds at a time when they were back in the Premiership, back at the Valley and challenging for Europe. One sour note for the club was that

Scott Parker opted to make a £10m switch from Charlton to Chelsea against the wishes of manager Alan Curbishley. But for him, after 13 years at Charlton, the job was still as satisfying as ever, 'The club is in the black which is amazing and I'm still enthusiastic about coming in each day and happy to be here. What we have done is a fairy tale.' That turned into a bit of a nightmare in the next few weeks as they endured a spell of six defeats in eight matches.

When Newcastle beat Leicester 3-1 on 7 February Gary Speed became the first player to take part in 400 Premier League games, and Sir Bobby Robson made a special presentation to him before the match. Ray posed a related question in *Focus* when he challenged the pundits to name the six men who had played in at least one Premier League game for the same club in every year of the Premiership. They were revealed to be Martin Keown and Ray Parlour (Arsenal), Ryan Giggs and Nicky Butt (Manchester United), Jason Dodd (Southampton) and Darren Anderton (Tottenham).

Arsenal's 3-1 win over Wolves meant that they had established a new club record of 24

Opposite Southampton's Jason Dodd (right) was one of only six players to have played at least one Premiership game each season for the same club. He retired in 2005 after notching up over 400 appearances for the south coast club.

Below A 1-0 win at Everton saw Charlton move into fourth place in mid-January in what was the south London club's most successful ever season.

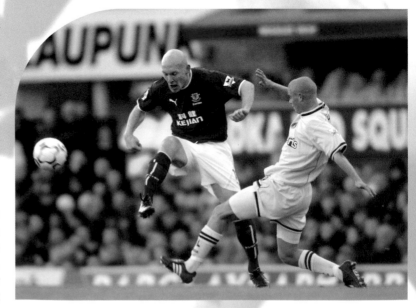

Above Thierry Henry scored his 100th and 101st Premiership goals for Arsenal in a 2-0 home victory against Southampton on 10 February to take the Gunners five points ahead of the chasing pack.

unbeaten games at the start of the Premiership season, and there were more celebrations for the Gunners a few days layer when Thierry Henry joined the 100 club, scoring both goals in their 2-0 win against Southampton. Things were less happy at the south-coast club and Gordon Strachan unexpectedly left his job. He was replaced firstly by their youth coach Steve Wigley and, a few weeks later, by Paul Sturrock, the Plymouth boss.

Eidur Gudjohnsen scored in the first 60 seconds of Chelsea's crucial home match against Arsenal but 14 minutes later Bergkamp struck a great pass with the outside of his left-foot to split the defence and send Vieira through to make it 1-1. Edu's winner followed shortly after and the North London team moved nine points clear. Arsène Wenger also confirmed that they would leave Highbury in two years' time for a 60,000-seater stadium at Ashburton Grove. 'It's vital for the evolution of the club and gives a good message out that the club is ambitious, brave and audacious.'

March

Arsenal beat Bolton 2-1 to equal the record of 29 games unbeaten at the start of a season held by Nottingham Forest and Liverpool. Dennis Bergkamp got the winner in his 255th league appearance for the Gunners, the most by any foreigner in the Premier League. It left Arsenal nine points ahead of Chelsea and 12 in front of Manchester United. Charlton, Liverpool, Newcastle and Birmingham were still chasing the fourth Champions League spot. Arjen Robben became the latest player to join Chelsea, moving from PSV Eindhoven for a reported £13m.

Middlesbrough's best score of the season came when they beat Birmingham 5-3 and Wolves also conceded five, against Chelsea for the second time this season. Hasselbaink celebrated his 32nd birthday with a hat-trick inside the last 13 minutes to increase his ratio to 102 goals in 200 Premier League games.

Sir Alex Ferguson conceded defeat in the title race after Manchester United had drawn 1-1 at Highbury to leave them 12 points behind with eight games left to play. 'I think they'll go on and win the league now. They're playing with great determination and are a very strong team.'

April

Having seen their treble dreams vanish when they were knocked out of both the FA Cup and the Champions League during the first week of the month, Arsenal hit back on their return to league duty, beating Liverpool 4-2 at Highbury. Henry's hat-trick meant that they needed just 15 points from their final seven games to be sure of the title as they were seven ahead of Chelsea and 15 in front of Manchester United.

It was a very different situation at the bottom where six clubs were still looking vulnerable. Wolves were 20th on 24, Leeds and Leicester each had 28, Portsmouth 30, Blackburn 31 and Manchester City 32.

Chelsea's title chase suffered a big blow when they lost 3-2 at Aston Villa and drew 0-0 at home against both Middlesbrough and Everton. Villa's win took them up to sixth in a season that truly had been one of two halves. Having won only three games in their first 15, they had recovered to collect maximum points in 11 of their 20 matches since December as David O'Leary began to get his squad working as a team.

Wayne Rooney scored his ninth goal of the season and his final league goal for Everton in their 1-1 draw at Leeds, but David Moyes' side couldn't repeat their form of last season when they finished seventh and, instead, took just two points from their remaining six fixtures to end up narrowly missing relegation, in 17th place.

When Chelsea lost 2-1 at Newcastle their title run-in had seen them drop ten points in four games. Shearer's 22nd goal of the season came when he held off Marcel Desailly, turned and shot across the box and into the top right-hand corner from 25 yards. Ranieri was still being criticised for the number of changes he was making but the manager was, as ever, unfazed. 'I don't change my way. I'm like Frank Sinatra.'

Arsenal won their 13th championship when they drew 2-2 at Tottenham and that evening Thierry Henry became the first player to win the PFA Player of the Year award in consecutive seasons. In their previous game, a 5-0 win over Leeds, he had scored four to take his tally to 29 league goals for the season.

May

The relegation places were soon also confirmed. Leicester failed to get the points they needed by drawing 2-2 at Charlton, Wolves went down despite beating Everton 2-1 and Leeds lost 4-1 at Bolton to all but condemn themselves. In theory they could have closed the six-point gap with Manchester City, but would have needed to make up a 37-goal difference!

Opposite Dennis Bergkamp set two landmarks in Arsenal's 2-1 home victory against Bolton on 20 March. He scored the winner, which meant that the Gunners equalled the record of 29 unbeaten games at the start of an English top-flight season, in a match that marked his 255th appearance, the most by any foreign player in the Premiership.

Above right A second-place finish, the club's highest for almost 50 years, was not enough to satisfy Chelsea's new owner Roman Abramovich, and it was clear that Chelsea's final home match of the season was the right time for manager Claudio Ranieri to say goodbye to the fans.

Sky Television

Sky transformed football broadcasting in the UK when they paid a £191m in a five-year deal for the rights to show live Premiership matches when the league began in August 1992.

The move saw screens go up in pubs and clubs all around the UK when live Sunday afternoon and Monday night matches became regular fixtures for many fans. Richard Keys has been the main presenter since the Premiership began and has fronted well over 1,000 games, assisted by Andy Gray who was given access to a wide range of new technology to take punditry to a new level. Martin Tyler has been Sky's commentator for the past 15 years and their Saturday morning show, *Soccer AM*, normally fronted by Helen Chamberlain and Tim Lovejoy, has been a popular and influential fixture since 1996.

With the title decided, attention turned to second place which carried with it automatic entry to the Champions League. With two games left Chelsea were in the stronger position with 75 points to Manchester United's 71, and the places were confirmed when the sides drew 1-1 at Old Trafford to give Chelsea their best finish since they won the title in 1955. Although they had already equalled their record Premier League points total with one match left it didn't seem that it would be enough to keep Claudio Ranieri in the job, but he still wanted it. 'I started the job. The foundation and a good floor is ready, and I'd like to finish it.'

On the final day of the season the main point of interest was whether Arsenal really could be the new Invincibles and remain unbeaten for the entire season. A 2-1 win against Leicester earned them their new tag and they were presented with the Premiership trophy on the Highbury pitch at the end of the game. They were the first team to survive an entire season without losing since Preston North End in 1888–89, although the old Invincibles had only played 22 games.

Chelsea's final match saw them beat Leeds 1-0 to finish second, four points ahead of Manchester United but 11 behind Arsenal, while United won 2-0 at Villa who came sixth, a ten-place improvement on the previous season for the Birmingham club. Liverpool and Newcastle drew 1-1 to end in fourth and fifth positions and both secure European competition, but that wasn't enough to save Gérard Houllier and his tenure in the Anfield manager's office ended shortly afterwards.

Final League Table

Team	P	W	D	L	F	A	Pts
Arsenal	38	26	12	0	73	26	90
Chelsea	38	24	7	7	67	30	79
Manchester United	38	23	6	9	64	35	75
Liverpool	38	16	12	10	55	37	60
Newcastle United	38	13	17	8	52	40	56
Aston Villa	38	15	11	12	48	44	56
Charlton Athletic	38	14	11	13	51	51	53
Bolton Wanderers	38	14	11	13	48	56	53
Fulham	38	14	10	14	52	46	52
Birmingham City	38	12	14	12	43	48	50
Middlesbrough	38	13	9	16	44	52	48
Southampton	38	12	11	15	44	45	47
Portsmouth	38	12	9	17	47	54	45
Tottenham Hotspur	38	13	6	19	47	57	45
Blackburn Rovers	38	12	8	18	51	59	44
Manchester City	38	9	14	15	55	54	41
Everton	38	9	12	17	45	57	39
Leicester City	38	6	15	17	48	65	33
Leeds United	38	8	9	21	40	79	33
Wolverhampton Wanderers	38	7	12	19	38	77	33

Leading Goalscorers league only

Thierry Henry	Arsenal	30
Alan Shearer	Newcastle United	22
R van Nistelrooy	Manchester United	20
Louis Saha	Manchester United	20*
Mikael Forssell	Birmingham City	17
Nicolas Anelka	Manchester City	16
Juan Pablo Angel	Aston Villa	16
Michael Owen	Liverpool	16
Ayegbeni Yakubu	Portsmouth	16

*including 19 for Fuham

Awards

Footballer of the Year
Thierry Henry, Arsenal

PFA Player of the Year
Thierry Henry, Arsenal

PFA Young Player of the Year
Scott Parker, Chelsea

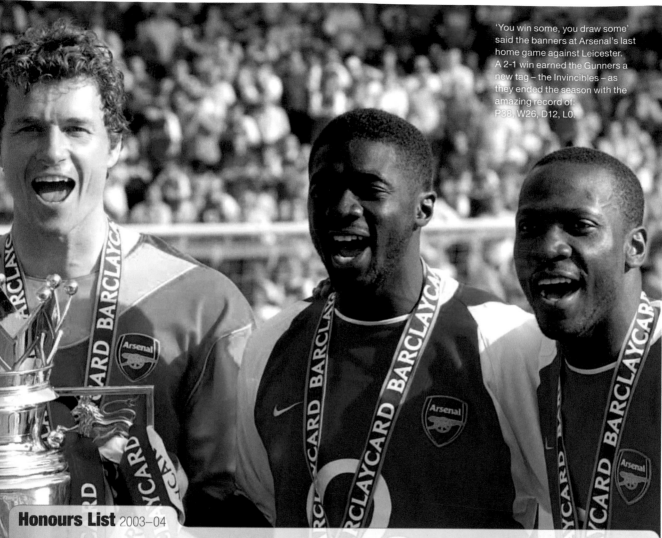

'You win some, you draw some' said the banners at Arsenal's last home game against Leicester. A 2-1 win earned the Gunners a new tag – the Invincibles – as they ended the season with the amazing record of: P38, W26, D12, L0.

Honours List 2003–04

Champions Arsenal

Runners-up Chelsea

Relegated Wolverhampton Wanderers, Leeds United, Leicester City

Promoted Norwich City, West Bromwich Albion, Crystal Palace

FA Cup Winners Manchester United

League Cup Winners Middlesbrough

League Cup

Middlesbrough won the first trophy in their 128-year history when they beat Bolton 2-1 in the League Cup final in Cardiff with two goals in the opening seven minutes from Joseph Desire-Job and Boudewijn Zenden.

FA Cup

Manchester United won the FA Cup for a record 11th time when they beat Millwall 3-0 at the Millennium Stadium. Ronaldo opened the scoring in the 44th minute and Ruud van Nistelrooy scored from the penalty spot 20 minutes later. In the 81st minute the Dutchman slid home his second goal to clinch the Man of the Match award and ensure that yet another piece of silverware went back to Old Trafford.

Fifty years of hurt show in the faces of Chelsea's Frank Lampard, William Gallas and Didier Drogba as the Blues take the lead in the title-clincher at Bolton's Reebok Stadium in late April. It was the Londoners' first championship victory since 1955.

FF **2004–05**

Programmes

With Premiership action returning to the BBC after a three-year break there were several changes to BBC football coverage with Manish Bhasin the new presenter of *Football Focus*. Mark Lawrenson remained alongside him and they were joined throughout the season by a regular panel, which included Lee Dixon, Gavin Peacock, Peter Schmeichel, Garth Crooks and Gordon Strachan.

Ray Stubbs fronted *Score* throughout the afternoon on the BBC's interactive service and also *Final Score* on BBC1, which was now, effectively, a separate show from *Grandstand*. Gary Lineker was back with *Match of the Day* on Saturday evenings, there were now commentators at all matches and a new show, *MOTD2*, on Sunday nights, fronted by Adrian Chiles.

Presenter
Manish Bhasin

Pre-season

The new season began with a rebranding of the entire football league. The Premier League became the Barclays Premiership, thanks to £57m of sponsorship over three years, Division One became The Championship, while Divisions Two and Three were now to be known as League One and League Two.

A trio of big name overseas managers had taken up residence in the Premiership as José Mourinho, Rafael Benitez and Jacques Santini all began their spells in charge at Chelsea, Liverpool and Tottenham Hotspur respectively.

Despite finishing as runners-up last season Roman Abramovich had still replaced Claudio Ranieri as manager of Chelsea. As had been widely predicted his job was taken by the flamboyant, confident and quotable Mourinho who had just won the Champions League with Porto. Once again, they played the most expensive game of footballing musical chairs and nearly 20 players left Stamford Bridge for varying reasons. However, Abramovich was still able to find almost £100m for new talent including £24m for Didier Drogba from Marseille, £10m for Tiago from Benfica and a further £19.85m to Porto for Ricardo Carvalho.

It was all change up-front for Liverpool as Michael Owen joined David Beckham at Real Madrid and Emile Heskey moved to Birmingham. Benitez brought in Djibril Cisse for £14m from Auxerre to replace them. Other strikers on the move included Leeds' Alan Smith who joined Manchester United for £7m while former United striker Andy Cole moved on to Fulham. Also leaving Old Trafford was Nicky Butt who joined Newcastle.

August 2004

The new season got underway fairly quietly on 14 August. An unmarked Cisse tapped in from six yards to score on his debut in

Liverpool's 1-1 draw at Tottenham and promoted West Brom gained a point when their trip to Blackburn also ended 1-1. Their fellow newcomers finished with the same scoreline when Crystal Palace travelled to Norwich.

Arsenal won 4-1 at Everton as they set off on the defence of their title with the first of five straight wins, and Mourinho had the perfect start to his new career when Eidur Gudjohnsen scored in the 15th minute of Chelsea's opener against Manchester United. Drogba headed it into his path and, with no one near him, he tipped it over Tim Howard. In contrast to the Gunners, United's only win in their first five matches came against Norwich. Their 2-1 victory included a spectacular first goal by Alan Smith who took the ball on his chest and struck a long-range, left-foot volley.

In the next two weeks Arsenal equalled and then broke Forest's record when they extended their unbeaten league run to 43 games by beating Middlesbrough 5-3 and Blackburn 3-0. John Motson described it as, 'another breathtaking benchmark and surely it will be another long-lasting landmark'. At the age of just 17 years and 113 days Francesc Fabregas became the club's youngest scorer when he struck Arsenal's second in the 58th minute against Blackburn.

Even though the season was barely a fortnight old, two clubs changed managers. Paul Sturrock was the first victim, leaving Southampton by mutual consent two games into the campaign and despite beating Blackburn 3-2. Steve Wigley, the coach, was his replacement. A bigger shock came at Newcastle where Sir Bobby Robson was sacked after five years in charge even though the club had finished in the top five in three successive seasons.

The other major story was the Wayne Rooney saga as, to the disappointment of Everton and David Moyes, he handed in a transfer request three days before the

deadline and subsequently moved to Manchester United for £27m. Despite the Russian millions at Chelsea it meant that in Ferdinand, Veron, Rooney and van Nistelrooy Manchester United were responsible for four of the five most expensive transfers in British history.

September

Graeme Souness quit Blackburn to take over at Newcastle having been at Ewood Park for four years. 'I'm joining one of the biggest clubs around and I'm very excited by it,' he told *Focus* but he inherited a side who were in 17th place, two above the team he left although both clubs had two points from four games. They were split by Norwich, with Crystal Palace bottom with only a single point.

Chelsea made their best league start for 76 years but Arsenal were still dominating the headlines and made it three straight wins when they won 3-0 at Fulham. The game was notable for Henry's skill in drawing six players to allow Freddie Ljungberg to score from his pass and for the Arsenal players' haranguing of referee Mark Halsey. He awarded a penalty against

Opposite top Newcomers Norwich City and Crystal Palace shared the honours in a 1-1 draw on the first day of the season.

Ashley Cole celebrates his winner for Arsenal at Manchester City. It was the last goal described by commentator Barry Davies who retired in September 2004 after 35 years with the BBC.

Ashley Cole for bringing down Andy Cole but after being surrounded by the visiting team he spoke to his assistant and changed his mind. 'Player reaction told me I'd made a mistake,' he said after the match.

Souness watched as his new team beat his old 3-0 at St James' Park to start a better period of form with four wins and two draws in their next six games and a few days later the Welsh manager, Mark Hughes, was confirmed as the new man in charge at Blackburn. He won his first match, 1-0 against Portsmouth, when Matt Jansen scored in the second half, but they then slumped, winning only one of their next 13.

In their previous game Pompey had beaten Palace 3-1 in a match that saw one of the strangest own goals of the season. In the 85th minute, Palace's veteran Australian, Tony Popovic, backheeled a volley into his own net to give the home team their third goal.

Arsenal dropped their first points of the season when they drew 2-2 with Bolton at Highbury. It was their best start in the league for 57 years and the Gunners had scored 21 goals in just six games including five by new Spanish midfielder Reyes. They stayed top with 16 points, two clear of

Cult heroes

Each week, from August 2004 to May 2005, *Football Focus* searched for the nation's all-time favourite footballing Cult Heroes.

During the season they put up three nominees for all 134 clubs in the main English and Scottish leagues, and invited viewers to vote for each club's winner. The results were published in a special BBC book by the show's editor, Steve Boulton, and viewers then voted for their all-time Cult Heroes XI. The

final line-up was as follows:
Neville Southall (Everton)
Willie Miller (Aberdeen)
Tony Adams (Arsenal)
Paul McGrath (Aston Villa)
Stuart McCall (Bradford City)
Stuart Pearce (Nottingham Forest)
John Wark (Ipswich Town)
Ian Holloway (QPR)
Tony Currie (Sheffield United *pictured*)
George Best (Manchester United)
Steve Bull (Wolverhampton Wanderers).

Chelsea with Everton third on 13. Having dropped as low as 11th place Manchester United achieved their second win of the season, beating Liverpool 2-1.

The following day's papers were full of tributes to the former Derby and Forest manager, Brian Clough, who had died aged 69. There was another farewell five days later when the man who had commentated on Clough's last home match retired from *Match of the Day* after 35 outstanding years behind the microphone. Arsenal's 1-0 win at Manchester City was Barry Davies' final game. During the post-match interviews he was presented with a signed shirt by Kevin Keegan and a large bottle by Arsène Wenger. On *Match of the Day* Gary Lineker remarked, 'I've most definitely got the best tan now.'

October

In midweek after a three-month injury lay-off Wayne Rooney had scored a hat-trick on his Manchester United debut in Europe but

Opposite Jimmy-Floyd Hasselbaink scored a second-half hat-trick as Middlesbrough beat Blackburn 4-0 at Ewood Park.

Premiership-winning manager José Mourinho

Fifty years after their only previous title win Chelsea found the right combination for success when they paired José Mourinho's confidence, style and coaching abilities with Roman Abramovich's millions and won the Premiership in successive seasons.

Mourinho was born in Setubal, Portugal, on 26 January 1963 and, after a short playing career, worked as Sir Bobby Robson's translator at Sporting Lisbon, FC Porto and Barcelona.

During 2000 he had a brief spell as coach of Benfica and spent a period with Uniao de Leiria before taking charge of FC Porto in January 2002. A year later he led them to the Portuguese League and Cup double, also winning the UEFA Cup. The following season he led Porto to win the Champions League before moving to Stamford Bridge in June 2004.

Mourinho made an immediate impact at Chelsea, and won the League Cup and the Premiership in his first season. He spent Abramovich's money freely and retained the title in 2006 to clinch his fourth successive championship victory. In his third season in charge he added two more tropies, winning both the League Cup and the FA Cup.

Above Another bad-tempered encounter between Manchester United and Arsenal ended in an alleged food fight in the tunnel at Old Trafford. United won 2-0 thanks to a penalty from Ruud van Nistelrooy and Wayne Rooney's first league goal for the Reds.

his stake in the club. United were sixth with 14 points and nine goals from nine games and Sir Alex admitted making too many changes to his format in their poorest league start since 1990–91.

Chelsea suffered their only loss of the season, at Manchester City, when Anelka's penalty was the difference between the two sides, Liverpool won 4-2 at Fulham and Jimmy Floyd Hasselbaink's second-half hat-trick helped Middlesbrough to climb to fifth place when they beat Blackburn 4-0 at Ewood Park.

With a quarter of the season already gone Arsenal had a five-point lead over Chelsea who, with 20, were one ahead of Everton with Bolton a further four back in fourth. Crystal Palace, Southampton and Blackburn were all in the drop zone and life was looking gloomy for Mark Hughes when Rovers were tonked 4-0 at Chelsea. Gudjohnsen struck a varied hat-trick, scoring with a volley, a right-foot strike and a penalty.

On 24 October Arsenal's long unbeaten run was ended at Old Trafford after 49 league games without defeat. It was yet another controversial encounter with Manchester United and there were allegations of food and drink being thrown in the tunnel. Alan Hansen thought that, 'Arsenal's players have let themselves down badly and Arsène Wenger has let Arsenal down badly.' Wayne Rooney scored his first league goal in United's colours when he made it 2-0 in extra time.

West Brom's Gary Megson was the next managerial sacking after he had announced that he would be leaving at the end of the season anyway and Bryan Robson took charge of the club that he had captained in the 1980s.

on the *Focus* sofa Gordon Strachan was still hard to impress, 'He's got a right foot, a left foot and he can head the ball. He's a big strong lad with great balance. Apart from that he's rubbish!'

United were the subject of a controversial takeover bid by the American businessman Malcolm Glazer who spent £45m to increase

November

Tottenham had spent nine months looking for Glenn Hoddle's successor but after just 11 games in charge Jacques Santini resigned, citing unspecified personal reasons. They had lost three games in a row, but things got worse as they were beaten twice at home, 3-2 by Charlton and 5-4 by Arsenal. When he saw the scoreline, José Mournho gave the view that, 'that's not football, 5-4 is hockey'.

Birmingham picked up their first win in nine games when Darren Anderton, who had joined the Blues after 12 seasons at Tottenham, scored at Anfield to give them a 1-0 victory and Fulham beat Newcastle 4-1 at St James' Park with heroics from their reserve goalkeeper Mark Crossley who kept out 26 shots and 19 corners from the home team.

Fulham came down to earth in the next home match when Chelsea won 4-1. The Blues drew their next match 2-2 with Bolton, and then put four more past Charlton at the Valley. Damian Duff's powerful push forward in the fourth minute ended with a goal when he put the ball low past the keeper. John Terry added

Presenter Manish Bhasin

Manish Bhasin was born in Leicester and worked on local BBC radio for five years before presenting a regional football show, *Soccer Sunday*, on ITV. After six months as a reporter on *Football Focus* he became the programme's fifth presenter at the start of the 2004–05 season. Manish is also the new front man for cricket on the BBC.

'The first thing I thought about when I got the job on *Focus* was the history of the show. I had watched it while growing up. It's the only programme of its kind on terrestrial television where you get to chew the fat over the week's issues and I'm really proud of that.

Focus has always been good at doing snazzy music pieces. It's a privilege to work with a production team that is always looking to find new music. We heard that Snow Patrol were delighted that we had used their track to front the programme.

The joy of *Focus* is that you get to talk to the biggest names in the game. The three standout interviews for me were with Pele, which was an amazing honour, Sven-Goran Eriksson and Tony Blair.

Sven was under a lot of pressure as it was at the end of the week when England had lost to Northern Ireland and we had him and Lawrie Sanchez on set. England were in a mess but he fronted it up. Lawro and I were almost playing "good cop, bad cop" as he was asking the questions that the person at home wanted to ask and I was letting Sven have his say and set the record straight.

Tony Blair's interview was surreal. He was all smiles, especially when we were meeting him in the production office beforehand and I had to ask what to call him. He just said, "Call me Tony." It was great to get him on the programme, although he was quite nervous to begin with but he had some nice stories and it was a fantastic day.

It is superb to work with Lawro as I remember him first and foremost as a player and then grew up with him as a pundit. He really helped me bed in on *Focus*, despite his corny jokes, and he is a thorough professional who is equally capable of giving the short answer or an in-depth analysis.

I was also privileged to receive Albert Sewell's legendary notes in the first year I presented. Three pages of tightly typed A4 with quirky bits of news and statistics and for me to have worked with him for a season was quite special as I'd always heard of the amazing Albert.'

the second with a leaping header from a corner at the start of the second half before he scrambled in a third and Gudjohnsen strolled through an open defence to complete the scoring with 30 minutes left on the clock.

Rooney scored twice in Manchester United's 3-1 win at Newcastle as Ferguson inspired his team to finally find their form and win 15 and draw three of their next 18 games. But it was Portsmouth's Harry Redknapp who was currently manager of the month, and the curse of the award struck again when he stunned supporters by walking out of Fratton Park after falling out with their chairman Milan Manderic. In a *Focus* interview in his local pub he told Garry Richardson that he planned a long holiday and a break from the game.

Crystal Palace keeper Gabor Kiraly saved a penalty from Wayne Rooney during a league match at Old Trafford in December. His heroics between the sticks were rewarded when he was the subject of the feature on *Football Focus* in January.

December

By the start of the month third-placed Everton had managed more wins than in the whole of the previous season and were seven points clear of Liverpool but still six behind leaders Chelsea. On 1 October Arsenal had a five-point lead but the power swung steadily across London from north to west and by 28 November Chelsea had a five-point advantage to complete a ten-point swing in six games. *Focus* called on Peter Snow and his swing-o-meter to demonstrate this sudden change from red to blue.

Manish opened the show on 11 October with the thought that, 'If a week is a long time in football then how about two weeks in the life of Harry Redknapp?' He had become Southampton's third manager of the season and risked the wrath of fans by making the switch along the south coast. Former Saints boss Gordon Strachan was surprised, especially as Harry had wanted a break. 'I'm four managers ago and I haven't finished my rest!'

Chelsea put four past Norwich in the start of a run where they took 40 points from an available 42. Petr Cech kept clean sheets in ten of those 14 games in a season where the club conceded only 15 goals, a new Premiership record.

When Arsenal beat Fulham 2-0 Thierry Henry scored his 128th league goal to equal Ian Wright's Gunners tally. He ended the season with 25 of Arsenal's 87 Premiership goals – this was 15 more than Chelsea and 29 more than Manchester United.

January

Liverpool's £6m signing from Barcelona, 26-year-old Luis Garcia, was the subject of the first *Focus* feature of the New Year, complete with the now regular subtitles. One of the beneficiaries of the Premiership's foreign invasion had undoubtedly been translators. 'Rafael Benitez told me he wanted a great team that would win trophies and the way of living football is very different here. People get behind the team. You hear them all the time and that is very important for a player.' Later in the month the Spanish contingent at Anfield was increased to five when Fernando Morientes signed for £6.5m.

But after 20 games Chelsea sat in top spot with 49 points and a goal difference of +32. At the opposite end of the table, in stark contrast, West Brom were on 11 points with a goal difference of -26.

Having been assistant and caretaker manager in his first few months at the club Dutchman Martin Jol became the ninth Tottenham boss in just 13 seasons when he agreed to assume control, but he couldn't halt the slump in form at White Hart Lane and they lost their next two games as well.

There was a *Focus* profile of Crystal Palace's Hungarian keeper, Gabor Kiraly. He had joined in the summer and became known for always playing in a grey tracksuit. 'At my first club in Hungary we were given two tracksuits, one black and one grey. I used the black for training and, as I always

prefer to play matches in tracksuit bottoms, I wore the grey ones for matches. They brought me luck so I have been playing in them ever since.' However, they didn't bring him a lot of luck at his new club as he picked the ball out of his net 49 times in the 32 league games that he played.

One of the best games of the season came when Norwich hosted Middlesbrough. With ten minutes remaining the visitors were leading 4-1, but Nigel Worthington watched his team recover in a style reminiscent of the great goalscoring side of the 1990s. Dean Ashton, on his home debut, scored his second of the match to make it 4-2, Leon McKenzie headed the third on the stroke of full time and, in the second minute of extra

time, Adam Drury headed the equaliser to save them from a fourth successive defeat and leave Steve McClaren furious at the way his side had caved in.

February

The opening weekend of the month was a good one for the top strikers. Alan Shearer notched his 250th Premiership goal with a classic left-foot drive in the ninth minute of Newcastle's 1-1 draw at Manchester City. His younger rival, Cristiano Ronaldo, scored twice as Arsenal lost 4-2 to Manchester United at Highbury. This was a bad result for the Gunners although they remained unbeaten from then until the final day of the season.

Above There was little for Southampton fans to cheer during the season. One of the worst days was 6 February when old boy James Beattie returned to St Mary's with his new club Everton and scored after four minutes. Despite taking a 2-1 lead, the match ended in a 2-2 draw when Marcus Bent scored a 90th-minute equaliser for the visitors.

Inset Norwich City director Delia Smith will try anything to help her team – from devising new diets to composing new terrace chants – but despite her best efforts the Canaries finished next to bottom and were relegated.

With 25 games played it was looking as though it would be three from a group of four for relegation as West Brom and Norwich were still bottom with 17 points, one below Southampton and five away from Crystal Palace. Norwich director and celebrity chef Delia Smith introduced a new diet to try and secure the Premiership status. The carbohydrate-rich diet was designed to help the players train longer and she gave a special demonstration for wives and landladies. Delia recognised that, 'Having the right diet and fitness doesn't help you score goals, but it ensures that your players won't get tired in the last 15 minutes.' Sadly, it didn't quite work as Norwich were relegated with the Premiership's worst goal difference of -35.

Undeterred by her failure with the players' diets, Delia tried rousing the fans. At half time in Norwich's home game against Manchester City, in which the Canaries had thrown away a 2-0 lead, she appealed to the supporters, 'A message to the best football supporters in the world. We need a 12th man here. Where are you? Where are you? Let's be 'avin you! Come on!' she yelled. It still didn't work as Robbie Fowler scored twice for the visitors, including his 150th Premiership goal, to secure a 3-2 victory. However, her words have gone down in history as many people now refer to Carrow Road at Letsby Avenue.

Commentator Barry Davies

Having begun his TV career with ITV during the 1966 World Cup Barry Davies joined the BBC three years later and spent 35 years as the longest serving member of the *Match of the Day* team.

'There was a lot of terrific football before the Premiership and when I thought about the favourite games that I had commentated on most were actually before it began. We live in an instant age and the past can disappear but I think that the attitude was very different and we could talk to managers and players more easily. Now everything is in a rush and it has become less personal.

However, from a TV point of view it has forced the coverage to be greatly improved. If we had more than four cameras we used to be doing well but there are now so many more and it has really helped the viewer move closer to the action. Ironically the game as a whole has moved further away from the people and the gap between the public and the player is now enormous.

I've always liked the artistic footballers who get you onto the edge of your seat and I certainly enjoyed commentating on Eric Cantona as he was invariably so different. There have been a heck of a lot of very fine players in the Premier League and I have always also been a fan of Ryan Giggs as I like wingers.

I had no idea that I was going to get a presentation at Manchester City after my last commentary. I was interviewing Kevin Keegan for *Grandstand* when he stopped answering questions and suddenly turned it around. He was very kind and complimentary and I've still got the shirt he game me. It was Anelka's No.39 as he said it was the nearest they could get to the number of years that I'd been commentating.

I didn't see any Premiership football for two years after that as almost straightaway I was asked to become president of Windsor & Eton FC but I started watching Premier League matches again in 2006. I still love the game after all these years.'

Manchester City had previously drawn 0-0 at Stamford Bridge as David James became the only goalkeeper to keep a second clean sheet against Chelsea. In contrast Arsenal's José Antonio Reyes scored an own goal when he was duped into saying live on the radio that he would like to move to Real Madrid by a journalist.

March

Things got even worse for Norwich when they lost 3-1 at home to Chelsea. However, at least they became the first team to score against the Blues after ten consecutive Premiership clean sheets and the goal finally came 1,025 minutes since the last one, a new record for keeper Petr Cech.

There was a change in the hot seat at Manchester City after a 1-0 defeat at home to Bolton. Kevin Keegan resigned after three and a half years in charge, leaving the team in 12th position. Stuart Pearce was asked to take them through to the end of the season.

With nine games remaining, Chelsea's 11-point lead looked unassailable. Manchester United had moved second, two clear of Arsenal with Everton a further ten back in

fourth. The gap in quality was illustrated by the fact that fifth-placed Liverpool were 30 points below the leaders but only 24 ahead of bottom-placed Norwich.

In the second Merseyside clash of the season Liverpool closed the gap with a 2-1 win. Steven Gerrard got their first in the 27th minute but five minutes later the crowd saw an incredible shot by Fernando Morientes from more than 30 yards out. It was high and

Match of the Day

The programme began on 22 August 1964 on BBC2 and has run, almost continuously, ever since although there were several years when the editions were infrequent and focused on live league or FA Cup matches when ITV held the rights to show league highlights.

Kenneth Wolsenholme (1964–69), David Coleman (1969–73), Jimmy Hill (1973–88), Desmond Lynam (1988–99) and Gary Lineker (1999–) have been the main presenters with

Bob Wilson and Ray Stubbs also fronting many editions. The show broadcast Premiership highlights from 1992–2001 and since 2004.

The latest three-year contract between the BBC and the Premier League cost £171.6m and ensures that the programme will be on air until at least 2010. A new Sunday evening version, *MOTD2*, has been presented by Adrian Chiles since 2004 and shows highlights of that day's games and a full round-up of the weekend action.

A hat-trick by West Brom striker Robert Earnshaw against Charlton ensured three more points as the Baggies avoided relegation on the final day of the season by one point from Crystal Palace and Norwich and two points from bottom-placed Southampton.

Opposite Chelsea's Frank Lampard ends a 50-yard run by rounding Bolton keeper Jussi Jaaskelainen and slotting the ball home to win the match and the title for the Londoners.

dipping and the back-peddling Nigel Martyn pushed the ball against his bar, but Luis Garcia came charging in to head home.

Chelsea's charge for their first title for 50 years continued when they beat Palace 4-1. But they continued to make the headlines off the field too when they were charged by the FA for illegally trying to tap up Arsenal's Ashley Cole at an alleged meeting with Mourinho and Peter Kenyon at a London restaurant in January. They were all later subjected to record fines.

Bryan Robson's influence was finally being seen at West Brom and, having only won twice in their first 27 games, they then beat Birmingham 2-0 and Charlton 4-1 in March, a match which included a second half-hat trick by Robert Earnshaw. In a remarkable turnaround, they lost only two of their final nine matches and narrowly avoided relegation.

April

Alan Shearer decided to stay with Newcastle for another season as player/coach after nine years with the club. He had previously announced that this would be his last campaign but the persuasive powers of Souness and the fact that he was only nine goals short of Jackie Milburn's club goalscoring record helped change the mind of the man who had been the leading scorer in the Premiership in five different seasons.

With the title seemingly wrapped up by Chelsea, attention was turning to the European qualifying places. In sixth spot, a point behind Liverpool, were Bolton whose manager Sam Allardyce aimed to be the first manager to take the club into Europe after an erratic season. 'We research a lot of people like Michael Johnson and Lance Armstrong who are dedicated to their sport and show the players what they do to achieve their ultimate goals. The difference between top and bottom is in the mind and we need to

work on that to get the best out of our players,' he revealed. Bolton hadn't finished in the top six since 1959–60, but they would match that this season, a major achievement for a man who had started as the manager of Limerick City in 1991.

James Vaughan, at 16 years and 271 days, became the latest teenager to claim the crown of being the youngest Premier league scorer when Everton beat Palace 4-0, having lost four of their previous five matches. Meanwhile the prolific Thierry Henry bagged his second-hat trick in three games in Arsenal's 4-1 win over Norwich as they began to move clear of Manchester United who had a poor run in, winning three, losing three and drawing two of their final eight games, starting with a goalless encounter at Blackburn.

At the bottom, Norwich had 25 points, Palace 26, Southampton 27 and West Brom 28. On *Focus* Alan Hansen thought that West Brom still had a chance to escape, 'If Bryan Robson keeps them up it will be remarkable but he's got them organised, fighting and playing, he's given the players belief and the supporters optimism'. The Saints were rocked when, despite being two up at half time, they conceded three goals to Aston Villa in a 17-minute burst and Palace and Norwich shared the points and six goals when they met at Selhurst Park. Andy Johnson scored Palace's third in a season where he would become the first Premiership player to score more than half of his team's goals. He was responsible for 21 of their 41 goals, which included 11 penalties, and he scored the only goal of the match in their surprise win over Liverpool.

Chelsea were crowned champions 50 years after their previous title when they won 2-0 at Bolton with both goals coming in the second half from Frank Lampard. His second, in the 76th minute, saw him run unchallenged for half the length of the pitch, round the keeper, score and then vanish under a scrum of his team-mates.

May

Arsenal secured second place when they beat Liverpool 3-1 and then achieved the season's highest score by putting seven past Everton. Manchester United were only able to draw 1-1 with West Brom and lost 3-1 at home to Chelsea, the champions' 29th win of the season. The club was then the subject of a formal takeover bid of more than £800m by Malcolm Glazier.

For the first time in Premiership history all three relegation places were decided on the final day and it made for thrilling listening all afternoon on Radio Five Live as they cut between the relevant matches. West Brom began the day bottom with 31 points, Palace and Southampton had 32 and Norwich were best placed with 33 knowing that their fate was in their own hands.

John Terry (left) and Frank Lampard (centre) celebrate the winning the Premiership title with Chelsea owner Roman Abramovich whose £100m summer spend went some way to helping the club win its first championship for 50 years.

Final League Table

Team	P	W	D	L	F	A	Pts
Chelsea	38	29	8	1	72	15	95
Arsenal	38	25	8	5	87	36	83
Manchester United	38	22	11	5	57	26	77
Everton	38	18	7	13	45	46	61
Liverpool	38	17	7	14	52	41	58
Bolton Wanderers	38	16	10	12	49	44	58
Middlesbrough	38	14	13	11	53	46	55
Manchester City	38	13	13	12	47	39	52
Tottenham Hotspur	38	14	10	14	47	41	52
Aston Villa	38	12	11	15	45	52	47
Charlton Athletic	38	12	10	16	42	58	46
Birmingham City	38	11	12	15	40	46	45
Fulham	38	12	8	18	52	60	44
Newcastle United	38	10	14	14	47	57	44
Blackburn Rovers	38	9	15	14	32	43	42
Portsmouth	38	10	9	19	43	59	39
West Brom	38	6	16	16	36	61	34
Crystal Palace	38	7	12	19	41	62	33
Norwich City	38	7	12	19	42	77	33
Southampton	38	6	14	18	45	66	32

Leading Goalscorers league only

Thierry Henry	Arsenal	25
Andrew Johnson	Crystal Palace	21
Robert Pires	Arsenal	14
Jermain Defoe	Tottenham Hotspur	13
Frank Lampard	Chelsea	13
J F Hasselbaink	Middlesbrough	13
Ayegbeni Yakubu	Portsmouth	12
Peter Crouch	Southampton	12
Eidur Gudjohnsen	Chelsea	12
Andy Cole	Fulham	12

Awards

Footballer of the Year
Frank Lampard, Chelsea

PFA Player of the Year
John Terry, Chelsea

PFA Young Player of the Year
Wayne Rooney, Manchester United

Things didn't go quite to plan for them, however, as they lost 6-0 at Fulham. Southampton went down 2-1 at home to Manchester United and Crystal Palace could only draw 2-2 at Charlton, but Bryan Robson pulled off one of the best results of his career when West Brom beat Portsmouth 2-0 to survive in the top flight for another season. It was the first time that the team who were bottom of the Premiership at the end of December had not been relegated.

Chelsea ended the season with a 1-1 draw at Newcastle to take them to a new Premier League record 95 points, Everton claimed the fourth Champions League spot and there was also guaranteed European football for Liverpool, Bolton and Middlesbrough.

Honours List 2004–05

Champions Chelsea

Runners-up Arsenal

Relegated Southampton, Norwich City, Crystal Palace

Promoted Sunderland, Wigan Athletic, West Ham United

FA Cup Winners Arsenal

League Cup Winners Chelsea

Champions League Winners Liverpool

League Cup
José Mourinho's first trophy as Chelsea manager came in February when they beat Liverpool 3-2 after extra time in the League Cup final to win the competition for the first time since 1998.

FA Cup
For the first time in the history of the competition the destination of the trophy was decided by penalty shootout after 120 minutes with no goals. Arsenal keeper Jens Lehmann saved Paul Scholes' attempt when he took the second penalty for United and, when everyone else scored, it left Patrick Vieira to put the ball past Roy Carroll to make the score 5-4 to Arsenal. It was the club's fourth FA Cup triumph under Arsène Wenger and their tenth in all.

Champions League
Liverpool beat AC Milan 3-2 on penalties as the final finished 3-3 after extra time. The Reds became European champions despite only finishing fourth in the Premier League the previous season. They staged a remarkable recovery, having been 3-0 down at half time, and won the shootout when Jerzy Dudek saved from Andrea Pirlo and Andriy Shevchenko.

FF 2005–06

It's that Premiership feeling.
New boys Wigan celebrate another
goal in a fine first season in the
top flight which saw them in the
top half of the table for almost the
entire campaign.

Programmes

The new season began with the *Football Focus* and *Score* sets on opposite sides of BBC Sport's Studio 5 at TV Centre as Manish presented the lunchtime show and Ray Stubbs, accompanied by a range of pundits, took the football coverage through *Grandstand*, on the interactive service and for *Final Score* on BBC1.

As well as the ever present Mark Lawrenson other regular faces on the *Focus* sofa included Graeme Le Saux, Lee Dixon, Gavin Peacock, Tony Adams and Lee Sharpe. Celia Hinchcliffe became the first woman to present the show and the production team also introduced a new 3G video messaging service called 'Your Shout' to supplement the texts, emails and website.

Presenter
Manish Bhasin

Pre-season

José Mourinho strengthened his Chelsea squad with the additions of Spanish left back Asier Del Horno for £8m from Athletic Bilbao and Manchester City's Shaun Wright-Phillips who cost £21m. City brought in veteran Premiership hit man 33-year-old Andy Cole on a free transfer from Fulham.

Liverpool began the season with the largest squad as Rafael Benitez had 42 players to chose from including the league's tallest player, 6-foot-7-inch striker Peter Crouch, who made the switch from Southampton for £7m, and goalkeeper José Reina who arrived from Villarreal for £6m.

There was a major clearout at Old Trafford as 18 players left United in the summer including Phil Neville who joined Everton, while Fulham's Dutch goalkeeper Edwin van der Sar was signed by Sir Alex Ferguson for a bargain £2m. However, the biggest story had been the controversial takeover of the world's most famous club by the American sports tycoon Malcolm Glazer and his sons in a £790m buyout.

In north London, Tottenham had secured the free transfer of Edgar Davids, the Dutch midfielder whose previous clubs included Juventus, which was the new home of Arsenal's inspirational skipper Patrick Vieira who left after nine years. Belarus midfielder Alexander Hleb was Arsène Wenger's main acquisition having moved from Stuttgart.

August 2005

As the season began the promoted teams, Sunderland, West Ham and Wigan, were the bookies' favourites to go straight back down and only the Hammers were able to celebrate a win in the opening weekend. Teddy Sheringham got their first goal back in the top flight as they beat Blackburn 3-1. Hernan Crespo scored in time added on to give Chelsea a 1-0 win over Wigan as the champions won the first of nine consecutive games. They also splashed out a club record £24.4m on Ghanaian midfielder Mickael Essien. Sunderland began their season in the way that they had previously signed off in the Premiership, with a defeat. Their 3-1 loss at home to Charlton was the first of 29 as they embarked on a shockingly unsuccessful campaign. By contrast, they had won 29 games when coming back up as Championship champions in May. Darren Bent scored twice on his debut for the Addicks.

Ruud van Nistelrooy and Wayne Rooney both scored for Manchester United in their 2-0 win at Everton. Theirs was to prove a fruitful partnership for Sir Alex as they added a further 35 league goals between them during the season, although they were once again outgunned by Thierry Henry whose 81st-minute penalty for Arsenal against Newcastle was the first of 27 in another prolific season for the Frenchman. Robin van Persie added a second to complete a 2-0 victory at Highbury.

West Brom made a promising start with four points from their first two games including a 2-1 win over Portsmouth, but their season's pattern was soon established as they lost eight of their next ten matches. Liverpool also struggled and Xabi Alonso's 25-yard free kick against Sunderland was their only goal in their first four games and their sole win in six. The blue side of the city was suffering as well with Everton losing seven out of eight, scoring just once, in their win at Bolton. Having finished fourth last season this wasn't the start that David Moyes had been expecting.

Newcastle were also having a rough time with just one point from a possible 12 in August before paying Real Madrid £17m for Michael Owen. During the transfer window Graeme Souness also sold Jermaine Jenas to Tottenham for £7m.

Opposite top Darren Bent (in the white shirt) scored twice on his debut as Charlton beat Sunderland 3-1 at The Valley on the opening day of the season. It was the first of Sunderland's 29 defeats of the campaign.

Opposite bottom Chelsea were the visitors to Anfield on the first Sunday of October. The Londoners left with the points and the bragging rights as they put four goals past José Reina, including this one by Didier Drogba.

Below Two goals from Morten Gamst Pedersen secured Blackburn's first win against Manchester United at Old Trafford in 43 years.

Just nine years after being in the bottom division, Wigan recorded their first Premiership victory, beating Sunderland 1-0. Their first goal in the top flight was a second-minute penalty, converted by Jason Roberts in front of an ecstatic crowd at the JJB stadium and the trigger for a great spell that saw them win eight and draw one of their next nine.

September

As the first full month of action began Chelsea were top with maximum points from their opening four games and Manchester City were a surprise second on ten, one ahead of Charlton and Manchester United who had each played a match fewer. Sunderland, Newcastle and Portsmouth were the early holders of the bottom three places.

Newcastle fans had to wait until the 78th minute of their fifth game to celebrate a goal and it came when debutant Michael Owen was tripped on the edge of the Fulham box and Charles N'Zogbia's curling free kick beat Tony Warner to level the match at 1-1. Owen scored his first for the club in their next match when he nodded in the second of their three goals at Blackburn as they finally collected maximum points.

Although no one realised it at the time, Manchester United's goalless draw at Liverpool proved to be the last match in their colours for their inspirational skipper, Roy Keane, who limped out of the game with a broken bone in his left foot. It left Liverpool in the bottom half of the table with only six points from 12, although newcomer Peter Crouch was making an impression and already had his own Kop chant of, 'He's big, he's red, his feet stick out the bed.'

Aston Villa's Luke Moore became the first player to score against Chelsea after the Londoners had kept six clean sheets, but two goals from Frank Lampard kept the home team's 100 per cent record intact. As José Mourinho acknowledged the Stamford Bridge cheers and celebrated 21 points, Sir Alex Ferguson was being booed off the pitch at Old Trafford where Manchester United had just lost 2-1 to Blackburn. Both goals came from Morten Pedersen to give them their first league win at the ground since October 1962. His first was a left-foot free kick from outside the area which went straight through the defence and past a static keeper in the 33rd minute and then, nine minutes from time, he was left unmarked to slam home the shock winner.

When Sunderland beat Middlesbrough 2-0 in the north-east derby at the Riverside Stadium to end 26 consecutive Premiership games without a win, their manager Mick McCarthy said that it hadn't been a monkey on his back but felt more like the planet of the apes. He also felt that it gave them the knowledge and belief to win in the division. Unfortunately that belief was only used on two more occasions all season and they only took two of their next 42 possible points.

October

In-form Tottenham moved into second place after winning 3-2 at Charlton and 2-0 against Everton before holding their own with 1-1 draws against Manchester United and Arsenal. Chelsea, meanwhile, just kept winning and left Anfield with a 4-1 victory over Liverpool before thumping Bolton 5-1 in London despite having been a goal down at the interval. Their rampant second-half display took them to a maximum 27 points, nine ahead of Tottenham, and meant that they had now gone 38 Premiership games, the equivalent of a whole season, without defeat.

West Brom's 2-1 result against Arsenal was their best win of the season and the first time in two and a half years of Premiership football that they had managed to come from behind to win a game. The winner came from 21-year-old Darren Carter who had only been on the pitch for eight minutes when he sent a left-foot volley flying into the top corner.

Thierry Henry became Arsenal's all-time leading scorer when he overtook Ian Wright's club record, but Arsenal had made their worst start to the season for years and didn't endear themselves to their home supporters when Robert Pires made an extraordinary botch of a penalty in their 1-0 defeat of Manchester City. Having already scored from the spot in the 61st minute, he tried to tap a second penalty to Henry but instead just touched the top of the ball allowing the City defence time to rush at him and prevent a goal. Pires later said that it was a move that they had practiced in training but at the crucial moment his mind went blank and he panicked.

Chelsea dropped their first points in a 1-1 draw at bottom club Everton who finally scored their second goal of the season and ended a losing run of six, but across Stanley Park Liverpool embarked on ten straight league wins when they put two past West Ham.

On the last weekend of the month Wigan, incredibly, went second after Pascal Chimbonda's injury-time header gave them a 1-0 win against Fulham, but Charlton's 1-0 home defeat to Bolton took them into a dreadful spell where they lost seven of their next eight.

November

With just over a quarter of the season gone, Chelsea were on 31 points from 11 games, nine ahead of second-placed Wigan. Tottenham, Manchester City and Bolton all had 20 and then came Charlton, Manchester United and Arsenal. Although 14 points separated their teams the managers of Chelsea and Arsenal were engaged in another verbal spat that seemed better suited to the school playground

than the boardrooms of a multi-million-pound industry.

Mourinho claimed that he possessed a 120-page dossier on Wenger who he alleged was a voyeur who was obsessed with Chelsea. Wenger responded that this was disrespectful and that he was considering a formal complaint and, on *Football Focus*, Mark Lawrenson probably spoke for the majority. 'Am I the only person thinking that the whole country is bored with this? Just get on with it.'

On 5 November the Prime Minister, Tony Blair, spent half an hour as a guest on the *Focus* sofa. Sat between John Motson and Mark Lawrenson he explained that he had met Motty recently and told him that he was a regular viewer of the show because, 'when you're in my business it's always good to go and watch a whole load of other people under pressure'. The Prime Minister went on to discuss some of the unsung stars in the Premiership, and surprised Manish by talking authoritatively about Fulham midfielder Steed Malbranque, Wigan defender Arjan de Zeeuw and veteran West

Arsenal's Robert Pires (left) and Thierry Henry look completely confused as their well-rehearsed penalty trick goes wrong in front of their own fans during the home match against Manchester City.

Opposite Prime Minister Tony Blair chats behind the scenes with Alan Hansen, Gary Lineker and Garth Crooks before his appearance on the *Focus* sofa in November.

Pundit Garth Crooks

Garth Crooks played for Stoke City before moving to Tottenham Hotspur in 1980 where he built a reputation as a prolific goalscorer, winning two FA Cups and the UEFA Cup as well as forming a legendary strike partnership with Steve Archibald.

'When I was at Tottenham we all used to try to get to the hotel to watch *Football Focus* as it was part of the Saturday ritual. We'd see the show, have our pre-match meal and then set off to the ground. If you got onto *Focus* you were considered to be doing well, especially in the late 1970s and early 1980s.

Overall, however, Tottenham have been disappointing in the Premiership as they have never been able to establish a consistent side or approach, especially with so many different people in charge, nine in 15 seasons so far,

and I think the managers have always characterised the teams at White Hart Lane.

Ossie Ardiles was cavalier and his sides had great flair going forward but they simply couldn't defend. Gerry Francis made a tremendous acquisition in Jurgen Klinsmann but couldn't take the club to the next stage, and if there was ever a moment when someone was out of his depth it was the day that Christian Gross came to White Hart Lane. Like Egil Olsen at Wimbledon, he didn't understand the club or its customs.

I think that Martin Jol has been Tottenham's best manager during their time in the Premier League. As well as taking them to their highest placing of fifth in 2006 he has been very good at blending the side. The heart of the team is English but there are a lot of good quality foreigners in the mix as well.'

Ham striker Teddy Sheringham. He also managed to give one straight answer. A viewer's email asking if he would back a national holiday if England won the world cup was met with an instant and firm 'no'.

The following afternoon Chelsea suffered their first loss of the season when Darren Fletcher's first-half header for Manchester United ended their run of 40 unbeaten games in the league. As a result United climbed six places to third, ten points behind but with a game in hand.

Chelsea shrugged off that defeat by starting another long run of ten consecutive wins by beating Newcastle 3-0, and when they defeated Portsmouth 2-0 the following week Frank Lampard set a new record of 160 successive Premiership appearances dating back to October 2001, beating David James' total of 159 during his time with Liverpool.

The following week a major chapter of Manchester United's recent history came to a close when Roy Keane announced that he was leaving the club after 12 years and 480 games. Gary Neville succeeded him as captain.

Paul Jewell's managerial skills were tested when the inevitable dip in form came for Wigan although they had a terrific buffer having climbed to second spot and conceded only five goals in their first 11 games. Unfortunately, they had to pick the ball out of their net 13 times in their next five matches as they lost to all the teams who would be in the top five at the end of the season.

Portsmouth manager Alain Perrin was the first to be sacked after eight months in charge and two wins in 13 games. Chairman Milan Manderic explained why he wielded the axe. 'I don't fire managers, I think they fire themselves. If I make a mistake I maybe make mistakes when I hire them.' Since 1999 he's been through six managers and a director of football.

The month ended with *Football Focus* joining the rest of the footballing world in paying tribute to George Best who had died at the age of 59.

December

Having spent several uncomfortable few months sharing the limelight with the former England rugby union coach, Sir Clive Woodward, Harry Redknapp quit Southampton and took the return journey along the south coast back to Portsmouth to resume the manager's job that he had left a year before. His first job was to take on a difficult relegation battle.

Despite only conceding 31 goals in the season, Arsenal lost 11 league games including a spell of three in a row that included a 2-0 defeat at Bolton, a 1-0 loss at Newcastle and a 2-0 home defeat by Chelsea, their first win at Highbury since March 1990. Charlton's fifth straight defeat came when Manchester City returned home from The Valley as 5-2 winners and Sir Alex Ferguson was also showing signs of pressure when he

walked out of a press briefing after a record 74 seconds.

But the following day his team put four past Wigan including goals from Wayne Rooney ten minutes either side of half time. He recovered from a fall in the box, skipped through the defence and made it look easy. Despite having eight Wigan shirts with him in the penalty box, Rooney simply ran through and chipped Mike Pollitt.

Football Focus showed pictures of a former colleague, Albert Sewell, as he collected his

Above Bolton's Senegalese midfielder Aboulaye Diagne-Faye powers a header past Arsenal keeper Jens Lehmann. Bolton's 2-0 win was the first of three defeats in a row for Arsène Wenger's men.

MBE from the Prince of Wales. The legendary football statistician had retired from the BBC at the end of the previous season after spending 37 years with BBC Sport.

Michael Owen's first hat-trick for his new team proved to be the last time that he and Alan Shearer appeared on a scoresheet together when Newcastle won 4-2 at West Ham. The club took just one point from 18 and Owen missed the rest of the season when he broke a metatarsal in his right foot when they lost 2-0 to Tottenham on New Year's Eve.

As the year ended, Chelsea led by 11 points from Manchester United. Frank Lampard's illness had caused him to miss their win at Manchester City to leave his new record of consecutive Premiership appearances at an impressive 164. Equally praiseworthy were the nine clean sheets in ten games for Liverpool keeper José Reina that had helped the Reds climb to third although, on 37 points, they were 15 behind the leaders but three in front of Tottenham.

January 2006

City beat United 3-1 in the latest edition of the Manchester derby, a game that saw Robbie Fowler's only goal of the season for the home team before he returned to a heroes' welcome at Anfield. Liverpool, however, were starting a mini slump in a strange season of four quarters. They scored five goals in their first eight games, 24 in the next 12, four in the following eight matches and 24 in the final ten.

After seemingly reverting to Old Arsenal with back-to-back 0-0 draws, New Arsenal re-emerged and walloped Middlesbrough 7-0 with three goals from Henry. Steve McClaren's Boro followed that with a 3-2 home defeat to Wigan, before heaving a sigh of relief and facing Sunderland against whom they registered their first win in ten with a 3-0 result. Arsenal looked to the future by signing 16-year-old Theo Walcott from Southampton for £5m, giving him instant celebrity status and allowing the tabloids to focus their frenzy on a new footballing girlfriend.

On 21 January Celia Hinchcliffe became the BBC's first female presenter of *Football Focus*. It was a red-letter day too for Sunderland, who collected their second win of the season when Anthony Le Tallec's shot took a big deflection from Steve Watson in the 72nd minute for the only goal against fellow strugglers West Brom. It was a surprisingly good weekend for the bottom two sides as Birmingham stunned their fans with a 5-0 win against Portsmouth. Those goals counted for almost 20 per cent of their entire tally for the season as they managed an embarrassingly low total of 28 in their 38 games.

February

Blackburn completed the double over Manchester United when Mark Hughes once again got the better of his former boss as David Bentley's hat-trick, his only goals of the season, saw them to a 4-3 win. On the same day Newcastle went down 3-0 at Manchester City and Graeme Souness was

Reporter Celina Hinchcliffe

Celina Hinchcliffe worked as a reporter at Radio Five Live before joining News 24. She is a regular reporter on *Football Focus* and became the first woman to present *Football Focus* and *Match of the Day*.

'Just to be associated with the programme and be the first woman presenter was a real honour. Our biggest problem is that access to players is so difficult but we managed to get a superb interview with David James in 2006. We took him to a gallery in Southampton because we knew he loved art. As a result we had more than three hours with him and the access and relaxed nature of the interview meant that it was so much better than most and he compared the commitment and discipline of an artist to that of a footballer.

I think that a good *Focus* piece will tell us something we didn't already know but the players are so media trained now that to get David away from the training ground was refreshing and gave us a real insight to the person behind the gloves.'

sacked. Since joining in September 2004 he had acquired a transfer deficit of £31.4m. He left the club in 15th place, only six points off the bottom three. Glenn Roeder and Alan Shearer took temporary charge.

With 24 games played Chelsea were racing away on 63 points with Manchester United on 48 and Liverpool 45, although they had two games in hand. Tottenham and Wigan were on 41 and 38 points respectively. United began to claw back the points with a 4-2 victory over Fulham, the first of nine successive wins, while the battle of their old boys saw Bryan Robson victorious as West Brom beat Blackburn 2-0. It was, however, the Baggies' last victory of the season and they managed just four points from their final 13 games.

Alan Shearer's 64th-minute goal in Newcastle's 2-0 win at home to Portsmouth gave them their first win in seven games and him a club record 201st goal to take him past Jackie Milburn's longstanding record.

When Chelsea beat Liverpool 2-0 it meant that they had conceded just six goals in 13 games. In total they kept 20 clean sheets and only let in 22 goals all season. It also marked an outstanding season for Czech keeper Petr Cech who played in 34 league games. Ironically, they lost their final game of the month 3-0 at Middlesbrough.

March

With ten games to go time finally ran out for Mick McCarthy and he was sacked by Sunderland. Despite coming up as champions they had only taken 10 of 111 possible points in the top tier since he took over. Kevin Ball was placed in charge as caretaker but was unable to change their form and they immediately lost 1-0 at home to Wigan. Henri Camara's turn and volley created a stunning goal when there seemed to be no options open to him.

Blackburn beat Aston Villa 2-0 to start a good run in, taking 20 of a possible 30 points to secure sixth place after finishing 15th in the previous two years. By contrast Manchester City lost nine of their last ten beginning with a 2-1 defeat at Portsmouth. It was Pompey's first win of the year and they had only scored seven times but conceded 35 in their previous 17 outings. Pedro Mendes got both as they began their survival bid.

On the day that the fans at Stamford Bridge remembered the legendary Peter Osgood, who had died suddenly, aged 59, Chelsea beat Tottenham 2-1 when William Gallas cut in from the left and drilled the ball past Paul Robinson two minutes into added time prompting their manager to charge out and join in the celebrations.

In the chasing pack Wayne Rooney scored twice as Manchester United beat Newcastle 2-0 and Robbie Fowler nodded in his first goal for Liverpool in five years as part of their 5-1 win against Fulham.

Portsmouth achieved back-to-back wins for the first time in the season when they won 4-2 at West Ham to close the gap to three points behind 18th-placed Birmingham City. It was the first time that Redknapp had been back to Upton Park as a manager since he'd left five years before and the first time that the 'Harry Houdini' tag started appearing in the press.

Fulham were only just above the drop zone but pulled off one of the shocks of the season when they beat west London neighbours Chelsea 1-0 at Craven Cottage.

Luis Boa Morte struck home after poor defending. Buoyed by the victory Chris Coleman's team picked up 16 points from their final eight games to ensure a fifth successive mid-table position when the season ended. It was some achievement just a decade after they were playing Third Division football.

Where once *Focus* would chat to players in their own homes, now they could only get to talk to the top names at events arranged by sponsors. When an audience of competition winners were due to meet Wayne Rooney in London at one such occasion organised by a soft drinks company, Ray Stubbs flew down from Manchester with him in a private jet and they were filmed for the programme in a

Jermain Defoe opens the scoring in Tottenham's 3-1 defeat of Charlton at White Hart Lane.

rare interview. Sitting in a branded shirt and in front of a branded backdrop, he perfectly illustrated the way that footballers have increasingly become commodities.

April

Arsenal were in sixth place and 28 points behind the leaders but their hopes of climbing above Blackburn and Tottenham to claim the fourth Champions League place were enhanced when they beat Aston Villa 5-0, their fourth consecutive win. Portsmouth made it a run of three out of three when they won 3-1 at Fulham and Birmingham managed to hold the leaders to a goalless draw at St Andrew's on the day that Manchester United won 2-1 at Bolton. The gap at the top was rapidly narrowing and had been reduced from 18 to seven points in just three weeks with six games remaining.

Although Chelsea were suddenly looking a tad vulnerable, José Mourinho remained calm and said that he was more worried about the swan with bird flu than the teams gaining on the leaders. They responded by beating West Ham 4-1 despite going a goal down.

Opposite **Kelvin Davis put in a magnificent performance in already-relegated Sunderland's goal during their 0-0 draw at Manchester United. After the game Sir Alex Ferguson conceeded that it was unlikely that the Premiership trophy was going to Old Trafford this season.**

Pundit Alan Hansen

Alan Hansen made 623 appearances for Liverpool and was captain between 1985 and 1990, winning eight Championships, three European Cups, two FA Cups and three League Cups. Now *Match of the Day*'s senior pundit, he has been an ever-present selection throughout the history of the Premiership and has also been known to appear on the *Focus* sofa.

'After 15 years of the Premiership I think that the product has probably never been better and it is very different from when I was playing. The speed, intensity, fitness and the number of absorbing games are unmatched anywhere in the world.

With more cameras and more technology the punditry has changed as well and nothing should escape us as we can look for things that 15 years ago we would never have seen. It would be very easy to just show the goals, but we try to get away from that and look for things the public might not spot.

One thing I would change is the offside rule. No one understands it, players, referees or spectators. There are so many grey areas with the indecision and uncertainty adding to pressure on referees and as the rewards are so much higher their job is becoming far more difficult and some games are impossible to referee. Managers and players have some responsibility, although I know it is easy for me to say, but there should be a penalty for the teams who surround the referee with maybe just the captain being allowed to speak to him as the minute you start penalising them it will stop.

The finest player in the history of the Premiership would be Alan Shearer. Henry and Cantona run him close, but Shearer played from the start and he epitomised everything you want in a centre forward as well as being a great team player.

As an outstanding defender I would pick Sol Campbell. He was fantastic for Tottenham and brilliant for Arsenal but everyone thought it was all over for him when he had his troubled spell but he came back with Portsmouth and proved to be one of the best signings in recent times. To come back and play so well was a great achievement for both Harry Redknapp and Sol and it's an amazing story.'

The first 70,000 Premiership crowd saw Manchester United beat Arsenal 2-0 and a few days later a new record 72,519 were at Old Trafford to see their title ambitions damaged by a goalless encounter with Sunderland. Sir Alex conceded that they now needed a miracle to become champions after Kelvin Davis had a superb game in goal for the visitors, but the result still confirmed their relegation. Just above them, only a point separated West Brom, Portsmouth and Birmingham.

Alan Shearer's career ended ahead of schedule at the Stadium of Light when he struck the 409th goal of his career in Newcastle's 4-1 win against Sunderland but, having scored with a penalty in the 61st minute, he limped off injured and was unable to play again.

The title race was settled on 29 April when Chelsea beat Manchester United 3-0 and were crowned champions on their own pitch at Stamford Bridge. It had been the two clubs' tenth meeting in all competitions in two seasons and the goals came from Gallas, Joe Cole and Ricardo Carvalho. In an act which endeared himself to Chelsea supporters, Mourinho threw his medal into the crowd, was given another and lobbed that in as well.

Portsmouth competed an improbable escape act when they won 2-1 at Wigan, meaning that West Brom and Birmingham joined Sunderland as the relegated clubs. Pompey had won six and drawn two of their last nine games and Matt Taylor's 70th-minute penalty ensured their safety and his status as a local legend.

May

Sunderland managed their third and final win of the season when they beat Fulham 2-1. But their season was a record of Premier League lows: fewest wins in a season (the worst tally in the top flight since Stoke City in 1984–85); lowest points tally of 15; they equalled Ipswich's record of most defeats in a season with 29; and although their total of 26 goals scored in the whole campaign didn't quite break the record, they already held that having scored only 21 in 2002–03.

Alan Curbishley retired as Charlton's manager after 11 years as his team finished 13th losing 4-0 at Old Trafford on the last day of the season. Manchester United were second, eight points behind Chelsea who lost their final game 1-0 at Newcastle who came in seventh. Chelsea had won 29 games – a new Premiership record.

Sport Relief

Sport Relief was a new fundraising initiative created by BBC Sport and Comic Relief in 2002 and in its first three outings has raised almost £50m.

The Premier League clubs contributed around £200,000 by donating 50p from every matchday programme sold in the final weekends of the 2004 and 2006 seasons, and many footballers and BBC presenters and pundits have been heavily involved.

Half of the money raised is spent on sports-based projects around the UK with the other 50 per cent going to support some of the most vulnerable young people overseas. In February 2006 Ray Stubbs, Eleanor Oldroyd and Mark Lawrenson (right) were among a group who visited South African townships to see how the money is being used.

Liverpool won 3-1 at Portsmouth to finish a point behind United but 15 ahead of fourth-placed Arsenal who managed to claim the Champions League place with a 4-2 win against Wigan. Thierry Henry's hat-trick took his total to 27, one more than the entire Sunderland squad, as Arsenal said farewell to Highbury after 93 years, 13 championships, 10 FA Cups and a movie. Their rivals for fourth spot, Tottenham, lost 2-1 at home to West Ham when ten of their team were struck by food poisoning.

Middlesbrough came 14th, losing 1-0 at Fulham in their final match under Steve McClaren who was appointed the new England coach as successor to Sven-Goran Eriksson who was standing down after the World Cup finals.

The season ended with the signing of a new Premier League television contract as even more money was pumped into the game. For the first time Sky lost the exclusive rights to show live games as a European Court ruling had insisted that no one company could have a monopoly. The total contract was a 66 per cent increase on the previous deal and was worth £1.76 billion over three years. Sky paid £1.314 billion for 92 live matches and four of the six available packages, while the Irish-owned Setanta Sports channel added a further £392 million for the remaining 46 games. There were also the additional terrestrial highlights, overseas, online and mobile deals to be struck which were expected to push the total to over £2 billion.

Chelsea's William Gallas shows his delight as Chelsea retain the Premiership title for a second season in a row.

Final League Table

Team	P	W	D	L	F	A	Pts
Chelsea	38	29	4	5	72	22	91
Manchester United	38	25	8	5	72	34	83
Liverpool	38	25	7	6	57	25	82
Arsenal	38	20	7	11	68	31	67
Tottenham Hotspur	38	18	11	9	53	38	65
Blackburn Rovers	38	19	6	13	51	42	63
Newcastle United	38	17	7	14	47	42	58
Bolton Wanderers	38	15	11	12	49	41	56
West Ham United	38	16	7	15	52	55	55
Wigan Athletic	38	15	6	17	45	52	51
Everton	38	14	8	16	34	49	50
Fulham	38	14	6	18	48	58	48
Charlton Athletic	38	13	8	17	41	55	47
Middlesbrough	38	12	9	17	48	58	45
Manchester City	38	13	4	21	43	48	43
Aston Villa	38	10	12	16	42	55	42
Portsmouth	38	10	8	20	37	62	38
Birmingham City	38	8	10	20	28	50	34
West Brom Albion	38	7	9	22	31	58	30
Sunderland	38	3	6	29	26	69	15

Leading Goalscorers league only

Thierry Henry	Arsenal	27
Ruud van Nistelrooy	Manchester United	21
Darren Bent	Charlton Athletic	18
Frank Lampard	Chelsea	16
Wayne Rooney	Manchester United	16
Robbie Keane	Tottenham Hotspur	16
Marlon Harewood	West Ham United	14
Ayegbeni Yakubu	Middlesbrough	13
Craig Bellamy	Blackburn Rovers	13

Awards

Footballer of the Year
Thierry Henry, Arsenal

PFA Player of the Year
Steven Gerrard, Liverpool

PFA Young Player of the Year
Wayne Rooney, Manchester United

Alan Curbishley is applauded by the fans as he looks around the Valley for the last time as manager of Charlton before the match against Blackburn.

Honours List 2005–06

Champions Chelsea

Runners-up Manchester United

Relegated Sunderland, West Bromwich Albion, Birmingham City

Promoted Reading, Sheffield United, Watford

FA Cup Winners Liverpool

League Cup Winners Manchester United

League Cup
Wayne Rooney scored twice as Manchester United beat Wigan 4-0. It was United's second success in the competition and the first major final reached by Wigan.

FA Cup
Liverpool won the FA Cup for the seventh time in the club's history following a thrilling final against West Ham. Having been switched to Cardiff, as Wembley still wasn't finished, the game was decided by a penalty shootout. After leading 2-0 and 3-2, the London side were thwarted by an amazing performance from the Liverpool captain Steven Gerrard, who made one and scored two including a 90th-minute equaliser volleyed from 30 yards. The goal prompted John Motson to ask if this was the best FA Cup final in history. José Reina then took centre stage and saved three of West Ham's penalties to enable Gerrard to lift the famous trophy.

FF 2006-07

Liverpool's Jamie Carragher challenges Manchester United's Wayne Rooney in the spring sunshine at Anfield. United's 1-0 win convinced many pundits that it was going to be their year.

Programmes

Focus began with new music and a fresh titles sequence that paid homage to the classic *Match of the Day* opening from the 1970s as fans in different grounds raised cards that displayed the programme's logo.

Jake Humphrey presented several shows while Manish was in Australia to host the BBC's coverage of the Ashes and, when he then travelled to the West Indies to front the Cricket World Cup highlights, his place on the *Focus* sofa was taken by Mark Pougatch.

Mark Lawrenson completed his tenth season as the Saturday lunchtime pundit king but his opinions were also aired on a Friday after *Focus* launched a new version of the show that was recorded on Friday afternoons and broadcast on BBC World and BBC Online.

Presenter
Manish Bhasin

Pre-season

José Mourinho had a major clearout at Stamford Bridge that included selling Eidur Gudjohnsen to Barcelona for £8m, but Chelsea's income was once again dwarfed by the club's summer spending. Although German captain Michael Ballack arrived on a free transfer from Bayern Munich, John Obi Mikel cost £16m and, at the apparent instigation of Roman Abramovich, Andriy Shevchenko arrived from AC Milan for an astonishing £30.8m.

Ruud van Nistelrooy ended his time at Old Trafford when he moved to Real Madrid for £10.2m and Tottenham midfielder Michael Carrick arrived at Manchester United for a fee of £18.6m. Martin Jol used that money to take Dimitar Berbatov and Didier Zokora to White Hart Lane for £10.9m and £8.2m respectively.

Liverpool spent just over £12m to add Jermaine Pennant from Birmingham and Craig Bellamy from Blackburn to their squad, and veteran wheeler-dealer Harry Redknapp demonstrated that he still had an eye for a bargain when Sol Campbell and David James both joined Portsmouth on free transfers.

August 2006

The first *Focus* of the new season saw Watford manager Aidy Boothroyd join Manish, Mark and Lee Dixon on the sofa and he revealed a pragmatic approach that would endear him to many during the season. 'We are not basking in past glories; we want to try and emulate clubs like Charlton, Bolton and Wigan but are under no illusions that it will be a very tough challenge.' Sure enough Watford were 1-2 favourites for relegation, and at the other end of the betting the dominance of the big four was demonstrated by the odds for the title: Chelsea were 4-9, Manchester United 6-1, Arsenal 7-1,

Presenter Jake Humphrey

Jake Humphrey became the youngest presenter of *Football Focus* when he began an eight week stint on Saturday 18 November aged 28. He has been one of the main faces on CBBC for several years and also fronts *Sportsround* as well as reporting on matches for *Final Score*.

'I got through the first programme on excitement, adrenaline and disbelief that I had Mark Lawrenson, Lee Sharpe and Lee Dixon alongside me. I've watched *Focus* all my life and just as I walked onto the studio floor and sat next to the logo it was amazing, and I really appreciated the fact that I was not just taking on another TV show but one of the BBC's flagship football programmes and that is a huge responsibility.

I've been a Norwich City fan since I was about six years old and have great memories of their golden run in the early days of the Premiership, especially that first season when we came third. There was so much excitement and looking at the way the Premiership is now it is almost unbelievable that we were so far ahead at the top at one stage during that season.'

Liverpool 8-1 and then a huge gap to Tottenham at 50-1.

Watford lost their opening game 2-1 to Everton and their tough start continued, taking 11 games to register their first win. In contrast Newcastle beat Wigan by the same scoreline on day one but Glenn Roeder was struggling to put together an attack without the retired Alan Shearer and the injured Michael Owen. On this occasion Shola Ameobi scored the winner but the Magpies struggled for goals all season.

Neil Warnock had steered Sheffield United back into the Premiership after a 12-year absence and was rewarded by an opening day 1-1 draw with Liverpool while newcomers Reading came back from a 2-0 deficit against Middlesbrough to win 3-2 at the Madejski Stadium. As well as marking Steve Coppell's return to the top-flight as a manager it was Gareth Southgate's first game in charge of Boro.

Chelsea opened their defence of the title with a 3-0 win against Manchester City and Manchester United thrashed Fulham 5-1 in front of a new record Premiership crowd of almost 76,000 at Old Trafford. Fulham boss Chris Coleman said, 'We had a game plan but it went out of the window after 10 minutes.'

It was the first of four successive wins for United and there was also a record on the opening weekend for one of their old-boys when Teddy Sheringham became the oldest outfield player in Premier League history at 40 years and 93 days. He came on as a substitute in West Ham's 3-1 win against Charlton, two teams who would share a lot of headlines in the coming season.

Below There was an even more exciting start for Reading fans. After 45 minutes of the new season they were 2-0 down at home to Middlesbrough. Three second-half goals, including this one from leading marksman Dave Kitson saw them to a 3-2 victory.

Above Everton manager David Moyes can't hide his delight as the Blue half of Liverpool triumphs 3-0 in the first Merseyside derby of the season at Goodison Park.

Arsenal drew 1-1 with Aston Villa in front of 60,023 spectators in their impressive new Emirates Stadium and four days later 37,000 turned out at Villa Park to witness Martin O'Neill's home managerial debut. Gareth Barry headed the 61st-minute winner in their 2-1 victory and, after the game, American millionaire Randy Lerner completed his purchase of the club from Doug Ellis.

Manchester City's goalless draw with Portsmouth became notorious for Ben Thatcher's atrocious foul on Pedro Mendes when he charged across the pitch and gave him a forearm smash to the head that rendered him unconscious and sent him to hospital. On *Focus* Lawro observed that, 'If that had happened on a Friday night in your local high street you'd have spent the night in a police cell.'

After three games Manchester United were the early leaders with maximum points, two ahead of Portsmouth, Aston Villa and Everton. Before the transfer window closed Ashley Cole moved from Arsenal to Chelsea in exchange for William Gallas and £5m, Andy Cole joined the old guard at Portsmouth and two Argentinian stars, Javier Mascherano and Carlos Tevez, joined West Ham from Brazilian club Corinthians. It was a controversial move for an undisclosed fee that was linked to the possible takeover of the club and was to prove to be a costly decision by the club's board.

September

There were three missed penalties in the closing 20 minutes of Sheffield United's 0-0 draw with Blackburn. Brad Friedel saved two for the visitors and United's Paddy Kenny stopped Lucas Neill's shot. There was another missed opportunity at Stamford Bridge when Frank Lampard's spot kick was superbly saved by Charlton's Scott Carson. Unfortunately for the Addicks it didn't affect the result as earlier goals by Didier Drogba and Ricardo Carvalho were enough to give Chelsea the three points in a 2-1 win and condemn Ian Dowie's side to their worst ever Premiership start with three defeats in their opening four games.

In contrast Everton made it ten points from 12 when they beat Liverpool 3-0 at Goodison Park, their largest Derby win for 42 years. That evening on *MOTD2* Adrian Chiles thought that, 'David Moyes smiled like it was Christmas, he was eight years old and he'd just been given the Subbuteo set he'd asked Santa for.'

Ryan Giggs headed Manchester United's winner against Tottenham to give them maximum points from their first four games. Watford, Blackburn, Sheffield United and, surprisingly, Arsenal with just two points from a possible nine, were atthe bottom.

Portsmouth briefly took over at the top when they beat Charlton 1-0 and Manchester United lost by a single goal from Arsenal's Emmanuel Adebayor in the 85th minute at Old Trafford. As ever, Harry Redknapp wasn't too carried away. 'We're not thinking we're going to win the championship, we're not that stupid, but we'll enjoy it while it lasts.'

With Tiger Woods applauding in the stands Mourinho made it five out of five in the league against Liverpool when Didier Drogba chested the ball down on the edge of the box, swivelled and volleyed past Jose Reina in the 42nd minute. Frank Lampard scored twice in Chelsea's 2-0 win against Fulham a week later to see the defending champions regain pole position.

On the weekend that *Focus* marked Arsène Wenger's ten years in charge of Arsenal his side won 2-1 at Charlton with both goals coming from Robin van Persie. The second was a stunning Cantona-style effort as he scored with a leaping left-foot shot from the edge of the box. In the studio Lee Dixon recalled that when the Frenchman first took over at Highbury 'he looked more like a geography teacher than a football manager'. Wenger told the programme that he was still ambitious for success. 'My desire is the same; it is just to win the next game.'

October

On the opening day of October 33-year-old Ole Gunnar Solskjaer scored his first goals at Old Trafford for 42 months after he returned from a two-year injury to score both for Manchester United in their 2-0 win against Newcastle. A deft backheel by Danny Murphy and a penalty from Jermain Defoe gave Tottenham their first win in five games when they beat Portsmouth 2-1 although Didier Zokora's blatant dive to win the spot kick led to calls for retrospective red cards.

Manchester United briefly moved three points clear at the top following their 3-1 victory at Wigan where they had to come from a goal down but, the following day, Chelsea once again narrowed the gap when they won 1-0 at Reading. It was, however, an expensive win as Blues' goalkeeper Petr Cech suffered a fractured skull and missed the next three months of the season following a challenge by Stephen Hunt.

Replacement keeper Carlo Cudicini also ended up in hospital after being knocked unconscious late on in the match.

Arsenal collected a fourth straight win when they put three past Watford, Bolton's 2-1 result at Newcastle was their first victory at St James' Park in 47 years and Andriy Shevchenko scored his first goal at Stamford Bridge as Chelsea beat Portsmouth 2-1. He was booked for running to be hugged by the crowd before Michael Ballack scored with a header, promptly did exactly the same thing and suffered the same punishment.

Paul Scholes scored in his 500th appearance for Manchester United as they beat Liverpool 2-0 but he was still only the third longest serving player in the side as Gary Neville was in his 515th game in a red shirt and Ryan Giggs his 679th. In their next match one of the relative newcomers, Wayne Rooney, ended a ten-match drought in all competitions with a hat-trick in United's 4-0 win at Bolton.

Arsenal won by the same scoreline at Reading and Liverpool beat Aston Villa 3-1 after a week dominated by an anonymous director claiming that Rafael Benitez was underachieving, wasting money on sub-standard players and didn't know his best side. It was the 99th consecutive game that

Opposite El Hadji Diouf in action for Bolton at Newcastle. Wanderers' 2-1 win at St James' Park was the club's first in almost 50 years.

Long-server Steve Coppell

Sir Alex Ferguson and Steve Coppell are the only managers from the first Premiership season to be in charge of top-flight clubs 15 years later.

However, whereas Sir Alex has remained rooted at Old Trafford, the former Manchester United midfielder has had an eclectic 15 years.

Coppell resigned as manager of Crystal Palace when they were relegated at the end of the first season of the Premier League just two years after he had led them to third spot in Division One. However, he returned for three more spells in charge at Selhurst Park in 1995, 1997 and 1999. He also had brief periods managing Manchester City, Brentford and Brighton before joining Reading in October 2003 and steering them into the top flight for the first time in their 135-year history.

the manager had changed his line up and they were in eighth place after ten games, 11 points behind the top two, Manchester United and Chelsea who each had 25 points. Bolton were five points back in third, just ahead of Portsmouth and Arsenal, while Charlton, West Ham, Sheffield United and Watford filled the bottom four places.

November

This was the month of the manager and it began with another anniversary as Sir Alex celebrated 20 years in charge of Manchester United. *Focus* carried a series of tributes from other managers and former and current players but he only came fourth in the programme's poll to find the greatest ever British manager as the Liverpool fans voted in force for Bob Paisley with Brian Clough second and Jock Stein third.

But Sir Alex's team gave him a 3-0 win against Portsmouth as the perfect gift and

they utterly dominated the game with 70 per cent of the possession. Another celebrating manager was Aidy Boothroyd, who saw his Watford side finally win a Premiership match, at the 11th attempt, when they beat Middlesbrough 2-0.

Charlton's Ian Dowie seemed to have bought some breathing space too when Darren Bent's glancing header in the 28th minute against Manchester City gave his team their first win since August. It wasn't enough, however, and following their 3-2 defeat at Wigan the bottom-placed south London club sacked Dowie after just 15 matches in charge. First-team coach Les Reed was elevated to the manager's office.

Tottenham hadn't beaten Chelsea in the League in 32 meetings since 1987 but that finally changed when Aaron Lennon's second half goal sealed a 2-1 at White Hart Lane. There was more drama in another London derby after West Ham's Marlon Harewood had scored the only goal of their match against Arsenal. Arsène Wenger took exception to Alan Pardew's celebrations. The two managers were involved in a touchline scuffle and Wenger later refused to shake hands.

He was subsequently fined by the FA and on *Focus* Lawro observed that 'Arsène Wenger is a really good manager and a really bright and intelligent person but he's a bad loser.' West Ham were also in the news when they became the latest club to be bought by an overseas consortium. The £85m-deal was led by Eggert Magnusson, the president of the Icelandic FA, who became club chairman and publicly backed their manager, Alan Pardew.

Liverpool's 3-0 defeat at Arsenal meant that they had scored just one goal and taken one point from six away games, Didier Drogba struck a hat-trick of tap-ins in Chelsea's 4-0 drubbing of Watford and *Focus* interviewed Ryan Giggs after he picked up his first ever Player of the Month award.

The top two teams produced a 1-1 draw when they met at the end of the month at Old Trafford. Louis Saha opened the scoring for the home team on the half hour with a well-placed left-foot shot that went low past Carlo Cudicini. Forty minutes later the Frenchman deflected a header from Ricardo Carvalho onto the bar and into the net to level it up. United finished the month on 38 points from 15 games with Chelsea three points behind them.

December

Following the takeover at West Ham *Focus* featured the views of several club chairmen including Reading's John Madejski who felt that all Premiership clubs would be foreign-owned within 20 years. Five were now majority owned by a foreign investor although Mark Lawrenson sounded a note of caution when he recalled the maxim that, 'The only way to make a small fortune out of football is to start with a large one.'

A busy month for Newcastle saw them win four, including a 3-1 victory at Blackburn, and lose three as they lifted themselves out of the relegation zone despite having an entire team out injured. West Ham had lost five out of their previous six games when they produced a surprising 1-0 win against Manchester United. It came just a week after the club had sacked Alan Pardew as manager and replaced him with the former Charlton boss Alan Curbishley who saw his new team respond by beating the Premiership leaders in his first game in charge.

But, under Les Reed, Charlton were still struggling. A 5-1 defeat at Tottenham was followed by a 3-0 home defeat to Liverpool and a 2-0 loss at Middlesbrough and they sank to second from bottom with only Watford below them. After only 41 days in charge, Reed left the club and was replaced by Pardew who became their third manager of the season.

Chelsea and Arsenal drew 1-1 after a scorching shot by Michael Essien six minutes

Presenter Mark Pougatch

Mark Pougatch's broadcasting career began with GLR and BBC Essex and its 15-year span matches that of the Premiership. The last seven have been spent as the voice of *Sport on Five* on Saturday afternoons on *Radio Five Live*. He also presented *Football Focus* for several weeks in 2007.

'When I was a child I couldn't always see *Match of the Day* as it was on so late but I knew that if I lost my bargaining attempts with my parents then there was always *Football Focus* the following week where I could see the goals and I always had to be back home on a Saturday to watch Bob Wilson present it.

As a fan I think that, although the Premiership is not the best league in Europe technically, it is extremely exciting and completely different to the game I watched as a lad. It is horrifying how expensive it is now and I'm astonished about the sacrifices that people make to watch the game.

On *Radio Five Live* we now cover every Premiership match in some way and it is very different to the old days on Radio 2. Now that the major tournaments spill over into the summer, from both a personal and professional point of view I have to make sure that I don't allow football to smother all my other sporting interests, especially cricket and golf, and it would be very easy to let that happen.'

Liverpool's Craig Bellamy found his goalscoring touch in December netting four times in wins over Wigan, Charlton and Watford.

from time cancelled out Mathieu Flamini's 78th-minute goal. The Gunners followed that with a 1-0 win at Wigan and a 2-2 draw with Portsmouth before registering their highest score of the season with a 6-2 thrashing of Blackburn.

When Liverpool beat Watford 2-0 it meant that they had played ten hours and 40 minutes without conceding a goal and after the game the visitors' boss, Aidy Boothroyd, summed up the experience as 'competing against Muhammad Ali while we are featherweights'. The Reds' record was extended by a further 49 minutes until Benni McCarthy scored the only goal of the game in Blackburn's 1-0 win at Ewood Park.

Manchester United returned to form after their blip against West Ham and put three goals past each of Aston Villa, Wigan and Reading to finish the year on 53 points, six clear of Chelsea. Bolton were in third place with 39 points, followed by Liverpool, Arsenal and Portsmouth.

January 2007

A new year, a new Premiership TV deal for overseas rights and even greater potential riches for the clubs and players. The extra income meant that the Premier League champions would get £50m from next season with even the bottom placed team expected to collect in the region of £30m. The new £625m three-year agreement covered the domestic and Internet rights for 208 countries and when added to the UK deals meant the Premiership rights for the seasons 2007–2010 would be generating income of more than £2.7 billion.

Sir Alex Ferguson and José Mourinho both saw their teams open the year with a point away from home as Manchester United drew 2-2 at Newcastle and Chelsea finished goalless at Aston Villa. Liverpool and Arsenal closed the gap at the top beating Bolton 3-0 and Charlton 4-0 respectively, but it was Steve Coppell's Reading who made the biggest impact when they demolished West Ham's defence with a 6-0 win to end a run of six games without one.

Focus featured interviews with two of the longest-serving Premiership stars, Paul Scholes and Andy Cole. Scholes felt that his stunning 25-yard volley against Aston Villa in December had been the best goal of his career and Lee Dixon suggested that he was the best player in the Premier League this season. Portsmouth was Cole's sixth Premiership club and, at the age of 35, he remains the second most prolific goalscorer in the competition's history.

Chelsea had been the subject of a lot of speculation about the future of their

Below A season that started badly for Charlton got slightly better when a goal from Darren Bent against Manchester City at The Valley earned them their first win in eight games.

manager but following a 4-0 win against Wigan the club publicly backed José Mourinho prompting him to tell *Focus* that, 'It is important for a manager to know and to feel that the club want and like and support him and that is much more than just spending money on a player.' His mood won't have been improved when they lost 2-0 at Liverpool in their next match.

On the same afternoon Charlton managed their first away win of the season when Amady Faye's first goal for the club gave them victory at Portsmouth, and a brace from Mark Viduka helped Middlesbrough to a 5-1 win over Bolton.

The following day Arsenal briefly upset the leaders when a stoppage-time header from Thierry Henry gave them a 2-1 victory, but United recovered to put four past Watford at Old Trafford and maintain their six-point lead over Chelsea, despite their 3-0 win at home to Blackburn.

February

Liverpool became the latest Premiership club to come under foreign ownership when they were taken over by the American tycoons George Gillett and Tom Hicks in a deal thought to be worth £220m. It didn't make an immediate impact on the team's form as they drew 0-0 with Everton on a weekend that produced more gloom for the sides struggling at the bottom. Two goals by Morton Pedersen gave Blackburn a 2-1 win over Sheffield United, West Ham lost at Villa Park to a goal by 27-year-old John Carew on his home debut and Charlton and Watford each went down 1-0 at home to Chelsea and Bolton. At the top Manchester United equalled their best away win of the season when they beat Tottenham 4-0.

On *Focus* the Bolton boss, Sam Allardyce, expressed his concerns about the lack of good young English players coming through. He felt that there was a lack of sport being played in schools and that, 'We are becoming a fat, lazy nation.'

A fourth successive league win fuelled terrace talk of a place in Europe at Reading after Steve Sidwell scored two cracking goals in their 2-0 victory over Villa. Steve Coppell was, as ever, taking a realistic approach despite being only three points off the Champions League places. 'Where you are in February is meaningless,' he told the show.

West Ham's plight worsened as they allowed Watford to gain their first away win of the season when Darius Henderson scored with a 12th minute penalty at Upton Park. That was followed with a 4-0 defeat at Charlton, a devastating result for Alan Curbishley against his old club after his job swap with Alan Pardew. It left the Hammers in 19th place and six points adrift from safety having also played a game more than Wigan, the side immediately above the drop zone.

Manchester United came from behind to beat Fulham 2-1 thanks to a stunning 88th-minute winner by Cristiano Ronaldo who collected the ball in his own half before accelerating upfield and scoring his 16th Premiership goal of the season. It left his team with a nine-point lead over Chelsea at the end of the month and Sir Alex felt that it was their toughest game so far as the Champions League campaign was also taking its toll on his side.

March

The month began with the creation of a new cult hero when former *Focus* presenter Ray Stubbs opened up a whole new set of career options as the star performer on *Comic Relief does Fame Academy* on BBC1.

The response was more muted in his hometown when Liverpool's 30-match unbeaten home run ended in a 1-0 defeat against Manchester United. John O'Shea nipped in for the winner in the 90th minute

John Carew joined Aston Villa from French champions Lyon in a part exchange deal for Milan Baros. The lanky Norwegian striker endeared himself to the Holte End by scoring the winner against West Ham on his debut at Villa Park.

The supporters Phil and Avril Lidster

The received wisdom in the Premiership is that Newcastle are most fans' second choice team, an assertion based largely on the excitement and passion of the Keegan years. The club have had the largest crowds outside of Old Trafford, produced the Premiership's best English player in Alan Shearer, and took part in its greatest match when they lost 4-3 to Liverpool in 1996, but have remained trophyless. For the club's devoted supporters it has been an incredible journey, and here two of its loyalists, Phil and Avril Lidster (right), give their perspective on the Premiership, having been regulars for more than 30 years.

Phil 'Grounds and facilities have improved tremendously with good views of the game and there are very rarely any signs of trouble now but many of the fans are more middle class than working class. Overall the Premiership has meant a tremendous atmosphere, good entertainment and marvellous footballers as the huge influx of foreign players allows us to see the best in the world. On the downside some teams have not one single Brit playing for them, which is a disappointing trend and I think that the standard of refereeing is low at present and has spoilt a number of matches.

Some people would say it has all become a little too predictable with a couple of teams dominating but I think football has always been like that and we live in hope that one day it will be Newcastle that dominates! It is good to see teams like Reading come up to the Premiership and make go of it, giving the so-called big clubs a run for their money. But it is a fact that money dominates.'

Avril 'The great thing about the Keegan years was that we used to score heaps of goals. Every match was exciting because you knew we would probably score more than we would let in (we never had the best defence). Andy Cole was unstoppable and other marvellous players included Ferdinand, Asprilla, Ginola, Beardsley and, of course, Alan Shearer. He gained my admiration by turning down undoubted glory at Manchester United to wear the No.9 shirt for his hometown team and it was a gutsy decision. We all loved Kevin Keegan for his sincerity and passion and for rekindling the spirit of our club.

Most clubs try to send reduced price tickets out to local schools, which is a great idea to attract the younger generation. Family areas are also a good idea. Language hasn't improved, although thankfully you don't hear many racist comments any more. The facilities have got better too and in some grounds there are nearly as many female toilets as male!

Football has always been an obsession in the North East as it was a release from the toil of Monday to Friday working in heavy industry. Expectations are high; we are all optimists and never give up hope. In recent years we have been so close but we still look forward to that Premiership trophy being in the St James' Park cabinet one day.'

Long-server Gary Speed

When Bolton beat West Ham 4-0 on 11 December 2006 their 37-year-old midfielder, Gary Speed, became the first player to clock up 500 appearances in the Premiership.

The former Wales captain, with a reputation for strong tackling and skill at set pieces, is regarded as a model professional. He won the title with Leeds in 1992 and also represented Everton and Newcastle in the Premier League before joining Bolton in 2004. He is one of only two players to have scored in all 15 Premiership seasons, the other being Ryan Giggs. Speed was appointed first team coach at the Reebok in May 2007.

when Jose Reina fumbled Ronaldo's free kick. Sixteen years and a day after his club debut Ryan Giggs made his 700th appearance for United.

Despite Carlos Tevez scoring his first goal for the club West Ham looked doomed when Tottenham beat them 4-3 at Upton Park. Paul Stalteri struck the winner in injury time after the Hammers had led 3-2 with only five minutes remaining and to add to their troubles the Premier League charged them with fielding two ineligible players in Tevez and Javier Mascherano.

Things went West Ham's way in their next match, however, in a controversial 2-1 win at Blackburn when Bobby Zamora was credited with a late winner despite his flick hitting team-mate Tevez who stopped the ball from crossing the line. As a result Blackburn boss Mark Hughes became the latest to call for the use of video replays but West Ham then began an astonishing turn around and won seven of their final nine games.

Stuart Pearce was also under pressure at Manchester City as they suffered a fifth straight defeat when losing 1-0 at home to Chelsea. Their main problem was that they simply couldn't score. City's end-of-season league statistics made grim reading: they established a new Premiership record with only ten goals in their 19 home games, managed none at the City of Manchester Stadium after 1 January and only scored a paltry 29 goals in total.

In complete contrast Paul Robinson became the first Tottenham goalkeeper to score a league goal since 'Tiny' Joyce in 1914 when he took a free kick some 95 yards from the Watford goal line. The ball bounced into the net over the head of his opposite number, Ben Foster, as part of their 3-1 home win.

April

Chelsea narrowed the gap at the top to three points when they beat Tottenham 1-0 and Manchester United lost 2-1 at Portsmouth. Pompey's second win in their last 12 games was helped by an 89th-minute own goal from Rio Ferdinand who mistimed a back pass from the edge of the box and put it past a stranded Van der Sar and into his own net.

Fulham were in 15th place with 35 points and had gone seven games without a win when they sacked Chris Coleman after four years in charge. Northern Ireland manager Lawrie Sanchez took over on a temporary basis but was confirmed as the full time boss at the end of the season.

A double dose of happiness for Sir Alex came when Ronaldo signed a new five-year deal with United and he watched his team join Chelsea and Liverpool in the semi-finals of the Champions League with a stunning 7-1 demolition of Roma.

Sheffield United beat West Ham 3-0 to open up a five-point gap between the sides as they went above Charlton and out of the bottom three. Everton moved into fifth spot the following day when they beat the Addicks 2-1 thanks to James McFadden's 20-yarder in stoppage time.

Shaun Wright-Phillips scored his first two Premiership goals for Chelsea in their 4-1 win at West Ham as they continued to chase down the leaders in the week that chief executive, Peter Kenyon, stated that the club had no plans to sack José Mourinho.

On the other side of London Arsenal were in turmoil when their vice-chairman David Dein suddenly left the club after 24 years on the board following a disagreement about foreign investment and the future direction of the club. Dein had supported the purchase of Arsenal shares by American billionaire Stan Kroenke who then increased his stake to just over 12 per cent. On *Focus* Lee Dixon felt that Arsène Wenger would miss Dein as he had looked after all the player contracts and details after the manager had made his decisions. The programme also looked at the issue of ticket prices, which had risen 500 per cent in the Premiership since 1992.

That afternoon Watford were relegated after drawing 1-1 with Manchester City and Jacqui Oatley became the first female commentator in the 43-year history of *Match of the Day* when she saw Fulham share two goals with Blackburn.

Portsmouth keeper David James celebrated breaking David Seaman's record of 141 Premiership clean sheets when they drew 0-0 at Aston Villa and at the end of the month West Ham were fined £5.5m by the Premier League for irregularities in the transfers of Tevez and Mascherano. *Focus* also paid tribute to Alan Ball who had died, aged 61.

Manchester United came back from a two-goal deficit to win 4-2 at Everton and open up a five-point lead over Chelsea who could only draw 2-2 with Bolton at Stamford Bridge leaving them on 80 points with three games to play. At the bottom Sheffield United beat Watford 1-0, Charlton lost 4-1 at Blackburn and West Ham won 3-0 at Wigan. These results left Sheffield in 15th place, ahead of Fulham and Wigan, and three points above West Ham who were in the relegation zone along with Charlton and Watford.

On 29 April Sam Allardyce shocked Bolton fans by resigning after eight years in charge of the club. His deputy, Sammy Lee, took charge with the team in fifth spot and chasing a UEFA cup place.

There were few highlights for Watford fans in a poor season at Vicarage Road. However, a week after they had beaten league leaders Manchester United, Portsmouth were on the end of a 4-2 hiding from the team sitting at the other end of the table. Goals from Gavin Mahon (below), Tamas Priskin and Hameur Bouazza giving the Hornets a slim chance of survival.

May

Manchester United clinched their first Premiership title since 2003 when Ronaldo's penalty gave them a 1-0 win at Manchester City, for whom Darius Vassell missed a penalty, and Chelsea could only draw 1-1 at Arsenal. It was United's ninth win in the 15 years of the Premier League and Ryan Giggs broke Alan Hansen's record of eight championship medals. Sir Alex Ferguson, who had seen his team lose to AC Milan in the Champions League semi-finals, was very happy. 'I used to have an obsession of winning in Europe but the Premiership has become a priority.'

West Ham moved out of the bottom three for the first time since December when two goals by Tevez helped them to a 3-1 win over Bolton. Charlton had their relegation confirmed when they lost 2-0 at home to Tottenham and the final weekend began with West Ham, Sheffield United and Wigan all trying to avoid the final place in the drop to the Championship.

Chelsea drew 1-1 with Everton to equal Liverpool's record of 63 home games unbeaten in the top flight and Bolton claimed the final UEFA Cup spot when Gary Speed, who has played more games than any other player in the Premiership, scored the opening goal of their 2-2 draw with Aston Villa. Another long server, Robbie Fowler, was captain for the day at Anfield in his last appearance for Liverpool as they drew 2-2 with Charlton to clinch third place ahead of Arsenal.

West Ham managed to pull off one of the greatest ever relegation escape acts when

Opposite Chelsea's Didier Drogba finished a superb season for him personally by topping the Premiership goalscorers list with 20 strikes and also getting the winning goals in both the League Cup and the FA Cup finals.

Final League Table

Team	P	W	D	L	F	A	Pts
Manchester United	38	28	5	5	83	27	89
Chelsea	38	24	11	3	64	24	83
Liverpool	38	20	8	10	57	27	68
Arsenal	38	19	11	8	63	35	68
Tottenham Hotspur	38	17	9	12	57	54	60
Everton	38	15	13	10	52	36	58
Bolton Wanderers	38	16	8	14	47	52	56
Reading	38	16	7	15	52	47	55
Portsmouth	38	14	12	12	45	42	54
Blackburn Rovers	38	15	7	16	52	54	52
Aston Villa	38	11	17	10	43	41	50
Middlesbrough	38	12	10	16	44	49	46
Newcastle United	38	11	10	17	38	47	43
Manchester City	38	11	9	18	29	44	42
West Ham United	38	12	5	21	35	59	41
Fulham	38	8	15	15	38	60	39
Wigan Athletic	38	10	8	20	37	59	38
Sheffield United	38	10	8	20	32	55	38
Charlton Athletic	38	8	10	20	34	60	34
Watford	38	5	13	20	29	59	28

Leading Goalscorers league only

Didier Drogba	Chelsea	20
Benni McCarthy	Blackburn Rovers	18
Cristiano Ronaldo	Manchester United	17
Wayne Rooney	Manchester United	14
Mark Viduka	Middlesbrough	14
Darren Bent	Charlton	13
Kevin Doyle	Reading	13
Dimitar Berbatov	Tottenham Hotspur	12
Dirk Kuyt	Liverpool	12
Ayegbeni Yakubu	Middlesbrough	12

Awards

Footballer of the Year
Cristiano Ronaldo, Manchester United

PFA Player of the Year
Cristiano Ronaldo, Manchester United

PFA Young Player of the Year
Cristiano Ronaldo, Manchester United

Right The sweetest feeling? Manchester United players celebrate as they show off the Premiership trophy for the first time since 2003. Among a stellar cast, Cristiano Ronaldo stood out in a season when he swept the board taking all three player of the year awards.

they won 1-0 at Manchester United and Wigan beat Sheffield United 2-1 at Bramall Lane to send the Blades back down on goal difference after just one campaign in the Premier League.

Glenn Roeder had quit as Newcastle manager just before the end of the season and was replaced by Sam Allardyce. Chris Hutchings was the new manager at Wigan when, after six years in charge, Paul Jewel resigned to take a break from the game, Neil Warnock ended his seven-and-a-half year tenure at Sheffield United and Stuart Pearce was sacked by Manchester City.

Eight Premiership managers had left their clubs since the start of the season but the man on top of the table, yet again, was the only manager who had been in charge of the same team and kept complete focus for all 15 years and 582 games of the Premiership, Sir Alex Ferguson.

Honours List 2006–07

Champions Manchester United

Runners-up Chelsea

Relegated Sheffield United, Charlton Athletic, Watford

Promoted Sunderland, Birmingham City, Derby County

FA Cup Winners Chelsea

League Cup Winners Chelsea

League Cup
Chelsea beat Arsenal 2-1 in an ill-tempered final at the Millennium Stadium in Cardiff. Seventeen-year-old Theo Walcott gave the Gunners a 12th-minute lead with his first goal for the club but Didier Drogba levelled the scores eight minutes later before heading the winner in the 84th minute. The match ended with John Obi Mikel, Kolo Toure and Emmanuel Adebayor sent off for taking part in an injury-time scuffle.

FA Cup
The top two teams in the country clashed once again when Chelsea beat Manchester United 1-0 in the first FA Cup final to be played at the new Wembley Stadium.

Almost 90,000 had watched 116 minutes of largely uninspiring football before Didier Drogba played a perfect one-two with Frank Lampard before poking the ball into the United net. It completed the domestic set of trophies for José Mourinho and was the club's sixth in three seasons.

A week in the life of *Football Focus* Steve Boulton

Steve Boulton joined the BBC as an engineer in 1990 joining BBC Sport several years later. He became one of the youngest editors of *Football Focus* when he took on the role at the start of the 2004–05 season at the age of 34.

Tuesday

'We have a *Focus* meeting at 10.15 with the production team, presenters, commentators and reporters. I send an email to all the production team a week before with a list of thoughts… they respond with additions and changes and that gives us a loose running order for the meeting.

We start with a review of the previous show and then try and identify the big stories of the coming week and discuss how we can tackle them in a better way than anyone else. It's crucial that the meeting is lively and my job is to keep the discussion at a level where it is charged and passionate making sure that everyone wants to produce the best possible programme. Motty will invariably be vigorously championing one story while Jonathan Pearce argues for another.

To get the big interviews you often have to put in the request several weeks in advance. We have a planning team who try and keep us ahead of the game, prompting thoughts for future features and interviews.

In the afternoon I'll sit down with the assistant editor, Shelly Alexander, who edits a third of the shows across the season, and we'll be joined by Andy Gilbert who has been *Focus*' director for the past three years.

There are usually about eight significant features on the programme each week and we'll look at the ideas we've come up with and start allocating staff to make each one. Once we've done that we'll start talking through the features in greater detail and discussing the different treatments.'

Wednesday

'Always the most uncomfortable day as this is when the answers to the interview requests start coming in and, of course, they don't always say yes, so there is usually a rethink at this point. Though I still worry every week whether or not we'll be able to fill the 49 minutes, the fact is that this is the day that the support of the team becomes crucial and the brilliant thing about the people we work with is that someone will always come up with a new idea and the show invariably begins to take on a different shape.'

Thursday

'Most of the films are shot and the interviews recorded. I'm usually at Television Centre until 9.30 in the evening but it is a privilege to be the editor of such a long running show and we are all aware of its history and the responsibilities that come with it.'

Friday

'It's always a busy day with the films being edited and approved. Manish and I also work on the script and he'll then go off and write it up in his own way while the sports sub-editors check all the facts.'

Saturday

8.00 a.m. 'Start with coffee and bacon rolls, and then go through the papers and the script and chat points with Manish.'
10.15 a.m. 'Rehearsal to practice the links'
Midday 'Reconvene in the TC5 gallery to have a final practice after Manish and the pundits have been into make up and we check that they can hear us through their earpieces.'
12.09 and 30 seconds 'Mark Lawrenson will wander onto the set'
12.10 'Tiles roll, Gilby cues Manish and another edition of *Football Focus* is live on BBC1.'

Steve Boulton took over as Editor of *Football Focus* at the start of the 2004–05 season.

The Premiership: 15 years in statistics

Individual records

Top 10 appearances
Gary Speed **519**
David James **476**
Ryan Giggs **464**
Teddy Sheringham **448**
Alan Shearer **441**
Gareth Southgate **426**
Sol Campbell **422**
Andy Cole **407**
Ray Parlour **378**
Nigel Martyn **372**

Top 10 goalscorers
Alan Shearer **260**
Andrew Cole **188**
Thierry Henry **174**
Robbie Fowler **162**
Les Ferdinand **149**
Teddy Sheringham **147**
Jimmy Floyd Hasselbaink **127**
Michael Owen **125**
Dwight Yorke **122**
Ian Wright **113**

Most Championship medals
Ryan Giggs, Manchester United **9**

Most goals in a season
Andy Cole, Newcastle United, 1993–94
34 in 40 games
Alan Shearer, Blackburn Rovers, 1994–95
34 in 42 games

Most goals in a game
Alan Shearer, Blackburn Rovers **5**
v Sheffield Wednesday,
19 September 1999
Andy Cole, Manchester United **5**
v Ipswich Town,
4 March 1995

Club records

Premiership titles won
Manchester United **9**
Arsenal **3**
Chelsea **2**
Blackburn Rovers **1**

Points in a season
Most Chelsea, 2004–05
95 in 38 games
Fewest Sunderland, 2005–06
15 in 38 games

Wins in a season
Most Chelsea, 2004–05
29 in 38 games
Fewest Sunderland, 2002–03
3 in 38 games

Defeats in a season
Fewest Arsenal, 2003–04
unbeaten in 38 games
Most Ipswich Town, 1994–95
29 in 42 games

Goals scored in a season
Most Manchester United, 1999–2000
97 in 38 games
Fewest Sunderland, 2002–03
21 in 38 games

Goals conceded in a season
Fewest Chelsea, 2004–05
15 in 38 games
Most Swindon, 1993–94
100 in 42 games

2003 — 2004

Most clean sheets in a season
Chelsea 2004–05
25 in 38 games

Biggest win
Manchester United
9-0 v Ipswich Town, 4 March 1995

Longest unbeaten run
Arsenal
49 games, 7 May 2003–24 October 2004

Left Gareth Southgate made 426 appearances in the Premiership for Crystal Palace, Aston Villa and Middlesbrough.

Above Arsenal players celebrate the (almost) perfect season in May 2004 having gone the entire season unbeaten.

Index

Entries in *italics* denote television and radio programmes.